About the author

Andrew Cumbers is professor of geographical political economy at the University of Glasgow. He has written extensively on the problems of uneven development in capitalist societies, responses on the left and the prospects for a more democratic and egalitarian politics. Recent publications include *Alternatives to Market Fundamentalism in Scotland and Beyond*, co-edited with Geoff Whittam, and *Global Justice Networks: Geographies of Transnational Solidarity* with Paul Routledge.

Reclaiming public ownership
Making space for economic democracy

ANDREW CUMBERS

Zed Books
LONDON | NEW YORK

Reclaiming public ownership: Making space for economic democracy was first published in 2012 by Zed Books Ltd, 7 Cynthia Street, London N1 9JF, UK and Room 400, 175 Fifth Avenue, New York, NY 10010, USA

www.zedbooks.co.uk

Copyright © Andrew Cumbers 2012

The right of Andrew Cumbers to be identified as the author of this work has been asserted by him in accordance with the Copyright, Designs and Patents Act, 1988

Set in OurType Arnhem and Monotype Futura by Ewan Smith, London
Index: ed.emery@thefreeuniversity.net
Cover designed by Baker
Printed and bound by CPI Group (UK) Ltd, Croydon, CR0 4YY

Distributed in the USA exclusively by Palgrave Macmillan, a division of St Martin's Press, LLC, 175 Fifth Avenue, New York, NY 10010, USA

All rights reserved. No part of this publication may be reproduced, stored in a retrieval system or transmitted in any form or by any means, electronic, mechanical, photocopying or otherwise, without the prior permission of Zed Books Ltd.

A catalogue record for this book is available from the British Library
Library of Congress Cataloging in Publication Data available

ISBN 978 1 78032 007 6 hb
ISBN 978 1 78032 006 9 pb

Contents

Tables and figures | vi
Acknowledgements | vii

Introduction: an unexpected guest – the return of public ownership. 1

PART ONE Public ownership and its discontents

1 Public ownership as state ownership: the post-1945 legacy. . . . 11
2 The neoliberal onslaught and the politics of privatization 38
3 Coming to terms with Hayek: markets, planning and economic democracy 62

PART TWO The return of public ownership

4 Financial crisis and the rediscovery of the state in the neo-liberal heartland 85
5 Public ownership and an alternative political economy in Latin America 108
6 Alternative globalizations and the discourse of the commons . 123

PART THREE Remaking public ownership

7 Remaking and rescaling public ownership 145
8 State ownership, deliberative democracy and elite interests in Norway's oil bonanza. 173
9 Decentred public ownership and the Danish wind power revolution 192

Conclusion 211

Notes | 221 Bibliography | 229
Index | 245

Tables and figures

Tables

2.1 Changes in salaries of directors following privatization 53
4.1 Privatization proceeds and left parties in power in European countries during the 1990s 91
4.2 Government support (loans) and share purchases of nationalized banks 97
5.1 Multinationals that have withdrawn from the Latin American water sector 112
7.1 An evaluation of the effectiveness of different forms of public ownership in achieving desired objectives 165
7.2 Schematic depiction of public ownership types by economic activity 168
9.1 Structure of the electricity power generation and distribution network in Denmark 199

Figures

2.1 Ownership of share capital in the UK's quoted public limited companies, 1963–2008 56
9.1 Wind power electricity generation (MW) in Denmark, 1986–2008 204

Acknowledgements

Although the responsibility for any flaws in the book is mine and mine alone, I do, nonetheless, owe a debt of gratitude to the many friends, family, colleagues and comrades who made it possible. Bob McMaster has provided a valuable sounding board for many of the ideas in the book over the years and I need to say a special thanks for his friendship, intellect and humour and much more besides. He has been an invaluable source of information and knowledge about heterodox economics in particular and has given unsparingly of his time in reading various drafts of chapters. Danny MacKinnon, too, has been an important and generous collaborator over the years with many insights and not a few drinks shared in late-night discussions. My colleagues in the Human Geography Research Group at the University of Glasgow have all provided much-needed collegiality, friendship and support, but Chris Philo needs a special mention as someone who commented wisely on some early writings and pointed me in the right direction. Dave Featherstone and Paul Routledge have also been important sources of knowledge and ideas about social movements, radical politics and left perspectives.

Outside Glasgow, Geoff Whittam has been an important influence and support to me in developing an Alternative Economic Strategy Network in Scotland, where I first aired some of the views expressed here. Thanks to other participants in the network, such as Mike Danson, Christine Cooper, Gesa Helms, Kean Birch, Phil Taylor, Peter Bain, Gerry Mooney, Molly Scott Cato, Owen Logan, Andy Pike and Tommy Sheridan, who were a critical but supportive audience. I also owe a debt of gratitude to the Geography Department at the Goethe University in Frankfurt, which hosted me for three critical months of writing in 2011, particularly Peter Lindner, Bernd Belina and Dorothy Hauser, who made my stay both enjoyable and productive.

On the publishing front, a big thank-you to Ken Barlow, my editor at Zed Books, for enthusiastically supporting and championing the idea of a book about public ownership. His editing skills kept me to tight deadlines in a quiet but determined manner, and his comments and suggestions improved the final text considerably. I would also like to thank the rest of the team at Zed Books for their professionalism and dedication in getting the book into print, especially Ewan Smith and Ian Paten.

Thanks to Anni, who has been a constant source of encouragement, advice and support, not least in her gentle prompting to get the thing started in the first place! Thanks also to Anna and David for putting up with my numerous absences during the writing of the book. I owe my parents an immeasurable debt for all their love and care over the years. I hope this book gives my mum some useful ammunition in her growing radicalism and activism. And finally, thanks to the other David Cumbers, my father, with whom I first had the kind of conversations that are the subject matter of the book. Without his quiet humanity, guidance and generous spirit, none of this would have been possible. The book is dedicated to his memory.

Introduction: an unexpected guest – the return of public ownership

On 17 February 2008, public ownership returned to the centre stage of British politics when the Chancellor of the Exchequer, Alistair Darling, announced that Her Majesty's Government was taking a 100 per cent stake in the bankrupt former building society Northern Rock. The Northern Rock nationalization came on the back of months of prevarication, following the government's initial £25 billion rescue package in September of the previous year. In the intervening period the Labour government had done everything in its power to avert nationalization, but not surprisingly there were no serious private investors willing to take on Northern Rock at a time of tightening credit markets and wider financial malaise. As Darling was keen to point out, nationalization was a last resort, and not something that should be countenanced in 'normal' circumstances. But these were not normal times. Northern Rock proved to be the first episode in a rapidly escalating drama as the entire global financial sector threatened to implode. Within months, the government was forced to intervene again with the full or partial nationalization of much of the rest of the UK's retail banking sector. Hitherto independent bastions of finance capital such as the Royal Bank of Scotland and HBOS, as well as the smaller former building society the Bradford and Bingley, were now owned by the British taxpayer. The country's main conservative broadsheet, the *Daily Telegraph*, proclaimed somewhat apocalyptically that 'October 13, 2008 will go down in history as the day the capitalist system in the UK finally admitted defeat'.[1]

Elsewhere, in two of the world's largest economies, the USA and Germany, governments were also forced into major nationalizations and a massive injection of public funds into the banking sector to avoid a series of catastrophic bankruptcies following the collapse of the US bank Lehman Brothers. Similar policies were pursued throughout the advanced economies to bail out institutions whose speculative adventures had brought the global economy to the brink of collapse. Huge government deficits were run up as a result. In the UK, for example, at the peak of the crisis, the government had committed the astronomical sum of £1.162 trillion of public money to provide loans, share purchases and guarantees to its errant banks (NAO 2011).

At the height of the financial crisis in 2008, there were some grounds for hope that the political tide had turned after three decades in which governments across the world – of both right and left – had signed up to a form of free market fundamentalism with its emphasis upon competition, individualism and market deregulation. Even arch-conservatives such as the Republican president George W. Bush or the evangelizing neoliberal government of Gordon Brown were forced to speak the language of state regulation and intervention. As the banking crisis began to ripple through to the rest of the economy, producing a collapse in the housing market, the freezing up of credit to business and a general downturn in consumer demand, it appeared that the political classes might be rediscovering the benefits of a more sophisticated form of economics. Hayek and Friedman might be about to give ground to Keynes, Polanyi and even Marx.

However, as the initial shock of the financial crisis wore off and state intervention appeared to have – at least temporarily – stabilized the banking system, it became clear that the grip of free market philosophy on the political mainstream was as strong as ever. Elite policy discourse remained cloaked in the language of better regulation and management of market forms with a continued commitment to private ownership as the more efficient form of service delivery. In the USA and the UK the appointment of private executives, often from the very banks that had caused the crisis, to run the nationalized companies in question reinforced this point (Brummer 2009). Not only did nationalization change very little but it was effectively used to save the banking sector from its own contradictions. In the words of one set of commentators, it was a 'band-aid nationalisation' (Panitch and Gindin 2009) with the public sector absorbing bad debts to allow private capital to restructure and get on with the job of accumulating profits and appropriating wealth. 'Socialism for the rich and capitalism for the poor' became a familiar but accurate refrain. Although there have been some more progressive voices in the mainstream – such as Paul Krugman, the US economics Nobel Prize winner, and the *Observer* columnist Will Hutton – who have argued that this level of state intervention has been necessary to correct for the mistakes of the private banking sector and that a better-regulated market economy can emerge from the ashes of the economic crisis, there has been almost no questioning of the underlying structures of the economic system that caused the crisis.

For many ordinary people, the most striking thing about these government interventions has been the failure of the political classes and of mainstream media commentators to ask more searching questions about the underlying nature of the economy and the values that drive it. The ideology of 'the market' and the other two tropes of 'private enterprise' and 'competition' seem to have emerged remarkably unscathed by events. But for seasoned and critical observers, there is no mystery to this at all. As the veteran economic historian Douglas Dowd points out, free market or neoclassical economics is useful precisely because it produces a set of theories regarding the links between private property, the rational individual and economic efficiency that serves the interests of powerful and established elites over the downtrodden and dispossessed (Dowd 2001). Its continuing grip on our ruling classes, despite its culpability in the financial crisis, should come as no surprise. In this book, when I refer to 'mainstream economics' I am referring to this seemingly intractable tradition of neoclassical economics.

In search of an alternative discourse

More surprisingly, debate on the left about alternative economic strategies and especially the role of public ownership in recent years has also been strangely muted. While there has been considerable analysis of the economic and financial crisis (e.g. Crotty 2009; Gowan 2009; Keen 2011; Harvey 2010), there has been little attempt to develop an agenda that might feed into mainstream discourses to counter three decades of market imperialism and a deeply ingrained sense of the benefits of private ownership. Although there have been some important recent theoretical responses to Hayekian concerns about the limits to planning, issues of liberty and democracy, under socialist forms of economy (O'Neill 2003; Burczak 2006), left thinking on the forms that public ownership might take in the context of globalization and neoliberalism has scarcely advanced since the last time nationalization was on the agenda in the economic crisis of the 1970s.

The dangers of this intellectual vacuum are clearly manifest as the free market right reasserts itself in the current economic crisis. In the UK, media discussion moved with a frightening and dizzying alacrity from the perceived immorality of the financial 'masters of the universe' and culpable individuals such as Fred Goodwin and Adam Appleyard (disgraced former CEOs of RBS and Northern Rock, respectively) to a renewed assault on the growing public sector deficit, which was partially attributable to the financial sector bailouts (Wray 2009). By the time of the 2010 general election all three major parties were agreed on the need for massive public spending cuts, the only subject for debate being over how much and where the axe should fall (education, health, transport, social services, etc.). Throughout Europe, too, there has thus far been little dissent from a mainstream consensus, although we wait to see what kind of socialist François Hollande will prove to be in France. Denmark's social democrat–left coalition is about the only government in the European Union proposing anything that Keynes might have agreed with. The Eurozone financial crisis meanwhile has brought with it an accompanying crisis of democracy as a general politics of austerity is steamrollered across the continent and imposed on reluctant electorates by supranational governance elites from the IMF and the European Commission. Similarly in the United States, both the Republican and Democrat parties broadly agree on the need for fiscal retrenchment, even if the extremes of the shared discourse are wider apart than in Europe. If anyone doubted the deeply entrenched hegemony of mainstream economic nostrums on the wider body politic, this dramatic shift in the discourse of the economic crisis has provided a timely reminder that neither neoliberalism, nor its underlying precepts, have been discredited.

Beyond the heartland regions of global capitalism, something more interesting has been happening. In Latin America a number of governments, municipal authorities and social movements have started down the path of attempting to reclaim their economies from multinational corporations and private profit to construct alternatives based around more collective ethics and values. Public ownership has returned to the fore as part of these debates, with strong nationalization agendas being pursued in Bolivia under Evo Morales and in Venezuela under Hugo Chávez's Bolivarian Revolution, but also with demands for the recuperation of common lands and rights by indigenous groups across the region. Although there is much discussion on the left about these developments, analysis tends to be either celebratory about some of the egalitarian and participatory practices being developed at the grass roots and among social movements such as the Zapatistas, or more critical of what are often perceived to be verticalist and anti-democratic tendencies emerging through the state projects of Chávez and Morales. There is little serious analysis in particular about the forms of public ownership that are being developed, what their prospects might be for constructing a more democratic and egalitarian type of economy, or what lessons might be learnt from past forms.

Critically, such struggles have all in their different ways identified public ownership and economic democracy as being central to left alternative projects today. Going beyond social democrat and centre-left concerns with distributional justice as the key means to develop a more egalitarian politics, they put questions of democratic ownership and control of the economy at the heart of their politics. They correctly recognize that current global inequalities and injustices are brought about as much by the appropriation of economic decision-making by elite groups as by distributional outcomes. In this sense, the quest for democracy means nothing if it does not include the ability to participate in the key decisions about economic life. Devising new forms of public ownership that address these issues therefore becomes critical.

My purpose in this book is to help fill this gap by addressing some hard questions about what type and forms of public ownership are relevant in the context of the global economy today. While the book draws mainly on experiences in western Europe, with the exception of Chapter 5, which reviews recent developments in public ownership in Latin America, the themes explored have broader resonance. The central argument is that past and existing forms of public ownership have done little to deliver genuine economic democracy and public participation because they were, on the whole, over-centralized, bureaucratic and lacking democratic participation. Public ownership and nationalization strategies have, more often than not, been used to stabilize capitalism rather than pursue more radical agendas. Even in the supposedly communist revolutions of the twentieth century, there are strong arguments that state-owned enterprises (SOEs) replaced exploitation by workers under private capitalism with state elites in regimes that are effectively better understood as 'state capitalism' (Resnick and Wolff 1994). In the 1980s such forms of public ownership were an easy target for a resurgent free market agenda under the new right. Hayekian critiques of nationalization and central planning, together with their conflation of markets, private property rights and individual liberty, gained widespread political support and still dominate the mainstream economic policy agenda today.

I engage with both Hayek's free market critique of central planning while highlighting also the limits of 'free market utopias' and privatization in particular in enhancing the goals of social justice and environmental sustainability. However, in a challenge to those on the left, as well as those social democratic and Third Way apologists for neoliberalism, it is important to go beyond older debates about the relative merits of free markets versus central planning to address the question of what organizational forms and institutions can foster public ownership and economic democracy in the twenty-first century.

In addressing these issues I draw upon critical literature to forge a renewed set of arguments for public ownership in the aftermath of the neoliberal onslaught on the state and the public realm. In particular, I argue for a more 'decentred' and pluralistic approach to public ownership which emphasizes the principles of openness, variety, democratic deliberation and even contestation, which should be at the heart of a socialist political economy (Cumbers and McMaster 2010). In doing all this, I draw upon a range of experiences both from the post-1945 period of active state policy and more recent initiatives from western Europe and Latin America.

Some definitional issues: public rather than common ownership?

What is perplexing in the current conjuncture is that public ownership – usually narrowly conceived of as the state takeover of private assets on behalf of the broader public – has few supporters on the left while many detractors on the right. Much recent left thinking, particularly that which has emerged out of the global justice movement, sets itself up as both avowedly anti-market and anti-state. Instead a 'global commons' is frequently invoked against both public (conceived of as a state always acting in the interests of capital accumulation logics or the totalitarian nature of state socialist projects) and private ownership, both of which are viewed as forms of ownership through which resources and knowledge are appropriated on behalf of certain powerful interests (either state elites or private corporations) at the expense of the 'common good' (e.g. Hardt and Negri 2009; De Angelis 2007; Holloway 2010).

The idea of common ownership as distinct from public ownership has been around for some time. As Anton Pannekoek, the leading council communist, put it:

> Public ownership is the ownership, i.e. the right of disposal, by a public body representing society, by government, state power or some other political body. The persons forming this body, the politicians, officials, leaders, secretaries, managers, are the direct masters of the production apparatus; they direct and regulate the process of production; they command the workers. Common ownership is the right of disposal by the workers themselves; the working class itself – taken in the widest sense of all that partake in really productive work, including employees, farmers, scientists – is direct master of the production apparatus, managing, directing, and regulating the process of production which is, indeed, their common work. (Pannekoek 1947)

In this vein, common ownership is seen as distinctive; a decentralized autonomous politics of the working class – however defined – which emerges either through workers' councils or through older forms of commons practice in traditional rural communities. Public ownership is associated with the state and a form of politics which might begin on behalf of an oppressed class but quickly becomes another means of managing society from above. Writing in the 1940s, Pannekoek, along with many others (George Orwell being one), was horrified at the creeping totalitarianism of the socialist state as evident in the Soviet experience. Later on, others were critical of the post-war state in many Western capitalist countries for similar reasons.

In this book, I argue against this distinction and use the term 'public ownership' in its broadest sense as encapsulating all those attempts, both outside and through the state, to create forms of collective ownership in opposition to, or perhaps more accurately to reclaim economic space from, capitalist social relations. If we understand capitalism as built upon the three pillars of the wage relationship, private property relations and the market, all forms of collective ownership that seek to disturb and intervene in these spheres should come into our analysis. Thus the concept of public ownership deployed here is deliberately broad and does not involve a totalizing vision of an alternative politics around a single dominant model or form. Rather, it is an attempt to 'work toward a way of thinking that might place us alongside our political others, mutually recognizable as oriented in the same direction even if pursuing different paths' (Gibson-Graham 2006: 8). Practically, this means embracing forms of common ownership outside the state (e.g. employee-owned firms, producer and consumer cooperatives) as well as those that involve state ownership. While the argument in this book recognizes some of the critiques of the dominant model of state ownership in the twentieth century, it nevertheless reaffirms the continued need to engage with the state as a space for progressive change and which, despite its problems, has delivered considerable improvements in the lives of the broad mass of people. The best example of this is the British National Health Service, a state institution which still conforms to the best socialist egalitarian principles despite its many flaws and attempts by recent governments of both the right and centre-left to turn it into a market-driven system.

Whatever the problems of binary thinking, the use of the term 'public' is here advocated in opposition to 'private' in relation to economic ownership and the social relations that underpin the economy. The point here is that the pursuit of public ownership in its broader sense implies that things are owned collectively and, more importantly, subject to collective forms of decision-making in opposition to private forms of ownership, which under capitalism involve the appropriation of both resources and labour for particular interests rather than in the general interest. Thus, public ownership and economic democracy are the two themes that run through this book. More equitable and socialist forms of economy have to be concerned not only with issues of distributional justice but also what has been termed 'productive' and 'appropriative justice' (Burczak 2006; De Martino 2000, 2003). In the past, many socialist experiments, however well intentioned, have often conceived of social justice too narrowly as about achieving distributive justice without being concerned with the issue of economic democracy. Forms of public ownership in the future must be imagined and constructed that have democracy at their heart.

PART ONE
Public ownership and its discontents

1 | Public ownership as state ownership: the post-1945 legacy

> What this war has demonstrated is that private capitalism – that is, an economic system in which land, factories, mines and transport are all privately owned solely for profit – does not work. It cannot deliver the goods. (Orwell 1982 [1941]: 73)

Introduction

In late July 1945, as the Second World War drew to a close, the British people rejected their wartime leader, Winston Churchill, and his Conservative Party and presented the Labour Party with a historic landslide victory and its first ever majority government. Under the new prime minister, Clement Attlee, Labour embarked upon the most radical and left-wing programme of economic reform of any British administration in history. With its commitment to tackle the poverty, deprivation and unemployment that had plagued the country in the years before war, Attlee's government embarked upon massive and unprecedented levels of state intervention in the economy. The centrepiece was an extensive programme of nationalization to take key sectors of the economy away from the oligopolistic private interests that the Labour Party and its supporters viewed as responsible for the economic anarchy of the interwar years.

> The great inter-war slumps were not acts of God or of blind forces. They were the sure and certain result of the concentration of too much economic power in the hands of too few men. These men had only learned how to act in the interest of their own bureaucratically-run private monopolies which may be likened to totalitarian oligarchies within our democratic State. They had and they felt no responsibility to the nation. (Labour Party 1945: 1)

For many on the British left, this was the moment when the long march along a parliamentary road to socialism took a massive step forward.

While the nationalization programme pursued in Britain reflected particular national concerns, it represented part of a much broader international shift in opinion away from the market as the key mechanism for economic development and towards the state and the use of economic management, planning and public ownership. For its part in fostering the economic, social and political conditions that had culminated in two world wars and a worldwide depression, the global capitalist system was firmly discredited. Additionally, through the contribution of the Soviet Union to the eventual defeat of fascism, the alternative economic model of communism and centralized state planning – whatever the developing misgivings about Stalinism – was firmly in the ascendant.

Laissez-faire (free market) capitalism was entirely discredited, to the extent that even some of its most avid and influential proponents severely doubted its ability to continue functioning in the aftermath of war. As Joseph Schumpeter, Professor of Economics at Harvard University, solemnly noted in 1943: 'The all but general opinion seems to be that capitalist methods will be unequal to the task of reconstruction' and it was 'not open to doubt that the decay of capitalist society is very far advanced' (Schumpeter 1943: 20, cited in Armstrong et al. 1991: 6).

Alongside the diminished standing of capitalism, the accompanying process of late nineteenth-century European empire-building was also unravelling with increased demands for political and economic independence among the colonized peoples. As Armstrong et al. put it in their authoritative account of the economic and political conditions of the time:

> Much more serious for the long term prospects of the capitalist system than the physical destruction was the challenge to its effective functioning as a social system. In the defeated countries the war had discredited the capitalist class: its association with the horrific consequences of fascism and war had undermined its authority in the political sphere and industrially ... Everywhere, with gathering momentum, people were demanding radical social change.
>
> Moreover, it was not only the internal structure of the capitalist societies which was in turmoil. The old hierarchy of nation states was overturned, the continued domination of the colonial order was under challenge, and capitalism was confronting a hostile social system, that of the USSR, whose prestige had been enormously increased by the war. (Ibid.: 6)

In almost every Western developed economy trade unions and workers were successful in building strong mass organizations in the immediate aftermath of the war, while varying shades of anti-capitalist politics were in the ascendant. Socialist and communist parties made substantial advances in the first elections in France and Italy, in part boosted by the significant role they had played in the wartime resistance to fascism, and in the defeated countries, Japan and Germany in particular, workers were already occupying factories and large corporations, calling for economic democracy and workers' control (ibid.).

While the more radical groundswell of the immediate post-war years was pushed back in North America and western Europe, as elements of the old order began to reassert themselves, and the geopolitical framing of the Cold War provided succour for embattled capitalist elites and moderate labour leaders to water down demands for more radical change, nationalization and state intervention became important parts of a new international economic policy paradigm which has among other labels been described as Fordism, the Keynesian Welfare State, Organized or Regulated Capitalism.

Central planning and nationalization were of course already in place in many parts of the world – notably in Latin America and the Soviet Union following various 'revolutions' – but it was in the period between 1945 and 1979 that they became hegemonic. They were also to the fore among newly independent countries throughout Asia and Africa, where they became an important part of a state developmentalist model in the 1950s and 1960s. Many countries rejected capitalism as part of the imperialist legacy, and turned instead to the Soviet Union for an economic model to imitate. Others at a more pragmatic level recognized that the absence of an indigenous capitalist class required the state to take on the mantle of economic development and entrepreneur (Chang and Rowthorn 1995). Ironically, even many of those countries that were to fall under the umbrella of US hegemony during the Cold War, notably South Korea, Singapore and Taiwan, used nationalization and state planning as integral components of national development agendas.

The British experience with nationalization

Between 1945 and 1951 vast swathes of the British economy were transferred out of the private sector and into public ownership. The nationalization programme of the Labour government extended to include the Bank of England, the civil aviation industry, the entire coal and rail industries, and public utilities such as electricity, water and gas. The final and most controversial nationalization was the iron and steel industry, eventually completed just after Labour left office in 1951 and subsequently reversed by the incoming Conservative government.

Referred to at the time by the government as 'socialization' (Saville 1993a: 38), nationalization brought around two million workers into new public organizations so that by 1951 the public sector (including local authorities) numbered around four million; around 18 per cent of the total workforce (ibid.: 37–8). Significantly, though, apart from the Bank of England, there was no attempt to nationalize the wider financial sector or redirect its activities towards a programme of industrial modernization.

As noted earlier, these changes need to be framed within the broader political and geopolitical context. The experience of the Great Depression and the war had fomented popular demand for radical social change in Britain. Even many Conservatives accepted the need for economic and social reforms in the post-war years,[1] and until the 1970s there was a broad consensus between Labour and Conservative governments regarding the pursuit of full employment and the role of the state in intervening to amelioriate trade cycles and boost the economy. Many sections of private business were supporters of limited nationalization, especially of industries such as coal and the railways, which were chronically inefficient prior to the war. Nationalization was expected to deliver improved performance and the potential for lower prices in key sectors that would confer advantages on the rest of the economy (Armstrong et al. 1991; Saville 1993a).

In these circumstances, the new Labour government was responding to a broader mood for change within British society, rather than having its own deeply rooted blueprint. While the Labour Party was committed to an agenda of social justice and redistribution of income, to the extent that the 1945–51 government founded a national health service and welfare state – considerable and lasting achievements which have rightly been widely acclaimed – there was a marked absence of a deeper socialist vision with regard to the economy. In this sense, the radicalism of the 1945–51 Labour administration should not be overstated.

Neither socialization nor modernization There was certainly no profound ideological or theoretical perspective informing government thinking (Saville 1993b). If there was a deeper motivation, beyond the need for some form of government intervention to rebuild an economy shattered and largely bankrupted by five years of war, it was an economic modernization agenda rather than a socialistic one. Labour Party pamphlets and documents in the 1930s were full of the need for national economic modernization and productivity agendas as a critique of the failure of private interests in the face of increasingly stiff competition from the United States, Japan and Germany (Fyrth 1993). In many sectors of the economy, private cartels were making monopoly rents[2] without making investments in new technologies and methods, while unemployment had remained high right up until the outbreak of war. Comparisons with US production methods by the newly created Anglo-American Council on Productivity (under Stafford Cripps at the new Ministry of Economic Affairs) in 1947 revealed strong American advantages in almost every industry (Saville 1993a). Nationalization, allied to greater strategic planning of sectors, was therefore considered a more effective means of securing economies of scale and the necessary modernization policies to make British capital competitive in world markets.

While some on the left were influenced by Oskar Lange's more radical vision of market socialism (where worker-owned enterprises might exist within an economy centred on the price mechanism), such radical agendas did not penetrate the upper echelons of the Labour establishment (ibid.). Although the party referred to its nationalization programme as 'socialization', this was largely a PR exercise for public consumption and belied the lack of radicalism underpinning nationalization either from a socialist or capitalist modernization perspective. The government was deeply suspicious of anything remotely 'syndicalist' that might provide more grassroots or shop-floor representation and influence on the councils of the nationalized industries.[3] While intellectual figures such as Evan Durbin, Barbara Wootton and the Webbs were advancing radical agendas around socialist planning, even these figures set their faces against more radical proposals for worker ownership or economic democracy (Cunningham 1993). Despite the famous Labour Party Clause 4 commitment to 'common ownership of the means of production', it was clear that it was the existing state establishment which was to be entrusted with the management and control of public ownership rather than 'the people' themselves. Although there was labour representation on most of the new national corporation boards, this usually came from the trade union establishment and right-wing leadership rather than directly elected worker representatives; for example, in the case of the National Coal Board, successive National Union of Mineworkers general secretaries (even under Conservative governments) were board members. In some cases, former trade union leaders even became chairmen of nationalized industries, such as Sir Joseph Hallsworth (NCB) and Lord Citrine (British Electricity Authority) (Fishman 1993).

At a more practical level, there had been little discussion or detailed thinking either about the way the different nationalized industries should be organized or what detailed criteria they should be judged by. Manny Shinwell, for example, the new minister for the coal industry, started with what he admitted was as 'an empty desk' (cited in Nove 1983: 168). The government opted for what has become known as the 'Morrisonian' model of nationalization.[4] The large centralized national public corporation, along the lines of the BBC – at arm's length from government control but at the same time providing no effective voice in decision-making for either workers, consumers or user groups – became the main working model. Morrison's model drew upon his own experiences before the war in setting up the London Passenger Transport Board (in 1931), where his emphasis had been upon the importance of a 'public corporation run by business and expert interests. Distance from local authority or government interests was even seen as a virtue' (Saville 1993a: 44). The lack of creativity or imagination surrounding the government's plans and its willingness to defer to established interests became particularly striking characteristics of the nationalization process as it unfolded.

Despite the government rhetoric, and subsequent criticisms from the right (see Chapter 3), nationalization altered remarkably little in the political economy of the United Kingdom, either in switching the country on to a new growth and modernization trajectory, or in changing the dominant power relations within the economy. Regarding modernization, while there was a clear will to introduce new management methods and develop more strategic planning agendas, the new government lacked the willingness to fundamentally challenge the private business lobby or the ability to reorganize the machinery of the main economic ministries (particularly in challenging the dominance of the Treasury and financial interests) (Cunningham 1993).

In comparison with other European countries, where the prestige of the ruling business and political classes had been severely damaged by the war – such that economic policy agendas had explicit political motivations that were directed against business interests that had colluded with fascism (see below) – the British ruling class, though weakened by the war, remained strong and intact in the machinery of government and industry (Armstrong et al. 1991). The wartime government – which had involved more state control and eventually the development of a planned economy – had been a coalition in both the political and economic senses (including representatives of business and labour). Most of the industry boards set up to coordinate the war effort came from private industry, the civil service and the universities and remained largely in the same hands after the war (Saville 1993a). To take one important example, the Capital Issues Committee, established during the war to administer and regulate government borrowing for investment through the capital markets, was staffed by seven representatives from private industry (bankers, industrialists and stockbrokers) and one from the Treasury (Saville 1993b: xxix). Such relationships also characterized many of the new national planning boards and corporations during the 1945–51 period (Rogow and Shore 1955).

The civil service also continued to be staffed by elite groups, while many of the leading Labour politicians were themselves from an upper-class background.[5] Those from a working-class background, such as Ernest Bevin, were either to the right of the party or, in the case of Manny Shinwell, the minister in charge of coal nationalization, showed a surprising complacency and lack of commitment to economic democracy (ibid.).[6] One of the few on the left who might have argued for a more radical stance, Nye Bevan, had his hands full with the setting up of a National Health Service. Even in the coal industry, and despite Shinwell's fiery rhetoric in Parliament, there was a remarkable degree of management continuity given the scale of reorganization, and despite the availability of a vast source of independent and trade union research into and knowledge of the economic and production conditions in the industry. Nine hundred separate companies and 700,000 miners were amalgamated into one national organization, the National Coal Board, with Shinwell appointing Lord Hyndley – the managing director of one of the largest private mining companies, Powell Duffryn, as well as a director of the Bank of England from 1930 to the end of the war – as its first chairman (Saville 1993a: 46). Regional officials were also appointed from the ranks of private industry or in many cases from the military (Fishman 1993). Meanwhile, employment relations changed little from those under private forms of ownership. Management was still heavily top-down and the development of large bureaucratic structures produced an alienating work environment for the average worker, while the lack of worker and broader citizen involvement in economic decision-making had created a significant democratic deficit in industries that were now owned and managed supposedly on behalf of the people.

Nationalization as life support for Britain's declining economic competitiveness The lack of commitment to economic democracy was matched by a failure to fundamentally challenge the underlying power relations within the economy as a whole, and in particular the relations between 'rentier' and 'productive' capital. Indeed, the manner in which nationalization was achieved actually reinforced existing imbalances in favour of the former over the latter. The underlying relationships between financial and industrial capital in Britain that were at the root of the country's long-term industrial decline – the short-term nature of financial interests, the increased tendency for British capital to invest overseas, the dominance of multinational interests over those of smaller domestically oriented firms and, underpinning all of this, the growing global role of the City of London as a financial centre independent of and often in opposition to a serious programme of industrial modernization – were replicated and even accentuated by the manner in which nationalization proceeded.

While there is not the space here to do justice to the broader debates around these issues,[7] two points were critical. First, the nature of the compensation given to the private owners was extraordinarily generous, largely justified by the need to ensure that investment continued in the run-up to privatization (Saville 1993a) – rather ironic, given the lack of investment in many sectors in the interwar years and the dilapidated state of much of the coal, iron and steel, and railway infrastructure in particular. The total payment has been estimated at just under £2.6 billion (ibid.: 48) and for most nationalizations was based on the principle of paying a total price that would give shareholders a yield just above the average for a given period prior to nationalization.[8] The general consensus at the time, even among the Tory press and the business sector, was that these figures were extraordinarily generous. As *The Economist* put it, following the publication of the terms relating to Bank of England nationalization: 'It would take a very nervous heart to register a flutter at what is contained in the bill. Nothing could be more moderate' (ibid.: 48).

Even with the benefit of hindsight, and accepting the government's concern to overcome resistance to implementing its programme, the payments still seem extraordinary given the vulnerable financial position that Britain found itself in at the end of the war. The country was virtually bankrupt in August 1945, and without warning the USA cancelled the wartime Lend Lease programme through which Britain had been able to service its war effort, replacing it with much tougher loan conditions which were also contingent on Britain continuing to meet its overseas and foreign military commitments in support of US foreign policy.[9] In short, the country could ill afford to be generous to the very class of people that had overseen its economic decline. Not only did the private owners escape responsibility for the costs of reinvestment in industries that had been neglected for decades,[10] but nationalization actually boosted their capital by converting decaying and depreciating industrial stock into highly liquid government bonds.

Secondly, the relations between the newly nationalized industries and the private sector were somewhat one-sided. On the one hand the nationalized industries were to be 'self-sufficient' (i.e. not allowed to run up huge debts over a given period) and on the other they were to provide cheap services to their consumers by not being able to set their own prices. In effect, and despite the rhetoric of commercial freedom independent of political interests, nationalized industries were denied two of the most important characteristics of commercial companies operating in market economies: being able to set their own prices and being able to borrow funds for investment from the capital markets. From the outset therefore they were operating in a severely compromised manner; unable to set their own agendas and firmly tied to the needs of the private sector (Fine and Harris 1985).

They were particularly constrained in their ability to finance new investment and yet they inherited infrastructure after the war that was badly in need of repair and in many cases – such as the railways and the mines – in need of a complete overhaul (Saville 1993a). The result of this and other restrictions placed upon them by Conservative governments in the 1950s and 1960s – such as preventing the National Coal Board's excellent research department from commercially exploiting any of the large volume of new mining equipment it produced (ibid.) – was that by the early 1970s the nationalized industries were running at a massive loss compared to the private sector. This has been attributed in particular to the low and unrealistic pricing policy put in place in 1945 and continued through the 1950s and 1960s (ibid.; Armstrong et al. 1991; Glyn and Sutcliffe 1972; Hughes 1960). While various governments did put considerable public resources into the nationalized industries, this was always for short-term fixes rather than for longer-term strategic and modernization efforts; a trend that was common to Conservative and Labour governments and continued into the 1980s (Fine and Harris 1985).

The history of British nationalization between the 1940s and the 1980s shows that, far from remaining 'hands off', governments constantly interfered with the running of the state-owned sector, particularly in relation to broader macroeconomic objectives such as addressing public sector and trade deficits and maintaining the value of sterling (Fine and O'Donnell 1985; Fine 1989). This was notable in the late 1960s during Harold Wilson's Labour government when important strategic investments in coal and rail industries were delayed to keep the budget deficit low and protect the position of sterling in international currency markets (Fine and O'Donnell 1985). To provide another example, in the early 1980s Margaret Thatcher delayed the proposed privatization of the British National Oil Corporation (BNOC) because of similar concerns about the weakness of the UK's trading position and the boon to Treasury coffers provided by North Sea oil and gas exports.

In effect, the nationalized industries, in their varying ways, provided large and continuous subsidies to the private sector while being severely constrained in their own operations. Even in the National Health Service, the most revolutionary and successful legacy of the 1945–51 government, opportunities remained for the private sector, through, for example, the continued agreement that consultants could undertake non-NHS work, and the continued monopoly of drug manufacture by the private sector, albeit with increasing public subsidy (King's Fund 2003). In the economy as a whole, the private sector returned a healthy profit throughout the 1950s and 1960s while the nationalized industries ran at a considerable loss (Saville 1993a; Glyn and Sutcliffe 1972). Ben Fine's summary of the relationship between the nationalized industries and the rest of the capitalist economy remains apposite:

> The major nationalisations that took place in the UK after the Second World War were the consequence of an erosion, partly during the war itself but over a longer period, of effective capitalist command of the industries concerned ... The subsequent history of these industries has been one of restoration of directly capitalistic forms of organisations and command, most noticeably in the increasing imposition of commercial criteria, but ranging across all of the other aspects as well. (Fine 1989: 229)

It should also be added that the constraints placed upon their operation by successive governments meant that they were being judged on capitalist criteria, particularly with regard to reducing costs, making efficiencies and returning to profit, but not being given the tools (through borrowing powers or the ability to undertake long-term strategic planning) to compete with the private sector. This made the nationalized corporations effective sinks that could disguise the poor performance (in terms of productivity and investment) of the wider British economy, which, on most measures, compared unfavourably with competitors such as Japan, the United States, Germany and France during this period (Williams et al. 1983; Fine and Harris 1985). Subsequently, the nationalized industries became the scapegoat for the wider deterioration of the British economy in an increasingly competitive world market and became easy targets for the resurgent right's broader attack on the role of the state in the economy.

A final word here needs to be said regarding the economic geography of the nationalized industries. The nationalization of the electricity, gas and other utilities resulted in the centralization of many activities that had formerly been locally or municipally owned and subject to a reasonable degree of local democratic control. One of the effects of nationalization as centralization was to significantly weaken the power and authority of local government vis-à-vis the national government to an extent far greater than in most other advanced countries. In his authoritative account of the effects of nationalization, Saville also notes how the national managements of the different nationalized entities gradually exerted more control over local and regional managements, so that power and decision-making became more centralized and driven by London-based bureaucracies, commercial and financial interests and metropolitan bias, overshadowing the regions. Not only did this eviscerate important traditions of municipal socialism and more democratic forms of public ownership, but it also led to an increasing number of costly and unaccountable decisions (notably the decision to invest in nuclear power) by nationalized entities. Strategic decisions regarding the country's economic interests were made without even a semblance of public debate and reflected the capture by particular fractions of the political elite: 'The lack of democratic controls meant little public, municipal or even parliamentary scrutiny of the activity of corporations; the colossal expenditures on the Magnox and AGR nuclear reactor systems were pushed through with virtually no proper debate with military considerations in mind' (Saville 1993a: 57).

But it also reinforced a growing 'spatial division of labour' (Massey 1984) within the UK that was already developing in the private sector with the concentration of corporate ownership in the south and east, particularly within the growing shift of headquarters and research and development activity to London, and the growing peripheralization of other regions from economic decision-making. Moreover, the geographical concentration of many of the nationalized industries – especially steel, coal and shipbuilding in old industrial regions such as the north-east of England, South Wales and west central Scotland – meant that the effects of this arrested modernization process were deeply felt through subsequent mass job losses and the destruction of communities – in particular places. In the north of England, for example, the publicly owned National Coal Board presided over a reduction in employment from 180,000 in 1952 to 49,000 by 1975 (Hudson 2000: 40–1). The victory of the Thatcher government over the miners in the pivotal 1984/85 strike, and the virtual destruction of the industry in its aftermath, was arguably made possible partly by the continued state ownership of the sector and the preceding rationalization process.

In short, the manner in which the nationalization programme evolved over time did little to challenge the existing unbalanced political economy of the UK and even accentuated such imbalances. Particularly important, given the broader themes of the book, was the evidence that state ownership did little to change the underlying power relations of the nationalized industries, and if anything had served to reinforce them. This was a significant missed opportunity for the British left which, however subsequent events might have turned out, had been presented with the opportunity to fundamentally remake the social relations underpinning the British economy in 1945. Its failure even to modernize British capitalism through effective planning and strategic management of the nationalized industries in the early post-war years (Fine 1989) meant financial and multinational interests were able to reassert themselves with new vigour from the early 1960s onwards as the global economy became increasingly integrated and the long-term structural problems of British industry mounted.

By the 1970s most critical observers viewed the nationalized industries as a subset of wider British malaise, characterized by inefficient management, a lack of significant capital investment and poor productivity performance (e.g. Williams et al. 1983). In its own terms, of significantly modernizing the British economy, the nationalization programme failed to live up to the hopes and aspirations of the more progressive elements of the 1945 Labour government. When nationalization was then used by both Labour and Conservative governments in the 1970s as a last resort to bail out failing private companies such as Rolls-Royce, British Leyland and the British shipbuilding industry (Fine and O'Donnell 1985) on the grounds that they were too strategically important to the economy to fail, it became associated with 'lame duck' industries, adding further grist to the mill of the free market right.

Nationalization elsewhere in the developed industrial economies

Beyond the UK, nationalization in the post-1945 era varied considerably, but on the whole enjoyed a more positive role in national economic development and in the public imagination. Outside the United States, where, with the death of Roosevelt and his support for a 'mixed economy', the post-war years reinforced a strong ideological resistance among the political and business classes to anything that had the faintest whiff of socialistic or communist forms of economic organization,[11] nationalization programmes elsewhere in the 'developed' economies played a pivotal role in reconstruction and modernization, particularly in western Europe.

Nationalization as state modernization in France Of all the other western European countries, France was the most comparable to the UK in experiencing a similar nationalization wave from 1945 onwards, but the political and economic forces were very different. Much of the French business class was ostracized at the end of the war because of its associations with fascism,[12] whereas socialists and communists were in the ascendant. Even on the political right, figures such as the wartime resistance leader Charles de Gaulle had called for the nationalization of the country's assets, including the banks, as part of the economic and social agenda of liberation. Nationalization played a fundamental role in changing the economic structure of France, with the largest banks and insurance companies also taken into public ownership in stark contrast to the UK, where finance capital (outside the Bank of England) remained untouched.

As the largest party in the first post-war election, the communists in particular exerted considerable influence in the development of the nationalized industries. Although by the late 1940s they were increasingly excluded by more centrist and social democrat politicians, communist-backed trade unionists from the CGT federation played an important role in the formulation of national economic policies in the critical period 1945 to 1947 and in the form that the nationalization process took (Sturmthal 1952; Bliss 1954). In their initial structures there was a greater commitment to the participation of diverse interest groups than in the UK. To give a few examples, the boards of the newly nationalized electricity and gas companies were composed of four members representing the state, four from technical and expert groups (two to represent the consumer interest), and four from the trade unions (Bliss 1954). Workers' representatives accounted for four out of twelve of the board members of the banks and one out of five of the committee to control the financial sector; in Renault it was six out of fifteen whereas in SNCAM, the aeronautical firm based in Toulouse, it was three out of eleven (Sturmthal 1952). According to

Sturmthal, the strength of the trade unions was such that they were able to subvert the principle of pluralism by having their members elected as consumer representatives. For example, in the case of the coal mining corporation, Charbonnages de France, they had fourteen out of eighteen members.

Although the democratic character of the French nationalization programme turned out to be rather superficial, the relationship between the nationalized industries and the rest of the economy was fundamentally different to that in the UK. A new technocratic political elite – epitomized by Jean Monnet, the architect of the European Union, but also appointed by De Gaulle in 1949 as the commissioner in control of planning – was concerned with the relative backwardness of the French economy in relation to its competitors and the subsequent imperative to modernize and industrialize. This involved a vision that fused state intervention, social progress and economic efficiency, although in the context of a relatively open economy and growing international trade: hence the commitment to the European project, which was perhaps the biggest departure from the protectionist political economy of the interwar years. This new elite coalesced around a determined programme of 'social compromise and more general public intervention congruent with the new "Keynesian and Fordist" mode of development' (Boyer 1987: 34). Subsequently, the setting of targets for particular sectors, and the close coordinating through central planning of industrial output, were critical to French economic growth and productivity improvements through the 1950s and 1960s (Armstrong et al. 1991). While the French nationalized utilities were subject to price controls similar to those of their British counterparts, the state control of banks and the existence of more effective planning boards for each industry meant a more thoroughgoing commitment to modernization could be backed by sustained financial investment. The success of Renault in producing popular, innovative and efficient models up to the 1970s – such as the CV2, Dauphine, Renault 4, 5 and 8 – in contrast to the faltering performance of its fragmented British private counterparts, showed what an efficient centralized model of public ownership could deliver in the most consumer-driven of industries (Chang 2007).

When France was faced with severe economic problems by the late 1970s, the narrative around the nationalized industries was very different to that in the UK; they were seen as part of the policy solution rather than a major source of the problem as they became depicted in the UK (possibly because of the continuing commitment of the right in France to state intervention). When the first left government, after twenty-three years of right and centre-right rule, was elected under François Mitterrand's coalition of socialists and communists in 1981, it included in its manifesto a commitment to a massive new nationalization programme as part of its mission to transform French society along more socialist and egalitarian lines (Ross 1987). Immediately on assuming office, the government nationalized thirty-six private banks, two finance companies and eleven industrial conglomerates (Hall 1987: 63). These included high-tech and emerging industries as well as mature ones,[13] in contrast to the British 'lame ducks' nationalization programme in the 1970s.

As is well documented elsewhere (e.g. Ross et al. 1987), Mitterrand's administration soon ran into problems, but there are strong arguments that these reflected the wider global economic climate, particularly growing international competition, the oil price shocks and the shift elsewhere (particularly in the USA and the UK) towards more austere economic policy retrenchment. In these circumstances, the hope among many on the left that nationalization would presage greater economic democracy, reforms of the employment relations system and the pursuit of more social goals were quickly dashed (Ross 1987; Moss 1988). Instead, the newly nationalized industries were 'effectively restructured' (Hall 1987: 64) along capitalistic lines with considerable rationalization and job losses, to the extent that all but one were restored to profitability by 1985 (ibid.). Subsequently, most of these industries were returned to the private sector during the 1990s, to such an extent that the use of state resources allowed most of them to regain profitability and develop their position in international markets.

Despite the caveats outlined above, the reversals faced by the Mitterrand government provided ammunition for those seeking to discredit 'socialism in one country' in the context of economic globalization, and presaged the acceptance by many on the left (not least subsequent French socialist governments!) of the neoliberal agenda in the 1990s (see Chapter 4). For both the new right and the 'Third Way' centre-left the experience became the textbook example of the supposed powerlessness of the state in the face of globalizing tendencies in the economy (e.g. Muet 1985; Ohmae 1990). However, as Glyn (1995) has pointed out, the French socialists' rapid retreat from their manifesto pledges had little to do with these globalization forces per se, but more to do with the particular problems the French economy faced from rising unemployment, the broader European recession (given that with European integration, other European countries accounted for most of France's export markets) and a severe inflation problem.

Nationalization and economic democracy in other northern European economies In Germany, nationalization policies were more limited than in either the UK or France, largely because of the influence of the post-war US and UK occupying authorities, which, for understandable military reasons, were opposed to the large-scale re-establishment of German industry in a centralized form, while at the same time being ideologically opposed to public ownership. The British trade union delegation to occupied Germany did not have its finest hour in supporting its own government's foreign policy to frustrate more radical local trade union agendas (Armstrong et al. 1991). This was in the face of a broad consensus among the German political parties at the end of the war – even the Christian Democrats (CDU) – regarding the need to socialize the economy and avoid repeating the mistakes of the unfettered capitalism that was held responsible for the country's pre-war economic crisis and the subsequent emergence of fascism.[14] Continuing divisions within the trade unions between more radical communist and moderate elements allowed the occupying forces to divide and rule; for example, frustrating attempts by some regions, most notably the largest in population terms, Nord-Rhein-Westfalen, to set up radical constitutions involving economic democracy and public ownership (ibid.).

As Cold War conditions intensified, and the fears of statism and socialism were used by moderate elements within the trade unions and Social Democratic Party to isolate the left, the Christian Democrats – after their brief flirtation with public ownership – were able to successfully reassert the principles of private ownership and markets in Finance Minister Ludwig Erhard's 'social market economy', which took precedence in the west, particularly in the face of Stalinism in the east (Schneider 1991). By 1959, with its Bad Godesberg Declaration, the Social Democratic Party also largely abandoned its commitment to nationalization as a policy goal (Hodgson 1999). Nevertheless, West German capitalism was transformed from the pre-war model by the decapitation of the political elite. As Anderson has put it:

> ... the fall of the Third Reich ... took down with it so great a part of the elites that had colluded with Hitler. The loss of East Prussia and Silesia, and the creation of the DDR, destroyed the bulk of the aristocratic class that had continued to loom large, not least in its domination of

the armed forces, during the Weimar Republic. The industrial dynasties of the Ruhr were decapitated, Krupp, Thyssen and Stinnes never recovering their former positions ... collective identity and power were decisively weakened. West Germany, bourgeois enough by any measure, felt relatively classless. (Anderson 2009: 22)

In these circumstances, the trade unions were able to assert themselves in other ways. Continued grassroots militancy and successive waves of strike activity in the late 1940s and early 1950s, for example, forced some important concessions from employers and the state in the broader area of economic democracy, especially with the rights of workers to co-determination in certain key industries and statutory recognition within large corporations of the role of the works council. This was broadened in 1976 to include all firms with over two thousand employees. Although union membership levels and influence in the economy have declined since the late 1980s, they remain a strong social partner in a continuing albeit fragmenting corporate system, while there remains in the population at large a sizeable majority who view Anglo-American-style capitalism and inequality as unacceptable moral norms (ibid.).

In other countries labour movements and social democratic parties were also effective in shaping the emergence of post-war state–economy relations, so that economic democracy and nationalization also became central to national economic development agendas. An important though seldom discussed case is Austria, which achieved one of the most impressive growth rates of any European economy between 1945 and 1987 and was second only to Japan in terms of the industrialized nations (Chang 2009). What is significant for our purposes here is the role of state-owned enterprises (SOEs) in achieving this growth (ibid.). Chang estimates that by the late 1970s Austria had the largest SOE sector in the OECD measured as a proportion of GDP; equivalent to 14.5 per cent in 1978/79, compared to around 13 per cent in France and 11.3 per cent in the UK (ibid.: 11). Like France, Austria also had a sizeable number of state-owned banks and investment funds to promote longer-term industrial development programmes. The other European economies associated with more 'social democratic' models of post-war economic success are the Nordic countries, although here it is difficult to find a common pattern in relation to nationalization and public ownership. Finland, Norway and Sweden all had traditions from the late nineteenth century onwards of state-owned enterprises being involved in the development of natural resources, but none experienced widespread nationalization programmes after 1945. In Sweden, a militant labour movement in the 1920s and 1930s was successful in forcing the private employers into a 'social pact' – the Saltsjobaden Agreement of 1938 – by which workers' representatives were given economic rights, both as social partners at the national level, and as members of boards within individual corporations, in return for allowing private ownership to persist and have control of strategic decision-making within corporations. Denmark, like Sweden, did not undergo a mass programme of nationalization after 1945, but arguably the Danish economy had a much longer-standing degree of economic democracy through a decentralized and associational model of development and a large number of cooperative enterprises in the economy (see Chapter 9). Norway, which we explore further in Chapter 8, had a strong tradition of state intervention and partnership deals with foreign companies that went back to the end of the nineteenth century, which was aimed at building up indigenous knowledge and expertise. Although many of the utilities were in state hands, nationalization policies were restricted elsewhere to particular strategic sectors such as oil in the 1960s.

The experience of state ownership under communist regimes[15]

In both the Soviet Union (after 1917) and China (after 1949), forms of state ownership were introduced following communist-inspired revolutions. Market mechanisms were also replaced by central planning, although in the Soviet Union Lenin had initially been pragmatic regarding the continued operation of markets and the private sector in some areas. While both systems have been the subject of considerable critique, and ideologically inspired assaults and post hoc dismissals by pro-Western and pro-market economists, it is important for us here to draw up a more sober critical assessment of the strengths and weaknesses of state ownership.

In the Soviet Union from the 1920s onwards both the agricultural and industrial sectors were brought under state control, often with considerable repression of particular social groups. Notably, the class of wealthier farmers, the kulaks, were effectively exterminated by Stalin's purges during the 1930s as part of the push towards the collectivization of agriculture. The number that were executed, died of starvation, or were sent to labour camps, is still a matter of dispute, and complicated by the effects of the great rural famines of the 1930s, but the total was almost certainly more than two million (Conquest 1986).

Contrary to popular perceptions, however, private property (in the sense of personal belongings) per se was not abolished, but 'capital' in the sense of the 'means of production' was brought into full collective ownership. Although most enterprises were state-owned, there were also some small cooperative associations in areas such as housing and in the sphere of consumption. However, in both the Soviet Union and China centralized state ownership became the predominant form of economic organization. The problem of resource allocation, which is at the heart of any economic system, and left to the market under capitalism, was resolved by the introduction of central planning. At the macro scale, both the Soviet and Chinese economies worked through a system of five-year plans with the setting of targets for industrial and agricultural output. Planning was introduced at lower scales into all sectors of economic life, one of the effects of which was to create massive bureaucracies charged with administering and monitoring 'the plan'.

As most critical observers now recognize, the effect of these communist 'revolutions' was to replace exploitation of workers by capitalists with an elite of communist party and state officials, referred to variously as 'bureaucratic centralisation' (Mandel 1986: 10) or 'authoritarian statism' (Wright 2010: 133). Resnick and Wolff (1994) consider these systems as forms of state capitalism on the basis that the situation of an appropriation of the surplus value from the direct producers by elite interests remains unchanged, and therefore the basic Marxist concepts of alienation and exploitation of labour also continue. What is clear from the experiences of these systems is that the combination of a one-party state, central planning and state ownership creates entrenched power hierarchies. However, as Nove (1983) points out, the excessive bureaucratization, inefficiencies and underperfomance that result are not the fault of public ownership per se, but rather the condensing of all economic activity into one system of central planning and into one monolithic form of ownership. The result is a system that is inflexible to changing economic circumstances, unable to sufficiently address consumer or user demands, and completely inadequate for taking into account diverse local conditions and circumstances (see also Chapter 3).

In both the Soviet Union and eastern Europe, the construction of vast state enterprises in particular sectors allied to the unwieldy system of planning created gross inefficiencies, waste and shortages (ibid.). It also did not eliminate business cycles but in many ways inflated fluctuations in the economy because of the delay with which economic shortages and deficiencies in one area of the economy could be addressed by shifting resources from elsewhere. A lack of knowledge and uncertainty about the operating conditions in the 'real' economy meant that central planners, however well intentioned, could make gross miscalculations about actual needs, leading to periods of dramatic over-investment in particular areas. Massive investment programmes to deal with future aspirations or needs could lead also to chronic shortages in the present, typified by Stalin's disastrous redirection of resources from agriculture to industry in the 1930s, but also present in Poland in the early 1970s and Hungary in the 1950s, which generated economic and political crises in both cases (ibid.: 92). Nove also cites the example of the Soviet chemical industry under Khrushchev in the 1950s. Belated recognition of the backwardness of the sector in providing important products such as fertilizers and plastics led to a massive campaign by Khrushchev to modernize the sector, but the scale of ambition was not matched either by the availability of trained staff or equipment, most of which had to be imported (ibid.: 96).

Other problems with the state socialist models resulted from decisions on broader macroeconomic questions over the allocation of resources, which inevitably led to conflicts between different sectional interests, with 'political pull' often being the decisive factor rather than any economic or social allocation of resources. Prestige projects in the military or high-tech areas could often take precedence over more mundane, but useful in an everyday sense, technical innovation. Nove cites a story from one Soviet newspaper of an inventor who had designed an efficient buttonholing machine for the clothing industry who was met with the official response: 'In an age of Sputniks, you come along with a button-holing machine' (ibid.: 93).

There was also no semblance of economic democracy in the state-owned enterprises. Although there were often formal elections, the tight control of managerial and administrative appointments in state enterprises by the party machine meant that ordinary workers had little voice in decision-making while trade unions were state controlled. This did not mean that workers' interests were not represented, but they were always secondary to the overall economic plan and strategy (ibid.). Workers could also exercise considerable economic power. In tight labour market conditions and with the relaxation of freedom of movement by the late 1950s, management's control over the labour process was often severely constrained. As Nove put it: 'The Soviet state may be a monopoly-employer but the state is for practical purposes a large number of separate units which compete with each other for labour. Influence from below, though unorganised, is therefore greater than it might appear' (ibid.: 83).

Some of the greatest problems arose in the agricultural sector, where the collective ownership of farms removed many of the incentive structures for peasants that existed under private ownership for productivity improvements and proper environmental husbandry. Additionally, under Stalin in the 1930s, the lack of freedom of movement effectively meant a new form of serfdom (ibid.).

Nevertheless, and despite all the problems, it is important to stress that forms of central planning and state ownership can be appropriate in particular sectors, especially those that are less concerned with quality and nature of output than with the right quantities of production (e.g. producing energy or steel). If there are centrally determined priorities, state ownership and planning can deliver much more efficient solutions in some cases than market-driven ones. Nove notes that in the Soviet Union sectors such as defence, oil and steel were relatively efficient in relation to Western capitalist standards. The Soviet Union did particularly well in its energy planning – although not based on any environmental considerations. Nevertheless, as Nove argues, Soviet planners in the 1980s were just as well equipped to make decisions about long-term energy needs and trends, when faced with the uncertainties of oil markets and prices, as those in Western multinational companies. Indeed, the energy and electricity sectors in particular are ones where planning and central coordination hold a distinct advantage over market-based forms. As Nove noted in his analysis of the Soviet economy:

> Electricity can also serve as a good example of 'planability'. It presents no product-mix problems (KWH are KWH are KWH), power-stations on a grid can be centrally controlled from a single control panel, and the information about need, now and in the future, is best assessed at the centre (and not only in Soviet-type economies!). In the planning of fuel and energy the USSR does well. A long view can be taken of this high-priority sector, and the necessary investments accordingly determined. Our own market-orientated economies accommodate themselves badly to supply shortages, for instance of oil. The USSR has responded to its own energy problem by massive efforts to develop oil and gas in Siberia, efforts which have achieved marked success in the face of formidable natural obstacles. The USSR's irrational prices matter little when decisions are taken which relate to energy supply in (say) 1990; none of us know what will be the prices and costs in 1990, and we must proceed on best estimates of future demand and supply largely in quantitative terms, which the Soviet central planners can estimate at least as well as, probably better than, any Western capitalist oilman. (Nove 1980: 5)

Of course, both Soviet and Chinese systems – in the case of the latter, both before and after the transition to capitalism – do not have the problem of dealing with the electoral cycle and can therefore commit to long-term investment and strategic decision-making. Overall, however, the basic problem with them is the centralization of power and decision-making within self-perpetuating oligarchies which dominates economic and social life. Even apart from the democratic deficit, this has perverse effects on the potential for the kinds of grassroots innovation that are essential to the health of any economy, while frustrating the development of alternative and deliberative forms of knowledge construction through a culture of conformity and the protection of vested interests. In the 1980s, while the Soviet system collapsed, the Chinese reformed through what Harvey (2005) has termed 'neoliberalism with Chinese characteristics'; in other words a freeing up of the economy, including the gradual relaxation of price controls, the introduction of private enterprise and foreign investment, though still with the attempt at strong central political control (Nolan 1995, 2001).

Eastern Europe after 1945 experienced some interesting variations from the centralized Soviet model. Hungary in particular attempted to decentralize economic decision-making power from the late 1950s onwards, and after 1968 introduced some modified market forms with relaxation of price controls and greater decentralization and autonomy for collective-owned enterprises and farms (Nove 1983). A relatively successful decentralization of finance also occurred through the setting up of investment banks which supplied credit to firms. Although there was little economic democracy, with no involvement of workers in management and decision-making, the reforms were judged a relative success in creating more autonomy, improving efficiency and going beyond the worst problems of central planning (see Kornai 1979). The reforms also allowed forms of cooperative and small-scale private ownership that injected some limited competition and innovation into the system.

Yugoslavia is the other interesting departure from the Soviet model through its decentralized form of public ownership based on self-managed worker enterprises or 'social ownership' (Estrin 1991). Having broken politically with the Soviet Union in 1948, Yugoslavian communism under Tito embarked on a different economic road from 1952 onwards with the shift from a centrally planned model to a more horizontalist structure based on worker enterprises within a market economy that was also open to international trade (Estrin 1983, 1991; Nove 1983). Under this scheme firms were self-managed by the workforce but without ownership rights, which remained with the state. As Estrin notes, the basic principle was that workers should have a say in economic decision-making, achieved largely through workers' councils, which had the authority to appoint managers, though often from an approved list. Nevertheless, there was what Estrin describes as 'a real degree of effective autonomy and decision-making power absent in other socialist economies' (1991: 189) with workers having considerable power over employment decisions, pay and welfare benefits.

While the Yugoslavian economy performed relatively well up until the late 1970s, averaging growth rates at 6 per cent per annum, which matched France and Germany – and were well ahead of the UK – for the same period, it suffered badly in the deteriorating international economic conditions thereafter. The country developed an increasing balance-of-trade deficit while its decentralized economic system, allied to its federated political system, meant that there was little effective central macroeconomic policy coordination to adjust to changing conditions. The absence of ownership rights for workers and managers also tended to encourage short-termism because there was little incentive to invest for the longer term (Nove 1983; Estrin 1991). The absence of a strong central authority allied to internal uneven development between the richer northern and western regions against the poorer southern and eastern ones and the resurgence of ethnic tensions created a tragically explosive mix. In general, the country's decentralized model of public ownership tended to encourage the development of vested and special interests and often a lack of coordination between the different republics, with a steady erosion of a commitment to a general interest. Nevertheless, as with the other state socialist models, this does not necessarily invalidate worker self-management as a policy option among a more diversified set of public ownership options. Rather it points to the need to have a balance between decentralized forms of ownership with some central coordinating bodies.

State-owned enterprises and developmentalism in the East Asian miracle

One of the ironies of the post-war period is that it was the anti-communist East Asian 'tiger' economies, under the US geopolitical orbit during the Cold War, that had some of the most positive experiences of state ownership. While Japan's dramatic post-war growth was achieved largely through the development of private corporations, albeit with a strong state-led industrialization strategy, Korea, Taiwan and Singapore all used state-owned enterprises to fuel spectacular economic growth (Chang 2006). Taiwan's industrial strategy in particular was state-dominated with nationalized entities playing the lead in all upstream sectors (ibid.). Singapore too, while not usually considered a hotbed of state ownership (but rather an authoritarian capitalist success story), actually has a vast number of state-owned or part-state-owned enterprises across a diverse range of sectors (Chang 2007), either through the state holding company, Temasek, or through government statutory boards in areas such as housing and the utilities. One of the world's leading airlines in terms of customer satisfaction, Singapore Airlines, is wholly owned by the government's Ministry of Finance, while a 1993 report suggested that as much as 60 per cent of the country's GDP was accounted for by the public sector (ibid.).

Korea, which has a lower share of state ownership than both Taiwan and Singapore, had both a system of five-year plans from 1961 onwards (Amsden 1989; Wade 1990) with a nationalized banking system and a financial sector tightly controlled by the government, able to provide long-term funds for industrial development. These were critical factors in the country's rapid industrialization, and the shift from a per capita income of $82 in 1961, which was half that of Ghana and Honduras at the time, to $12,020 by 2003 (twelve times that of Honduras and forty times that of Ghana) (Chang 2006). One of its most successful companies, POSCO (Pohang Steel Company), was set up as a state-owned company in 1968 – having failed to get World Bank funding – with the support of Japanese banks and technology transfer from Nippon Steel (Chang 2007). Within two decades it was the most efficient steel maker in the world (ibid.). Although Korean banks were largely privatized in the 1980s, the state retained some measure of control to ensure that their activities were channelled towards productive investment rather than financial speculation (Vartainen 1995).

While the East Asian economies exhibit all the deficiencies in democracy that characterized Soviet and Chinese experiences, at the same time they do demonstrate that state-owned enterprises can be just as effective in fostering economic development as privately owned ones, and as competitive over the longer term. The important factors behind their success seem to mirror the French experience, with clear planning objectives and criteria, and access to 'patient' financial capital, alongside a commitment to export markets plus an openness to new technology and best practice from overseas (Chang 2006). Vartainen (1995) advances the interesting proposition that state planning in the post-war period was more successful under moderate capitalist regimes than those with left governments, and in particular in the East Asian economies, where private ownership and business did not feel threatened but often collaborated with state modernization agendas. 'Late industrializers', in particular before 1970, were characterized by active state planning and management. Vartainen actually talks of a Nordic–East Asian model of industrial policy to highlight the parallels between recent Asian 'tiger' economy models and those of Nordic countries in the late nineteenth and early twentieth centuries. In both cases, rather than being concerned with issues of market efficiency and competitive conditions beloved of the neoclassical economic model, economic policy has been concerned with the 'productive efficiency of industries' (ibid.: 155) – often encouraging greater concentration and oligopoly rather than the neoclassical pursuit of welfare-maximizing outcomes through perfect competition across an entire economy.

Evaluating the legacy of state-centred public ownership

How can one sum up this vast and diverse legacy of state ownership that held sway over much of the world between 1945 and 1980? One obvious point is that it has been applied to different and often opposing political ideologies, both associated with forms of capitalist modernization and development, as well as with the nominally socialist projects of the Soviet bloc and China between 1917 and 1989. A second point is that, contrary to the current received wisdom, the experience and performance of statist public ownership was highly varied. In the UK, nationalization failed on two counts; first as a project of capitalist modernization, and secondly as the more radical agenda for social change that many on the left had aspired to. But this experience can be assessed only in the context of the ongoing evolution of British political economy and the continuing strength of powerful and vested financial and corporate interests alongside the lack of a coherent plan or evaluation criteria by which to drive forward and assess the nationalization process.

Elsewhere, however, state ownership in many countries was an important part of economic modernization agendas. In countries as diverse as France, Norway, Singapore and Korea, nationalization, allied to broader state intervention, led to sustained economic growth, improved living standards for the vast majority of the population, and massive improvements in productivity and economic efficiency up to the late 1970s. In many countries nationalization of the basic utilities brought cheap and affordable energy and decent water supplies and medical services to the mass of people for the first time in history. In the Soviet Union, many of the problems with the country's economic model were caused by an unwieldy system of centralized planning rather than public ownership. At the same time, in some sectors, state ownership actually helped to improve efficiency, deliver services and organize economic sectors on a large scale, with performance equal to or better than comparative experiences in privately owned sectors in the capitalist West (Nove 1983).

One element of the British experience that was shared more or less universally elsewhere was a growing democratic deficit as state projects became captured by dominant interests and increasingly removed from both the workers in state enterprises and the broader public. These nationalizations – with the possible exception of the Yugoslav model of self-management – failed to deliver the Marxist aspiration of giving the 'associated producers' the fruits of their labours. As we have seen, there was progress in the development of co-determination principles in many European countries, both inside state-owned corporations and in the private economy, but there were few examples of a shifting economic culture and practice in more progressive directions.

A common theme in this respect, across the diverse contexts described, was the link between public ownership and state-driven projects of national economic development which, in some cases, were about building a national consciousness and identity around dominant ideologies and centralizing tendencies at the behest of existing and more localized sets of economic relations and practices. In the process many older forms of collective and mutual ownership were extinguished, sometimes violently in the case of modernizing projects in the Soviet Union, China and many developing economies, but in other cases – such as the UK and France – through democratic processes which had the similar effect of eliminating local and municipally owned organizations.

With the economic crisis of the 1970s, such state projects gradually became discredited, so that by the early 1980s the idea of any kind of centrally planned form of economic development was everywhere in retreat, in terms of both macroeconomic intervention and regulation and of direct ownership and management of companies. For its perceived, rather than actual, failings – given the mixed historical record outlined above – and scorned by both the radical left and the new right for its undemocratic, hierarchical and bureaucratic nature, the centralized model of public ownership was under attack. The caricaturing of state ownership as a step on the 'road to serfdom' – in the words of Hayek – provided considerable grist to the mill for the ascendant neoliberal discourse. Although the left had its own critique and proposals for more decentralized and worker-centred forms of ownership, these were largely ignored by the political mainstream as the centre of gravity shifted rightwards.

2 | The neoliberal onslaught and the politics of privatization

Privatization, as the process of transferring public resources and assets to private ownership and control, has become one of the key instruments of global economic policy-making since 1980. It has been part of a broader assault by big business and its political supporters – commonly referred to as neoliberalism – on the state, and through it the gains made by labour parties and trade unions on behalf of the working classes in the 1945–79 period. Privatization, like neoliberalism, has mutated over time to the extent that the rationale and manner in which privatization policies have been justified and taken forward have changed and adapted to particular circumstances, not least its own contradictions. However, there has been an underlying set of dynamics that can be explained in part through Marx's term 'primitive accumulation' or what David Harvey has creatively and more recently referred to as 'accumulation by dispossession' (Harvey 2003). As a policy, privatization started in the 'heartland' of liberal capitalism – the United Kingdom under Margaret Thatcher in the 1980s – but it was soon adapted as a key policy plank of the International Monetary Fund and World Bank's economic governance agenda, subsequently referred to as the 'Washington Consensus'.

Many mainstream economists – particularly in regard to the way it is implemented in Third World or 'market transition economies' – tend to present privatization as free of normative considerations but somehow concerned only with securing more efficient outcomes. Privatization is part of a package to create more efficient market mechanisms to take the place of what are seen as inefficient state bureaucracies, corruption and restrictive institutions. Not only are such accounts blind to the underlying political and social processes that drive privatization, but they also tend to accept a rather simplified account of how economies work and develop over time, taking for granted the role that markets and private ownership should play.

In this chapter I use a different approach, drawing upon a political economy perspective to place privatization in a broader and more critical frame, viewing it first and foremost as a political project that emerged out of a particular context: the economic downturn facing western Europe and North America in the 1970s, the subsequent political crisis and discussions of policy alternatives that resulted. Privatization and neoliberalism emerged out of a battle between competing visions as the approach favoured by pro-business interests in opposition to a radical agenda emerging on the left articulating a more democratic and participatory approach to the economy, especially the greater involvement of workers in corporate decision-making. Reflective of a wider struggle by capital to restore its 'right to manage' (Hall 2003), it reflected real fears that a much more socialistic approach to the economy would take root in the years ahead, including the fulfilment of more radical demands for the takeover of whole industries and firms to be run by and for workers and their trade unions.

Putting privatization in context: neoliberalism as a project to re-establish class control

Privatization is a multifaceted process involving the opening up or transferring of publicly owned and managed parts of the economy to private ownership, control and profit-seeking initiatives. It involves three key elements: the contracting out of public services (such as health, education and social care) to private firms; the use of private finance initiatives to build and run public services; and the transfer of state-owned enterprises to private ownership, or what Ben Fine earlier termed 'de-nationalisation' (Fine 1989, 1990). Given the focus of this book, our interest here is with this third element, which developed as a counter-attack to the perceived threat of public ownership and democratic control.

There is not the space or the need to explore neoliberalism in depth and there is helpfully a vast literature on the topic.[1] Instead I provide a brief overview, focusing particularly on its ideological and political basis as a class project, usefully depicted by Rowthorn in his description of Thatcherism as a '*counter*-revolution whose primary aim has always been to turn the clock back and reverse the tide of collectivism, which at one time seemed to be engulfing the country' (Rowthorn 1989: 283). Most commentators agree on what the basic precepts of neoliberalism are, with the three most important being the markets/competition couplet in producing efficient, well-functioning economies, the centrality of private ownership and legally enforceable property rights, and the importance of a free trade regime to eliminate inefficient producers and allow Ricardian laws of comparative advantage to shape the distribution of economic activity. The role of the state should be minimalist (though not absent) and should be concerned with providing the legal and regulatory framework to enforce and protect the operation of free markets, private property and free trade. Where necessary, state reforms should be introduced to enable capital, labour and land markets to function smoothly and without unnecessary interference (from government, trade unions or other social institutions).

Neoliberalism fuses two elements of right-wing economic thinking in constructing its arguments. First of all, an attack on Keynesian macroeconomic management and the dangers of such interventions in distorting markets and stoking inflation associated with a Chicago school of economists, most famously Milton Friedman. Their solution was the withdrawal of government intervention, the unleashing of market forces and policies to control the money supply and inflation, usually referred to as monetarism. A second set of arguments attacked at a deeper philosophical level the state and all forms of state intervention in the economy as a threat to freedom and individual liberties. Associated predominantly with the work of Friedrich Hayek, this approach also highlighted the limits of central planning and public ownership in the efficient running of the economy because of what he saw as the restrictions placed on entrepreneurialism, innovation and the dynamic evolution of economies.

We will engage further with Hayek's critique of planning in the next chapter, as he offers some important insights into the problems associated with top-down, over-centralized forms of public ownership. Critical for us here is the way that Hayek's political critique of statism and bureaucracy was linked to the economic policy agenda of markets and freedom (defined in rather negative terms as the private individual) in the neoliberal project. His insistence that private ownership and competition were preferable to planning and collective ownership because they delivered more efficient solutions to the problems of economic coordination was used to push an aggressive agenda of privatization in the first instance by Margaret Thatcher, although the Chicago school of economists had considerable influence in the slightly earlier (and disastrous) neoliberal experiment under Pinochet in Chile (Harvey 2005).

The 1970s crisis and another radical moment In retrospective accounts of neoliberalism, the politics of the 1970s and early 1980s are often reduced to the battle between a Keynesian social democratic 'big state' apparatus and an increasingly ascendant neoliberal free market discourse. But it is important to recognize that these were not the only political currents – or even the most dominant – abroad at the time. As well as the emergent critique from the Hayekian right, attacks on the social democratic post-1945 consensus also came from the left. One outcome of the radicalization of the 1968 generation was a questioning of the post-war order in North America and western Europe and the top-down and overbearing welfare state that had developed, seen by many as an over-centralized and increasingly undemocratic regime of state control and alienation where the unregulated market capitalism of the pre-war period was being superseded by a state-managed capitalism.

Various currents were developing among a broad 'new left', critical of both the social democratic state and the centralized version of socialism of the official Communist Party, both in western Europe and in the 'socialist' regimes of the Soviet bloc. Although this was a very fragmented set of ideas and platforms, composed of a plethora of grassroots movements and tendencies, from Trotskyite, to anarcho-syndicalist, to autonomous Marxist, to situationists, to more prosaic 'rank-and-file' tendencies, as well as the beginnings of a radical green movement in response to the emergent environmental limits to capitalist growth projects, they did collectively amount to a set of fertile and rigorous critiques of the status quo which found their way into mainstream political discourse. A concern with workplace politics and economic (or industrial) democracy rose high on the political agenda of many liberal democracies in both Europe and even North America, so that as late as 1980 the president of the United Autoworkers Union, Douglas Fraser, gained a seat on the board of Chrysler, one of the big three US auto manufacturers, proclaiming this as providing workers with 'a voice in the highest echelons' (Åsard 1982: 158) of the company. In 1979 an article in the US *Academy of Management Review* reflected the mood of the day when it confidently proclaimed that 'It is unlikely that the trend toward industrial democracy and participative management is "a passing fad"' and that 'Rights to income, health, and education will be seen as more important than property rights' (Bass and Shackleton 1979: 402).

While in the USA most elite opinion, including among the conservative and staid trade union leadership, remained hostile to an agenda of workplace democracy (Zwerdling 1980), the latter gained serious credibility in much of western Europe. Germany and the Nordic countries already had strong elements of co-determination (as noted in the previous chapter) through works councils and statutory requirements for worker-directors on the boards of large companies, but the 1970s saw demands for even more radical change that would allow workers to take greater ownership and control of the economy. In the UK, the Labour Party, on re-entering government in 1974, committed itself to a radical programme of both further nationalization and developing economic democracy legislation, going as far as to launch a Committee of Inquiry on Industrial Democracy (as it was referred to at the time), the Bullock Report. This advocated much greater participation of workers in the management of companies as a way of dealing with the UK's deteriorating employment relations during the period.

Among the measures that the Bullock majority report advocated – there was a minority report by some of the businessmen on the committee – was that there be worker-directors and that the company interest be rewritten to take into account employee as well as shareholder interests (Davies and Wedderburn 1977). One set of critical left commentators felt confident enough to predict that this shift towards worker empowerment was the state of things to come.

> The land in which industrial democracy is built may well be one where the old maps of 'unitary' and 'pluralist' models are inadequate. The reality of conflict between workpeople and capital will remain and the powers of workers organised in their trade unions seem likely to increase. But both extended strategic bargaining and participation in the institutions of the enterprise are likely to bring us into a new land – a new social transition – where novel institutions of conflictual partnership are developed. The duty to dare to imagine that development is painful but inescapable. (Ibid.: 211)

Given the militant atmosphere of the time, these proposals were taken seriously by the big business lobby, which feared the growing power of trade unions and their grassroots members. Although it is difficult to imagine some thirty-five years later – following globalization and the undermining of the labour movement generally – some kind of accommodation with organized labour was viewed as inevitable. The mood of the times is captured in a response to the Bullock Committee by a group of lawyers representing London's financial elites:

> The more people are able to influence decisions which closely affect their work the more effective will that involvement be; the more effective the involvement the greater the commitment to the company's objectives which, in the final analysis, will be concerned with generating wealth or services for the community as a whole. (CCLC 1977)

The Bullock Report was a fairly moderate document and – with shades of the post-1945 rationale behind nationalization – was informed more by the Labour government's desire to stabilize employment relations during a period of considerable workplace conflict. It imbued more of a spirit of partnership in the interests of improving productivity for the ailing British economy than anything more radical, but it did raise the spectre of greater worker involvement in corporate decision-making. Even this, however, would have been a historic break with the trajectory of the UK's political economy since the time of Adam Smith.

The demand for economic democracy was felt particularly keenly by those working in the nationalized industries, for whom one set of elite managers under the original 1940s nationalization had been replaced by another, and systems of labour control became more heavily bureaucratized and subject to management supervision.

> I can remember standing at the pit with the banners, celebrating with my father and his friends. They thought, this was it. What a surprise they were going to get. They thought nationalisation would bring everything they'd fought for. But within a very short space of time they found out that they'd swapped one boss for another. The first boss we got was a major from the Indian Army, six months later followed by Captain Nicholson ... Later we had a banker!
>
> We really believed it would make a difference. We really thought it was the beginning of socialism, you know, almost time to hoist the red flag. I thought that we'd be working for ourselves, that we'd be in control. But in fact the supervision and bureaucratic administration became a hundred times worse. You'd get 10 foremen where you only had one; you'd have to use 10 pieces of paper where before you'd only have one. You'd always have to go through many more channels to get anything done. That approach killed nationalisation. A lot of us felt really frustrated. Mind, I still think nationalisation is the only way, but next time it will have to be different. (Former coalminers discussing the 1940s nationalization in Beynon and Wainwright 1979: 180)

A more radical set of proposals was being articulated in the grass roots of the Labour Party with the publication of the Alternative Economic Strategy (AES) (London CSE Group 1980) and the movement for workers' control.[2] Initially developed by Labour Party subcommittees and prompted by dissatisfaction with the moderate stance of Labour governments in the 1960s and 1970s, the AES subsequently broadened to include the Communist Party, left-leaning labour MPs (the so-called Tribune group), the Cambridge Political Economy Group, the Conference of Socialist Economists, and some trade unions, among others (Callaghan 2000). Addressing the perceived unpopularity of the nationalized industries, the AES stated:

> Widespread nationalisation is simply not popular ... the experience of nationalisation, however much we may condemn the failure to 'socialise' the public sector, has not been such as to give support for a socialist case for public ownership. The way that nationalised industries have in practice operated, particularly in so far as the socialist criteria of production for social need and democratic forms of management are concerned, has not greatly differed from firms in the private sector. Public ownership is identified, however unjustified this may be, with inefficiency and bureaucracy. (London CSE Group 1980: 74)

The radical mood for a change in the UK was also fuelled by the recent discovery of North Sea oil and gas, and public debate, at least in Scotland, over the ownership and control of natural resources. The setting up of a state oil company, the British National Oil Corporation (BNOC), in 1975 was intended to provide a bulwark against the power of foreign multinationals, although despite the more radical rhetoric of the Labour Party, particularly in its 1979 Scottish election manifesto, it was run for its brief history as a 'corporatist vehicle that might – in other circumstances – have become the champion for the British industrial lobby' (Woolfson et al. 1993). Although the Labour Party continued to press for nationalization and a left agenda up to the 1983 election, its loss of power to the Conservatives in 1979 forestalled further nationalizations.

Surprisingly, the most significant threat to the established order came from Sweden with the ruling Social Democratic Party's proposal to introduce wage-earner funds (WEFs) (Armstrong et al. 1991; Glyn 1995; Blackburn 1999; Whyman 2004). Minns has described this as 'The most explicit attempt to transfer the control of corporate capital to labour' (Minns 1996: 44), although the final scheme that was adopted by the government in 1984 was heavily diluted as a result of an effective right-wing campaign against the proposals and the timidity of the centrists in the government, such as Prime Minister Olaf Palme. The original proposal would have fundamentally transformed the nature of Swedish capitalism. Its basic premise was that over time firms would give workers – through their unions – controlling shares of all large corporations, but held collectively rather than as private individuals. Under the original proposals, companies would have been obliged to pay a certain amount of their profits into WEFs that were to be organized on a regional basis. Although the primary aim of the proposal was to continue the Swedish trade union movement's Solidarity Wage system,[3] which had successfully reduced wage inequality between high-paid and low-paid groups, its second and third aims were stemming the growth of private ownership and strengthening employee participation in the workplace through the principle of 'co-ownership' (Meidner 1993: 224). In the context of the 1970s, these aspects of the proposal were the ones that met with most approval from both the grassroots and union leadership, as Rudolf Meidner himself reflected in an article twenty years later:

> The proposal was discussed intensively in the union movement, mainly in a large number of rank and file study circles which reacted in a surprisingly positive way. Many active unionists hailed the wage earner fund issue as an important step on the road towards economic democracy. The original motive – to lend support to the wage policy of solidarity – was overshadowed by the broader anti-capitalist aspects of the proposal which had a vitalizing effect on the union movement.
>
> The LO leadership which originally had taken a rather neutral position vis-à-vis the working group report, was influenced by the positive, even to some extent enthusiastic reception by the union elite and decided to present the report with minor changes to the 1976 LO convention. It was adopted by acclamation followed by the singing in unison of the Internationale. An issue had been created capable of mobilizing and activating the union movement. (Ibid.: 224)

Although Sweden was at the forefront of such plans for economic democracy, it was indicative of a wider and growing grassroots desire for a greater say in the economic decisions affecting their lives. This was in part a response to two decades of full employment which in many countries had undermined the position of employers, fulfilling Kalecki's long-standing prognosis on how such conditions radicalize workers and as such are always discouraged by business and its political supporters (Glyn 1995). This of course contrasts with the views of many Marxists, who argue the opposite: that economic recession and unemployment provide the conditions for revolution.

Although, as the British and Swedish examples demonstrate, the extent of left radicalism in the 1970s varied considerably, there was nevertheless a broader trend which implied a threat to capitalist class power, particularly in western Europe, of which the French government nationalization – discussed in the last chapter – was originally seen as the harbinger of things to come (Ross and Jenson 1994). Despite the (often poisonous) internal battles within the labour movement and the wider left that took place within every country, and the continuing ability of moderates to water down more radical proposals when in government, the perceived threat to private ownership was very real to many business leaders and right-wing politicians at the time.

In Sweden this led to the employers' federation's (SAF) decision to break with their long-held national collective bargaining agreement in 1984, typifying a trend that was to develop in many other countries in an emerging counter-offensive. The anti-union and anti-state politics of Margaret Thatcher and Ronald Reagan in the UK and the USA were at the forefront of these developments,[4] but employers were also helped by the emerging economies in the global South, particularly the Asian tiger economies and China, which offered a low-wage non-unionized workforce as an alternative 'spatial fix' to deal with Western corporations' domestic workplace troubles (Harvey 1982, 2005). Privatization became another important element of this counter-offensive.

The Thatcherite privatization project: from property-owning democracy to the private accumulation of public wealth

With good reason is the UK referred to as one of the 'heartlands' of neoliberalism (Peck and Tickell 2002). While privatization was 'road-tested' first on Chile, the UK was the battleground for the first sustained series of denationalization measures that were soon to be copied and adapted around the world. Between 1980 and 1996, the UK was responsible for 40 per cent of the total assets privatized by OECD countries (HM Treasury 2002: 4), over twice that of the second-largest privatizer, France. State-owned enterprises went from accounting for more than 10 per cent of GDP in 1979 to virtually nothing by 1997 (Megginson and Netter 2001: 324).

The UK thus played a pivotal role first as the testing ground for a full-frontal assault on state ownership and organized labour, and also as the launch pad for the spread of privatization as a discourse and practice, contributing considerably to the setting up of frameworks and instruments to advise on privatization and marketization in other countries. In a 2002 self-satisfied retrospective, Her Majesty's Treasury extolled British expertise in delivering privatization: 'The UK was among the first countries to adopt privatisation and UK-based firms are now recognised as leaders in this field, having helped transform privatisation from an academic concept into practical policy which has been applied throughout the world' (HM Treasury 2002: 4).

However, it is important to emphasize that privatization – like the wider project of neoliberalism – has always been an ongoing, iterative and contested process. Indeed, although it is often perceived as the central plank of the Thatcherite programme during the 1980s, it emerged very tentatively as a policy instrument, becoming an explicit element of Conservative policy only after the second landslide election victory and the division of the opposition in 1983 (Fine 1989). In this respect, a rereading of the Conservatives' election manifesto for the 1979 general election is very illuminating. As one would expect, its analysis of the British economic crisis lays most of the blame at the feet of the governing Labour Party between 1974 and 1979, but it is the terms of the critique which are significant here. In her foreword to the manifesto, Margaret Thatcher's comments could have been lifted straight from the work of Hayek, when she homes in on the growth of the state as a threat to 'individual freedoms' and also the importance of liberty under the law to protect these freedoms (Conservative Party 1979).

Although the Conservatives felt no compunction to engage with demands for greater economic democracy in the workplace, they did nevertheless feel compelled to offer their own competing vision of how economic decision-making could be removed from the state and put into the hands of individuals, very much in terms that Hayek would have approved. Conservative thinkers such as Nicholas Ridley (a key minister in both the Edward Heath and Thatcher governments) were developing anti-statist perspectives that envisaged the emergence of a property-owning democracy that could be an important bulwark against the perceived threat of socialism. Thus, Ridley, in his memoirs, noted how in preparing the 1970 manifesto he had hoped that a privatization policy would be adopted to address the socialist threat: '[Edward Heath] even asked me to chair the small policy group he was setting up to work up the privatisation policy. Suitably disguised, the policy went into the Manifesto ... All seemed set to embark on the privatisation programme and the dismantling of the socialist state' (quoted in Stevens 2004: 49–50).

As early as 1968, and very much against the contemporary tide, Conservatives such as Russell Lewis, director of the Conservative Political Centre, were pushing privatization not just in terms of rolling back the threat of socialism but also of offering a competing democratic vision, which 'if adopted by the next Conservative Government, would have momentous consequences for British society ... It would create a "popular capitalism" in every sense' (ibid.: 51).

In the first Thatcher government, the key proposal in this alternative democratic vision, which proved a great electoral success, was the proposal to sell council (public) housing to create a new 'Property Owning Democracy'. This was an important part of the electoral appeal of the Conservatives to more traditional working-class voters, especially the skilled working classes in southern England, whose switch from Labour was pivotal in the 1979, 1983 and 1987 election victories. Over 2.2 million council houses (around 30 per cent of tenancies) were sold between 1979 and 1996, creating considerable private wealth for many families during a period in which house prices rose significantly, despite a fall in the early 1990s (Jones and Murie 1999). Such 'aspirational' working-class voters were a key part of the electoral coalition assembled by Thatcher during the 1980s, although as the negative effects of privatization and other neoliberal-inspired policies became apparent in the 1990s, it had evaporated decisively by 1997.

By the time of the Conservatives' second election victory, privatization had become a much more explicit part of their agenda, as they promised 'to continue our programme to expose state-owned firms to real competition' (Conservative Party 1983). Once again, the trade unions were demonized as largely undemocratic organizations that retained unaccountable power to hold the country to ransom, and nowhere did their grip remain so strong as in the nationalized industries, where they continued to prove troublesome in obstructing the nation's economic progress:

> few people can now believe that state ownership means better service to the customer. The old illusions have melted away. Nationalisation does not improve job satisfaction, job security or labour relations – almost all the serious strikes in recent years have been in state industries and services. We have also seen how the burden of financing the state industries has kept taxes and government borrowing higher than they need have been. (Ibid.)

Countering Labour's own manifesto commitment to bring new sectors and industries under public ownership, the 1983 manifesto repeated the association between private ownership and democracy, this time through a share-owning democracy – employee ownership not as a collective enterprise but devolved to individual workers:

> A company which has to satisfy its customers and compete to survive is more likely to be efficient, alert to innovation, and genuinely accountable to the public. That is why we have transferred to private

ownership, in whole or in part, Cable and Wireless, Associated British Ports, British Aerospace, Britoil, British Rail Hotels, Amersham International, and the National Freight Corporation. Many of their shares have been bought by their own employees and managers, which is the truest public ownership of all. (Ibid.)

While the significance of manifesto documents can be overstated, they are important reminders of the political currents and tensions of the times that political parties feel obliged to respond to. They also underline the importance of the Hayekian vision that was driving the Thatcherite agenda.[5] It was of course a highly idealized view of how a modern advanced capitalist economy works, predicated on decentralization of ownership, individual decision-making and the belief in a system of common law and property rights to safeguard democratic interests. It had, however, powerful discursive appeal to many people at the time, particularly after the economic and political uncertainties of the 1970s, and was mobilized successfully by the Conservatives in their own electoral interests. But of course it was a flawed vision that wilfully neglected the underlying power relations at work in a capitalist economy, namely the centralization of decision-making occurring in the private sectors of the economy as a result of competitive forces and the normal imbalance between employers and employees in the workplace that propels the latter towards forms of collective organization. It also emphasized Hayek's rather simplistic conception of the independence of legal institutions in a capitalist economy and their ability to safeguard justice and the common good (Burczak 2006).

Despite the ideological rhetoric and the invocation of individual freedom, traditions of democratic governance and the rule of law, the privatization programme in the 1980s was driven as much by an assault on the trade unions and a restoration of capital's 'right to manage' the economy, which was perceived to be under so much threat in the second half of the previous decade. That this was largely achieved by the third election victory of 1987 is evidenced not only in the emasculation of the trade unions and the rightward shift in the Labour Party after 1983, but more fundamentally in the marked turnaround of the share of profits relative to wages in income distribution, as well as in the return of a large surplus army of labour in the form of 3 million unemployed, up from 1.5 million in 1979, and representing around 8–10 per cent of the adult population (Glyn 1989).[6] Allied to the proceeds coming ashore from North Sea oil, the Conservatives' discovery of privatization also had the handy electoral advantage of providing them with considerable revenue to help pay for tax cuts for electoral purposes.

In terms of the goal of addressing the UK's longer-term structural economic problems, and despite the rhetoric of the time of a new spirit of competitiveness and entrepreneurialism, there is also a persuasive argument made by Fine (e.g. Fine 1989, 1990) that the privatization programme of the 1980s was far from the radical break with the past presented by both sides of the political argument. Seen from the longer-term perspective of the evolution of the UK's economy, the '(re-)capitalization' of public assets marks considerable continuity with the absence of a coherent industrial strategy and the prioritization of financial interests over productive concerns in the evolution of the national economy. Indeed, as another commentator at the time noted: 'In industrial policy I do not believe the government's policy has been that different from its predecessors ... Britain's relative economic decline under Margaret Thatcher continues much as before, despite being cushioned by the revenues from North Sea oil' (Rutherford 1983: 43). Indeed, without the impact of North Sea oil revenues, the level of investment in the country's industrial base between 1979 and 1987, compared to the amounts of capital flowing into the financial, consumption and housing sectors, would have been even more dismal (Glyn 1989: 73).

The effects of British privatization policy

The UK Treasury paper of 2002, extolling the virtues of privatization, stated with the kind of brash self-confidence that the Treasury does so well:

> Privatisation in the UK has led to greater commercial freedom for companies no longer controlled by the Government, allowing them to raise funds on the capital markets, and make decisions on staffing levels, investment requirements and the management of their particular business on a commercial basis. They are no longer subject to political control which may delay or distort investment. In the majority of cases, restructuring, competition, and price regulation have led to reduced utility charges – and in those cases where competition is most firmly established, for example the telecommunications industry, the falls in costs have been most significant. Most indicators of service quality have improved despite the price reductions. (HM Treasury 2002)

The report did note that there had been some unfortunate side effects, such as the loss of jobs and the end of cross-subsidization for lower-income consumers, but suggested that these were temporary problems that would be resolved with a proper competitive structure and the operation of market forces, not only reducing prices further but also helping to create new jobs, although the report was rather vague about how this would occur.

A second claim made consistently by the proponents of privatization is that it has delivered better services for consumers at lower cost. BT in the telecommunications sector is usually held up as the archetypal example (ibid.), although its relative success has been bought at the cost of considerable job losses.[7] Elsewhere the evidence is at best mixed. For example, research by Waddams Price and Hancock into the effects of UK privatization on households in the mid-1990s revealed that the main impact has been one of 'considerable redistribution between different groups' (Waddams Price and Hancock 1998: 68). Their study of the telecom, gas, electricity and water industries found clear evidence that, rather than increased competition driving prices down for all consumers, it was leading privatized companies to operate strategies of 'monopoly exploitation' (ibid.: 68). In the simplest terms, companies were changing their pricing structures, shifting away from charging on an average-cost price basis, which allowed cross-subsidization of lower-income groups, to one that gave price reductions based around quantity used, thus favouring higher-income groups or larger companies. While prices may have come down in real terms across the board, the restructuring of the pricing regime had allowed firms to increase profits at the expense of the most vulnerable groups. One effect in the gas and electricity sectors was that prices can rise during periods of peak demand – during wintertime – precisely when the poorest and most vulnerable groups need heating supplies the most.

The findings of these earlier analyses have been confirmed over the longer term by research undertaken by the Public Services International Research Unit at the University of Greenwich (www.psiru.org), which has spent over a decade undertaking forensic examination of the effects of privatization both in the UK and overseas. With regard to the privatized electricity sector, their research has revealed that although prices to consumers fell up until 2002, this was during an era of relatively benign prices in energy markets, which cast doubt upon whether consumers were benefiting from a 'privatization effect', particularly since consumer prices had fallen similarly in France, where the sector remained nationalized (Hall et al. 2009).

Water privatization became something of a national scandal in the mid-1990s, to the extent that even the bastion of 'Middle England' and loyal supporter of the Conservative Party the *Daily Mail* felt compelled to run a front-page headline on 'The Great Water Robbery' in 1994. Between 1991 and 1998, the ten privatized companies made 147 per cent profits, coinciding with a period of price rises of between 36 and 42 per cent (between 1988 and 1998) (Lobina and Hall 2001: 7). Rather than improved efficiencies and productivity, privatization also resulted in deteriorating levels of investment, such that the antiquated infrastructure began to suffer some severe breakdowns in some areas.

In other ways, privatization has exacted huge economic and social costs, particularly through a massive phase of job losses, bound up with a shift in emphasis from a public service rationale to that of providing profit for shareholders. Tickell (1998) has estimated that as many as 200,000 jobs have been lost in the privatized industries since 1984. In the energy industries, in the period 1991–96, the number of jobs declined from over 220,000 to less than 110,000 (Sadler 2001). For those remaining in work, the effect has often been a deterioration in working conditions, employment security and health and safety standards. Nor are health and safety concerns confined to the workforce. The inquiry into the Hatfield rail disaster, in which four people lost their lives, was particularly critical of the company responsible for track maintenance, Balfour Beatty, in the post-privatization regime. Many of its failings were down to a lack of skilled labour used by the company during inspections (*Guardian*, 9 May 2001, p. 20).

So, who were the winners out of privatization?

The obvious group to benefit directly from privatization was the elite group of managers who enthusiastically presided over the transfer of assets from the public sector, making windfall gains in the process from stock options and salary increases (see Table 2.1). Privatization has in this way created a class of extremely wealthy managers and directors as well as a set of companies increasingly driven by profit and less by providing services to satisfy a public need.

However, the main winners from privatization were the private shareholders that bought the assets of the nationalized companies. In the early years, there was some substance to Thatcher's claim of creating a popular capitalism, with privatization boosting the number of shareholders in the UK from 3 million to 10 million by the end of the 1980s (HM Treasury 2002: 20), and at the height of the privatization boom in 1986, around three million people bought shares in British Gas. This undoubtedly contributed to her government's electoral success in 1987 and that of her successor, John Major, in 1992, but the

TABLE 2.1 Changes in salaries of directors following privatization

Company	Increase in directors' salaries (%)	Number of years after	Date privatized
Amersham International	329	3	1982
Associated British Ports	67	2	1983
British Aerospace	181	5	1985[1]
BP	101	5	1987[2]
Britoil	36	2	1983
Cable and Wireless	352	3	1981
Enterprise Oil	215	2	1984
National Freight Cons.	93	2	1982
British Airways	242	2	1987
British Gas	68	2	1986

Notes: 1. Privatized in two stages – 52 per cent sold 1981, remainder sold 1985
2. 51 per cent state-owned until 1979, remaining stock sold in period 1979–87
Source: Derived from Sawyer and O'Donnell (1999)

longer-term ambition of turning Britain into a shareholding democracy was short lived. Most of the smaller and individual investors sold their shares quickly, taking advantage of the rising share prices that were the result of undervaluation; for example, 500,000 of the 2.2 million initial shareholders in BT had sold their shares within six months (Parker 2004: 8).

The main longer-term beneficiaries of privatization were the banking and financial institutions in the City of London, alongside foreign investors who were able to take advantage of the underpricing of national assets (ibid.). The first major privatization, the £3.9 billion sale of 51 per cent of BT shares in 1984, was six times greater than any previous stock exchange issue (HM Treasury 2002: 15), while the British Gas privatization was even larger. There is also considerable evidence that state assets were sold off at remarkably cheap prices, given subsequent profits that were made in privatized utility sectors (Parker 2004). BT shares in 1999 were worth around £15 at the height of the stock market boom, compared to 130p at issue (author's own research). The stock market valuation for Railtrack in 1998 (prior to the Hatfield tragedy) was £8 billion, compared to its sale price of £1.9 billion two years earlier. Similarly, the rolling-stock companies on privatization were sold off for £1.8 million, although originally valued at £3 million (Cumbers and Farrington 2000). The privatized electricity companies saw their shares rise at almost double the rate of the FT Index in the four years following privatization (Tickell 1998), and on and on. This is not surprising given the political rationale driving privatization; indeed, in his memoirs the former Chancellor Lord Lawson revealed that undervaluing the shares in successive stock market flotations became a stated aim of Conservative strategy from the time of one of the first privatizations, Amersham International, onwards (Stevens 2004; Lawson 1992).

It is instructive at this point to reflect upon the contrasts between privatization and the nationalization process forty years earlier. In both cases, the public sector has been the loser and the private sector the gainer, but for different, even opposing, reasons. As I noted in the previous chapter, the industries nationalized by the Attlee administration had experienced many years of neglect and underinvestment. In contrast, the majority of those industries privatized in the 1980s and 1990s had undergone considerable rationalization and restructuring in the lead-up to privatization, making them quite attractive prospects, especially in many of the utility sectors, such as water and electricity generation, where there was a natural monopoly. For example, employment in the regional public water companies was reduced from 80,000 to 50,000 between 1974 and 1989, and it was the previous public restructuring of local and municipal water concerns into regional companies undertaken in the 1970s which created the scale of operation to attract private investors (Hall and Lobina 2010: 5). The one exception was the rail industry, where over three decades of underinvestment had left the infrastructure in poor condition. Nevertheless, even here, the rationalization and restructuring of employment pre-privatization – employment was reduced from over 250,000 in 1974 to 120,000 by 1994 (Cumbers et al. 2010) – allied to increasing managerial attempts to increase productivity and commercialization under the Conservatives gave a significant boost to the newly privatized firms. Thus, not only had privatization massively enriched financial and corporate interests but there were also considerable hidden subsidies from previous public sector operations.

The City and the wider business services sector also benefited considerably as the main recipients of fees paid by government for advising in various ways on privatization. Around £780 million was paid out for a range of business services activities by 1994 (Parker 2004: 17), and in the case of the PR industry, privatization played a major role in its expansion with the need to 'sell' the benefits of the policy to the broader public, resulting in massive publicity and advertising campaigns. Ironically, the Conservative government had felt the need to invest heavily in PR and advertising to counteract their own negative campaigning about the nationalized industries in the 1970s (Miller and Dinan 2000). It had neglected to mention the fact that BT was actually a relatively healthy and profitable public organization during this period.

All in all, privatization in the UK added up to a massive transfer of resources and appropriation of wealth from the public realm to financial and corporate interests, referred to famously by one former Conservative prime minister as 'selling off the family silver'.[8] In the process, it had extended the power of financial interests by creating a block of institutions and social groups that had not only done well materially out of the privatizations that had taken place, but were to become cheerleaders for the promulgation of privatization to the rest of the world.

The globalization of privatization

In Doreen Massey's excellent account of the emergence of London as a global city in the 1980s and 1990s (Massey 2007), she makes the point that as a 'World City' it is both the producer and recipient of global flows of money, power and information owing to its pivotal position within wider global economic networks. Through the processes of financial deregulation and privatization that occurred from the late 1970s onwards, London's financial and business elites played an important part in both globalizing the UK through internationalizing the ownership structure of the economy and contributing to the global privatization drive elsewhere.

Over time, shareholding in Britain's privatized entities has become increasingly concentrated in line with the broader trends apparent in the ownership structure of Britain's largest firms, with the proportion of share capital held by individuals diminishing considerably. Indeed, as Figure 2.1 shows, the growth of foreign ownership of British companies in the past five decades far outweighs any turn towards a share-owning democracy of private individuals produced by privatization processes in the 1980s.

The increasingly globalized nature of Britain's privatized companies was commented on with pride by the UK Treasury in 2002; the ability to attract foreign capital being regarded as a virility symbol for 'UK plc' as a country open for wealth accumulation. At this point, any concerns about developing a yeoman-like share-owning democracy seemed to have disappeared, along with the rhetoric of individual

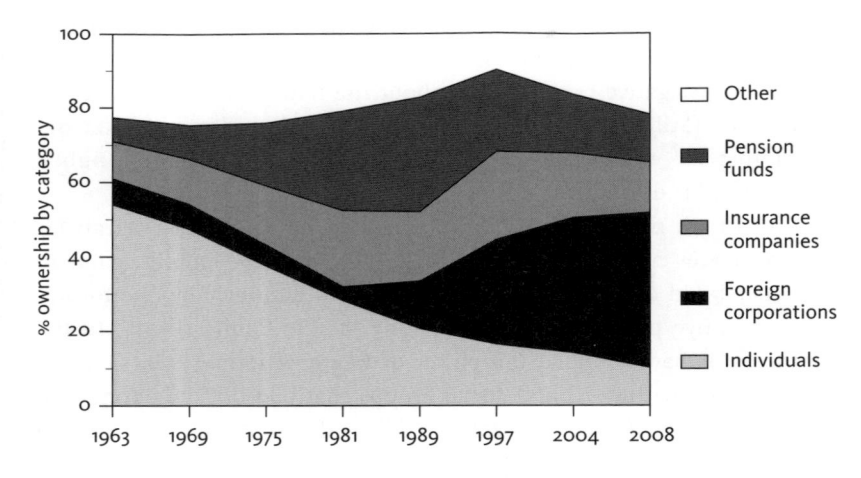

2.1 Ownership of share capital in the UK's quoted public limited companies, 1963–2008 (*source*: Derived from ONS 2010: Table A, p. 4)

freedoms, being replaced by a more naked desire to promote private profit-making, particularly from cash-rich foreign investors:

> The emergence of banks with the capacity to sell shares worldwide and the adoption of a more global approach to the marketing of shares has allowed the UK to reduce the number of banks in selling syndicates from over 100 (on the secondary sale of BT in 1991) to 8 for the British Energy sale in July 1996. Banks have been appointed in later sales either on the basis of their ability to sell to investors worldwide, or because they can access high-quality investors in specific markets in, for example, Continental Europe or the Far East. These developments have demonstrated the ability of UK-based firms to access investors in key overseas markets, in particular the crucial US market. (HM Treasury 2002: 15)

What the Treasury document failed to mention was the way in which the ownership of privatized companies was becomingly increasingly concentrated and monopolistic, particularly with the takeover by foreign concerns (many, ironically, state-owned or partially state-owned corporations in their own home countries) (Hall 2003). Even in the telecommunications market, where increased competition has had most effect on reducing prices and spreading customer choice, the lead firm BT still dominates the telephone market with 70 per cent of domestic residential calls and 60 per cent of business calls (Parker 2004: 23).

Elsewhere, the exposure of privatized firms to internationalization and foreign investment has not produced highly competitive sectors with a plethora of firms offering customer choice, but a growing concentration of ownership, facilitated by merger and acquisition activity; what one set of commentators refer to as 'commercial imperatives [having] re-integrated markets' (Hall et al. 2003: 26). To take the example of the water sector in England and Wales, it has shifted considerably from its original structures of regional privatized entities to a sector dominated by foreign multinationals and private equity groups. Of the twenty-three local and regional water companies in 2010, ten are under direct foreign ownership, eight are owned by private equity groups (these first two categories are not mutually exclusive), one small company (Cholderton Water) is family owned, and there is one not-for-profit mutual (Welsh Water/Dwyr Cymru) (Hall and Lobina 2010). The remainder are listed on the London stock exchange. Concerns about the privatized water and energy sectors in particular have grown within the European Union in recent years with several of the largest multinationals being fined by the European Commission and national anti-competition authorities (ibid.).

Scaling up privatization to a global policy paradigm

Despite the emerging problems with privatization in the UK and elsewhere, the 1990s was a decade in which the policy was 'rolled out' (Peck and Tickell 2002), both in the functional sense of opening up public services to marketization and private profit-making activities, and in the geographical sense of becoming a key part of the policy-making apparatus of international financial institutions such as the World Bank and the IMF. At a global level, privatization has become the main component of a restructuring strategy demanded of former state socialist and Third World countries. Impoverished and desperate states are offered market liberalization 'quick fix' packages by international lending agencies, such as the World Bank and the IMF, which they must sign up to before qualifying for financial aid. Privatization became an important mechanism for transforming the Soviet Union and eastern Europe to market economies with devastating effects in the former in particular.

Privatization has also become an important part of the development agenda for countries in the global South under the policies of the 'Washington Consensus'. The implication is that only increased competition and free trade can improve countries' economic and social prospects. However, there is scant evidence to justify this. Ecuador represents a salutary tale. In return for IMF assistance, the country was forced to agree to 167 loan conditions that included raising the price of cooking gas by 80 per cent, eliminating 26,000 jobs and halving the wages of remaining workers. The package also insisted that the government transfer ownership of its largest water system to foreign companies, and allow Arco – a subsidiary of BP – the right to build and operate an oil pipeline through the Andes. As Gregory Palast – who broke the news of the deal in an *Observer* article in October 2000 – noted, Ecuador's problems stemmed from an earlier round of IMF-inspired market liberalization policies. Palast also cites the example of Tanzania, where GDP had fallen by over 30 per cent in the previous fifteen years with the country on the receiving end of World Bank and IMF policy advice. Recent advice includes charging for hospital visits (in a country where 8 per cent of the population are suffering from AIDS) and imposing school fees (resulting in school enrolment falling from 80 to 66 per cent). As Palast wryly observes: 'Yet somehow the bank has failed to win over the hearts and minds of Tanzanians to its free-market gameplan. Last June, the bank reported in frustration: "One legacy of socialism is that most people continue to believe the state has a fundamental role in promoting development and providing social services"' (Palast 2000).

A central problem is the lack of economic pluralism within organizations such as the IMF and the WTO, and the belief that one economic model can be applied to all countries, irrespective of the individual circumstances. Privatization, for example, was even linked to the Drop the Debt Campaign by Jubilee 2000, in cases where the IMF has been allowed to set the terms by which debt is cancelled. For example, Honduras was ordered to privatize its electricity sector, prior to having its debt reduced (*Guardian*, 21 July 2000).

The overwhelming weight of historical evidence from the global South suggests that privatization has been a massive failure. To take one study that compares the economic performance of Latin America and Africa since 1950, it is clear that privatization has made material conditions much worse for the ordinary citizen. The two regions performed far better in the years between 1950 and 1980 than they did between 1980 and 1995. In Latin America, during the earlier period, per capita income rose by 73 per cent, while Africa's rose by 34 per cent. During this period: 'virtually every nation in the survey was either socialist or welfare statist. They were developing on the "Import Substitution Model", by which locally-owned industry was built through government investment and high tariffs, anathema to the neoliberals' (Palast 2000).

In contrast, in the latter period, Latin American per capita income grew by 6 per cent, while Africa's actually declined by 23 per cent. Additionally, life expectancy, which had risen across the board in the earlier period, fell in fifteen African states. Significantly, this period coincided with a shift towards market liberalization and privatization policies.

Nowhere have the effects of privatization been as pronounced and catastrophic in terms of the general appropriation of wealth by a small minority as in Russia. Here, the plunder of public assets, especially some of the world's richest energy and mineral resources, by an elite of oligarchs adds up to one of the greatest transfers of wealth ever seen, to the extent that it has been referred to by one commentator as 'piratization' (Goldman 2003).

Despite this weight of evidence, privatization remains a popular policy among global economic elites. During the 1990s and 2000s privatization and market liberalization were increasingly enshrined as the policy agenda within the European Union too, as part of the broader project towards an integrated European market. Privatization has subsequently been given a new lease of life with current Eurozone austerity measures, whereby new privatizations are being demanded in countries such as Greece, Spain, Portugal, Ireland and Italy at the same time as many bankrupt banks are being taken into public ownership to prevent their collapse (see Chapter 4).

At one point, the OECD even produced a list of over-regulated 'sinners' (OECD 1998), an 'index of product market regulation', which evaluates countries according to the level of 'state control', 'barriers to entrepreneurship' and 'barriers to trade and investment'. Interestingly, the OECD data at the time showed almost no relationship between regulation and long-term economic performance in the countries surveyed (ibid.). Wealthy countries that had managed to maintain relatively equitable levels of income distribution over time, such as Norway, Denmark and France, were regularly chastised because they were regarded as over-regulated and stifling market-led restructuring. In contrast, countries such as the USA and the UK that have deregulated the most are celebrated as models for the rest, even though they display widening income disparities between rich and poor, together with growing evidence of the problems caused by privatization and marketization. The UK also continues to lag in meeting climate change objectives and expanding renewable energy.

The ongoing politics of privatization: continuing struggles to reclaim the economy

There is a tendency among some commentators on both the left and the right to view neoliberalism and privatization as some kind of inevitable 'end state' of global capitalism. Yet this is to ignore both the historical record and the ongoing contestation of economic policy agendas that continues to this day. As one authoritative survey of privatization has put it:

> It is tempting to point to the spread of privatization programs around the world during the past two decades and conclude that the debate on the economic and political merits of government versus private ownership has been decided. But such a conclusion is flawed, since 25 years ago proponents of state ownership could just as easily have surveyed the postwar rise of state-owned enterprises and concluded that their model of economic organization was winning the intellectual battle with free-market capitalism. (Megginson and Netter 2001: 321)

Although privatization has become a dominant part of the wider global economic policy architecture, it has always met with opposition and resistance wherever it has been tried, and no doubt this will continue. Even during the heyday of Thatcherism in the UK, there remained considerable resistance to some of the sectors being privatized. The proposals to privatize the water industry in 1984, for example, were shelved after an effective public campaign, only to be reintroduced following re-election in 1988. Even then, water privatization has never been proposed in the more politically sensitive regions of Scotland and Northern Ireland.

Resistance to privatization continues today, as later chapters will demonstrate, and there is a trend in certain countries to return sectors to public ownership, often under more democratic forms than previously (see Chapter 5 in particular). At the same time, many of the privatizations that have occurred throughout the world often involve publicly owned corporations – of different hue – from other countries. This is particularly the case with many French and German utility multinationals; partial or even full public ownership has provided the base for taking advantage of privatization waves elsewhere. There is therefore a complicated politics of ownership in the global privatization process. What all this means is that a critical analysis of privatization must begin to raise questions about the continuing and unfolding relationships between different forms of private and public ownership and their effects. While it is important to the way the global privatization process has involved a massive transfer of wealth from public to private hands, and with it an important source of increasing global inequalities, it is not just a tale of the misdemeanours of private ownership. We also need to question the way that publicly owned and nationalized entities are operating, as well as to critique the use of state resources to subsidize (both explicitly and implicitly) and, in times of crisis, bail out private capital. To begin to democratize the economy, we need to give as much consideration to reclaiming public ownership and arguing for new forms as the equally important task of continuing to contest privatization processes. However, before doing so we must engage a little more substantively with one of the key intellectual inspirations behind the neoliberal project, the Austrian economist Friedrich von Hayek, and address some of his original objections to public ownership.

3 | Coming to terms with Hayek: markets, planning and economic democracy

If we can agree that the economic problem of society is mainly one of rapid adaptation to changes in the particular circumstances of time and place it would seem to follow that the ultimate decisions must be left to the people who are familiar with these circumstances, who know directly of the relevant changes and of the resources immediately available to meet them. (Hayek 1948: 26)

Hayek's big idea [is] that each of us sees the world a little differently and thus each of us has a comparative advantage in the use and application of our knowledge. It is an insight economists might reach if they were to apply postmodern notions of indeterminacy, open-endedness, incompleteness, and social constitution to the study of ordinary life and the knowledge of ordinary people. (Burczak 2006: 389–90)

Introduction

While the limitations of privatization and the broader neoliberal project have been all too evident in recent years, past forms of public ownership associated with systems of central planning have also been disappointing, if not disastrous, in promoting economic democracy and social justice. As we saw in the last chapter, 'privatization' has involved the mass appropriation of collectively owned resources and their capture by private and corporate interests. The result has been a growing centralization of economic power and wealth; extreme in the case of Russia, but the same prevailing theme is evident in the UK too. The promotion of unfettered and deregulated markets, meanwhile, has promoted a regime of financialization and speculation where the single-minded tendency to realize greater profits acts to the detriment of other human and social goals, notably achieving environmentally sustainable development, tackling poverty, and creating more egalitarian societies. To reverse these trends, economic decision-making needs to become re-rooted in collectivist institutions that can pursue more progressive ends through more democratic means. However, as Hayek and others have noted, the forms of public and collective ownership pursued by alternative 'socialist' regimes, as well as the state-centred projects in Western democracies, in the twentieth century also have a poor record in this regard.

Hayek's central critique of the pathway from state-driven development to totalitarianism is difficult to dispute given the historic record of China and the Soviet Union. However, it is something of a caricature when applied elsewhere. While the argument has been made here and elsewhere that Hayek's cherished relationship between markets, individual liberties and the rule of law is no guarantor against similar concentrations and hierarchies of power emerging under a capitalist system, we need to consider what the key concerns and issues remain over centralized forms of public ownership in a planned system to begin to rethink more democratic and appropriate forms of public ownership for the twenty-first century.

Hayekian-inspired critiques of public ownership as state centralized planning

Hayek's basic arguments against socialism and planning are that they inevitably lead to the centralization of economic power and decision-making, and, as a result, the crushing of individual freedoms and even democracy. As invoked in his famous book, *The Road to Serfdom* (1944), Hayek believed that once attempts were made to consciously plan and strategically design the economy, however progressive the intention, the unintended consequences would be tyranny and authoritarianism. Market individualism, voluntary exchange and free markets are therefore preferable in the achievement of economic democracy. The historical record of actually existing state socialisms in the twentieth century, from China to Cuba, to the former Soviet Union, does much to bear out Hayek's warnings with regard to the relations between central planning and democracy. Additionally, as we have seen with regard to the nationalizations undertaken under more social democratic auspices in Britain, France and elsewhere in the post-1945 era, the record of more centralized forms of public ownership in devolving economic decision-making power away from elites towards workers and citizens is also a poor one.

Hayek's thesis, highly influential in recent times and underpinning the political rhetoric of mainstream politicians of the links between markets and private ownership on the one hand and liberty and democracy on the other, is premised on a set of arguments and relationships between knowledge and economic decision-making that are an important challenge to many traditional versions of socialism, planning and public ownership. Hayek disputed the ability of socialist planners to effectively organize an economy because of the limits to their knowledge about the everyday practices and conditions of economic life. Following Hayek, 'social engineering' has become an associated and pejorative term for socialism and planning:

> The application of the engineering technique to the whole of society requires ... that the director possess the same complete knowledge of the whole society that the engineer possesses of his limited world. Central economic planning is nothing but such an application of engineering principles to the whole of society based on the assumption that such a complete concentration of all relevant knowledge is possible. (Hayek 1942–44: 173, cited in O'Neill 2003: 187)

In contrast, markets and private ownership can solve such knowledge problems because they involve dispersed decision-making and experimentation, independent of centralizing authorities and impulses. It is precisely the anarchy of the market order which is the key both to innovation and to the preservation of more democratic societies.

An important critique of the traditional socialist vision of an economy, where markets and private ownership disappear completely, comes from the British institutional economist Geoff Hodgson. Arguing himself from a left progressive perspective, Hodgson draws partially upon Hayek's arguments about the problems arising from knowledge construction in socialist planned economies. For our concerns here there are three elements to these knowledge problems that central planners face. The first concerns 'the problem of ignorance' (O'Neill 2003: 185) of consumer needs and demands. How can central planners have all the knowledge needed about the individualized demands of millions of consumers in advanced economies (see Hodgson 1999: ch. 2; Cumbers and McMaster 2010)? This criticism was commonly applied to the Soviet Union, even to the point of caricature by many Western economists, in highlighting the failure of Soviet economic managers in state-owned enterprises to understand the variegated demands of their own citizens in even the most basic consumer products. Because of the vast and complex information needed – for example, in matching supply and demand for shoes given the very different needs of individuals – planned systems simply cannot cope. Alex Nove, in his analysis of the inefficiencies of the Soviet system, calculated that in 1977 the absence of markets to set prices and allow spontaneous decision-making meant that planners had to produce plans for around twelve million products, which put impossible burdens on the system and on managers tasked with meeting centrally driven targets:

> According to the logic of the centralized planning model, the central organs know what society needs, and can issue and enforce plan-orders to ensure that these needs are effectively and efficiently met. This requires multi-million instructions as to what to produce, to whom deliveries should be made, from whom inputs should be received, and when. All this must be made to cohere with plans for labour, wages, profits, investment financing, material utilization norms, quality, productivity, for each of many thousands of productive units. In practice this task can never be completed, plans are repeatedly altered in the period of their currency, supplies and output targets fail to match, there are numerous instances of imbalance and incoherence. This is due not to the lack of commitment of officials, or to stupidity, but to the fact that the magnitude of the task far surpasses the possibility of fulfilling it. (Nove 1980: 4)

A second and related set of concerns relates to what knowledge is and how it is distributed within society. Much of the important knowledge through which economies function is of the tacit variety – bound up in social practices and routines within different parts of the economy, between producers and consumers, between local managers and employees and between workers themselves – which is not easily codified and appropriated by central state managers or planners. This point has also been made by economic geographers to justify the continuing existence of spatial clustering of specialist functions of industries in particular places despite high production costs (e.g. Maskell et al. 1998). The other side of Hayek's point about the nature of knowledge is that it is widely dispersed in society, through highly developed (and under advanced capitalism increasingly complex) divisions of labour, and indeed, because much important knowledge for the running of economies is tacit knowledge, it is decentralized and localized in particular forms of production and sectors of the economy. Again, the point is that such forms of dispersed knowledge are not easily appropriated by central managers.

A third point relates to the fact that, even if it were possible for central planners to absorb all the appropriate information and knowledge across a dispersed knowledge economy, economies are not static but are dynamic and evolutionary and therefore the processes of economic development and knowledge production are ever changing and unpredictable. Planners face problems of predictability in the face of the realities of economic uncertainty, not only in relation to changing patterns of consumer demand and need but also in relation to the changing nature of the production process itself. Thus, there are knowledge problems that central planners face – they cannot be fully cognizant of both consumer needs and production conditions at the local level.

The efficiency problems are actually multiplied if an autocratic and hierarchical system of planning such as those in the post-1945 communist states is replaced by a more genuinely democratic socialism – advocated by some in response to the criticisms of centrally planned models (e.g. Devine 1988; Adaman and Devine 1996) – because of the need to reach agreement, even by a simple majority (which of course has its own tyranny in the marginalization of minority groups) on every economic decision:

> That collective planning creates a situation in which it is necessary for us to agree on a much larger number of topics than we have been used to, and that in a planned system we cannot confine collective action to the tasks on which we agree, but are forced to produce agreement on everything in order that any action can be taken at all, is one of the features which contribute more than most to determining the character of a planned system. (Hayek 1944: 46, cited in Hodgson 1999: 32)

These criticisms are evoked powerfully in Hodgson's critique of Adaman and Devine's recent proposals for an alternative socialist economy based upon negotiated coordination, where key decisions are referred to democratic committees to adjudicate. His point is that a system of democratic planning becomes unfeasible because of the impossibility of having to make so many collective decisions which will inhibit spontaneity and creativity.

In practice, if economies are to continue to function under systems that have a strong bias towards central planning over markets, the tendency towards a small elite making the key economic decisions is a strong one, whether the system is run by the Communist Party as in China or the Soviet Union, a French dirigiste technocratic cadre or a modernizing state elite, as in the case of Asian tiger economies. Hodgson, for example, explicitly links the development of totalitarian regimes in nominally socialist planned economies to the flawed premises of planning:

> The fact is that the Russian, Chinese, Cambodian and other revolutions were inspired by a vision of an economy based on common ownership

of all means of production and subject to an all-embracing plan ... As this economic project was based on misunderstandings concerning the role of key economic mechanisms and institutions, then these revolutionary movements, despite their noble intentions, were headed towards some form of impasse. Such an impasse would precipitate a severe economic crisis. A revolutionary movement would attempt to consolidate its power. One possible outcome would be totalitarianism and terror. (Ibid.: 61)

Although Hodgson does concede that there is no inevitable link between planning, socialism and tyranny, his conclusions are that actually existing forms of socialist planning and public ownership have been unworkable without the centralization of decision-making power because of the contradictions and flaws inherent in the basic model. Hodgson's solution for socialists is to overcome their 'agoraphobia' or fear of markets and 'learn to inhabit open systems and spaces' (ibid.). While the importance of openness and diversity in economic thinking is a conclusion that I would endorse here in developing new thinking around public ownership, Hodgson, like many other left economists who have taken Hayek's arguments seriously, ultimately goes too far in his embrace of market forms and his rejection of public ownership. These are issues that we return to below.

Addressing Hayekian concerns from the left

In the previous chapter, the limits to Hayekian market utopias were exposed through detailed examination of the effects of privatization policies. Rather than producing greater economic democracy, unrestrained market forces usually lead to an increased concentration of decision-making and in many cases greater exploitation of both workers and consumers. Hayek viewed markets under capitalism as voluntarist forms of equal exchange that could be regulated by legal contracts, which would serve the interests of society as a whole, by organizing resources and production efficiently. Private ownership and the wage relation are viewed unproblematically in these terms because all economic actors have the freedom to choose whether to engage in economic relations or not. For Hayek, the market is preferable to socially planned models because it is seen as arbitrary and not underpinned by moral or ethical presumptions (see O'Neill 1998: ch. 2 on this point). Of course, this view was already open to criticism from a Marxist perspective when Hayek was writing in the 1940s, for its neglect of the underlying power relations that drive capitalist economies and indeed inform its mainstream discourse (Dowd 2001). The past three decades have certainly reinforced Marx's analysis of the workings of capitalism and markets rather than those of Hayek. Neoliberal economic policies inspired by Hayek's vision have produced an ever greater concentration of wealth and economic power in which the private appropriation of public assets, as we have seen, has played an important part.

It is also extremely doubtful whether the increasing monetization and commodification of all areas of economic and social life are contributing to the open-ended and decentralized forms of knowledge production that Hayek would have envisaged. Indeed, Hayek's quote with which I started the chapter could equally be levelled today at a global corporate and political elite which makes highly erroneous and undemocratic decisions about the running of the economy, often divorced from conditions on the ground. We are a long way from the devolved market utopia of innovation, knowledge discovery, diversity and experimentation that Hayek envisaged. In this respect, a key argument that I am advancing here is that public ownership, in the sense of forms of democratic collective ownership, is an important part of the solution to achieving greater equality and social justice and in overturning the growing inequalities under free market capitalism. The question, however, following the critique of Hayek and others of these earlier socialist models of collective ownership around the state and central planning, is what forms should this take?

Despite the problems inherent in Hayek's celebration of the market and private ownership in promoting individual liberty and democracy, his critique of planned economies under universal state ownership remains prescient. For an economic system to be democratic requires a level of devolved decision-making, variety and choice which is simply not present under centrally imposed planning regimes. As Hodgson puts it:

> No convincing scheme for durable economic decentralisation has been proposed, without the equivalent decentralisation of the powers to make contracts, set prices, and exchange products and property rights, through markets or other forms of property exchange. This does not mean that markets are regarded as optimal or ideal, nor that an entire economy is made subject to 'market forces'. It does mean, however, that markets and exchange are necessary to sustain genuine economic pluralism and diversity. (Hodgson 1999: 31)

While I am not fully endorsing Hodgson's enthusiastic embrace of the market in resolving these issues, the underlying point he makes here is inescapable. A system of completely centralized planning contains serious flaws, in terms of economic efficiency, social need and democratic accountability. Economists who have been sympathetic to socialist ideals have long recognized the limits to central coordination and the need for 'decentred' and more spontaneous mechanisms for day-to-day decisions. In developing the critique and alternative proposals here, Hodgson's (1999, 2005) observations on and criticisms of various models of socialism, particularly Adaman and Devine's (1996, 2001) participatory model of socialism, provides a valuable reference point.[1]

Adaman and Devine have, in various publications, advocated limits to the market mechanism, proposing instead greater recourse to a democratic system of participatory planning (Devine 1988). They state:

> Democratic participatory planning is envisaged as a process in which the values and interests of people in all aspects of their lives interact and shape one another through negotiation and cooperation. In the course of this process tacit knowledge is discovered and articulated and, on the basis of that knowledge, economic decisions are consciously planned and coordinated. (Adaman and Devine 1996: 531–2)

While the objective of participatory planning and 'negotiated exchange' is very much in the spirit of the arguments being made here, Adaman and Devine make the same mistake as earlier forms of socialism in assuming that all knowledge can be unproblematically codified to become available for democratic planning committees, devoid of its social context (Hodgson 1999, 2005). In this regard Hodgson (1999, 2005) provides a compelling critique, noting how:

> The idea that this [tacit] knowledge can be readily extracted from its institutional carriers, and freely codified and processed by a committee ... perpetuates a fatal error of Enlightenment thought: that such matters can largely be made subject to reason and deliberation; and that the mind may soar free of all habits, preconceptions and institutions – of which in fact it is unavoidably obliged to make extensive use. (Hodgson 1999: 60)

This is important when considering what forms of public ownership are most appropriately geared towards delivering economic democracy and participation. Relegating considerations of the social context through which knowledge develops in practice – as both mainstream economists and some Marxists do (ibid.) – is not only flawed in understanding how innovation and social creativity operate (Cumbers and McMaster 2010), but is fundamentally undemocratic, as it creates restrictive information channels reflecting rigid hierarchies, rather than allowing new forms of knowledge to emerge and develop through a freer flow and exchange of ideas.

Moreover, the main technical flaw in central planning is not that it is more inefficient in allocating resources than market-based systems but rather that it stymies innovation and human creativity in the context of the evolution of real-world economies. The work of Murrell (1991) in particular has shown that Soviet bloc countries performed as well as Western capitalist states in the short term in resource allocation. Where Soviet economics lagged, however, was in long-term dynamic efficiency, which involves 'not the allocation of existing resources but the potential for dynamic and transformative growth' (Hodgson 1999: 59). This is because the forms of knowledge that lead to new innovations in products, services and processes do not arise in the main from formal planned research, administered by committees (whether of multinational companies or state bureaucracies), but take place through social interaction in the coming together of individuals in a free, open and democratic exchange of ideas. Taking seriously the dynamic and evolutionary nature of the economy and its implications, in terms of tacit institutions, rules, habits, customs and deeply engrained practices of economic life, is critical in devising new socialist ideas around economic democracy.

The foregoing does not in any sense mean that planning or deliberative processes should not be heavily involved in addressing socioeconomic problems. Indeed, my argument here (see also Cumbers and McMaster 2012) is rather the contrary. The failure to treat knowledge production and economic action as socially embedded and interactive processes also applies to most of mainstream economics with its focus upon atomized individuals and market exchange (see Fine and Milonakis 2009; Keen 2011). Another important point to make is that the same tacit knowledge problems facing central planners under Soviet-style economies also confront multinational corporations operating in pyramidal systems of management and coordinating vast globally dispersed supply chains.

Countering agoraphobia through appropriative justice: Burczak's new theory of market socialism

A common response for those socialists and Marxists that have been prepared to engage with Hayek has been to develop theories of market socialism which seek to mesh more collective and egalitarian forms of ownership and social relations with the continued use of markets in economic governance and resource allocation (e.g. Lange and Taylor 1938; Hodgson 1984; Nove 1983; Burczak 2006). One of the most sophisticated and compelling variants is Theodore Burczak's recent proposal of a market economy consisting of employee-owned firms (Burczak 2006). Given the limited space available I will simplify Burczak's arguments greatly, but in essence his account fuses the traditional Marxist concern with the exploitation and alienation of the worker that exist under unfettered capitalism with Hayek's critique of a centralized model of socialism. In doing so, he seeks to rescue concepts of liberty and democracy from the right, while still being concerned with issues of equality and social justice.

Burczak's response to Hayek is to take up Hodgson's challenge to go beyond agoraphobia while remaining true to the socialist goal of abolishing exploitation. To do this and to tackle social injustices stemming from capitalist work practices, he argues, following De Martino (2000, 2003), that we still need to address 'appropriative justice' alongside distributive justice. Distributive justice can be dealt with through proposals such as minimum income guarantees and wealth taxes that provide individuals with the resources that allow them to make 'choiceworthy' decisions (Burczak 2006: 95). More interesting for the argument here, however, is the concern with what is termed 'appropriative justice'.

For Burczak, exploitation under capitalism occurs not because capital is privately owned and we have a market-based society per se, but rather because these forms of ownership are not democratic and a minority appropriate resources and surplus value produced by the labour of others. This exploitation is at source a threat to human dignity and is thus a strong critique of liberalist conceptions of liberty advanced by Hayek, Rawls and others before them, most notably Locke. Put very simply: 'a prerequisite for universal human dignity is that people cannot treat others as tools to achieve their ends' (ibid.: 117). In effect, then, the concern is with economic democracy and control of resources in achieving social justice rather than being fixated with ownership forms per se.

The solution for Burczak is a system of worker-managed firms operating in competitive markets. Markets are still able to perform the Hayekian functions regarding discovery, knowledge production, innovation and the stimulation of entrepreneurship, and even competition, but worker-managed firms would eliminate the basic source of exploitation under capitalism: the wage relationship. For Burczak, the source of capitalist exploitation is not private ownership but rather the 'ability of the owner of the means of production to appropriate the entire output of an enterprise that employs wage labour' (ibid.: 110). His solution is therefore the abolition of the wage relation that permits exploitation in the labour process, rather than abolishing private ownership. Importantly, this focus upon production and the labour process also enables us to identify why exploitation of workers does not go away – but can even intensify – in centralized socialist models or indeed in state-driven forms of capitalism. Capitalist forms of disciplinary power can even be reinforced by the domination by the state of all other spheres of social and economic life. But the basic point is that private managers and capitalists are replaced by state managers and Communist Party elites in the appropriation of the fruits of labour. The fundamental social relations of the economy remain unchanged.

Burczak's proposals would meet Hayek's objections about the limits to planning, yet are revolutionary in providing workers with ownership and decision-making power in the economy. Burczak views his approach as an element of a postmodern Marxism. He rereads Hayek in postmodern terms because of the latter's convincing arguments about the imperfectibility of knowledge, the limits to scientific rationality and the universalism of Enlightenment thought, which have informed both socialist and (though this has not been acknowledged by Hayek and his followers) market utopias.[2] Grand socialist theories evoking universal models of collective ownership and totalizing economic projects around planning as a solution to the contradictions of capitalism are flawed because of the knowledge problems and deficits described earlier. Burczak's response is to accept the market as an organizing device that is best able to deal with these problems; the market is defended here as a 'discovery process' rather than the neoclassical view of markets as price mechanisms that provide optimum outcomes under equilibrium conditions. It is Hayek's insistence on the ability of markets to deal with tacit knowledge more effectively than planned systems that socialists such as Burczak, Nove and Hodgson have taken on board.[3]

But where Burczak departs from Hayek is around questions of ownership (or rather the collectivization versus the individualization of ownership), democracy and social justice. Where Hayek viewed private capitalist forms of ownership backed up by legal contracts as sufficient to promote a 'thin' version of the common good, Burczak retains the Marxist insight about the uneven nature of power under capitalist institutions. Using Hayek's own arguments against him – with regard to the context-dependent nature of economic life over the shared rationalisms of neoclassical and orthodox Marxist perspectives – Burczak suggests that legal institutions under capitalism are not capable of arbitrating neutrally between economic agents (e.g. manager and worker) but will themselves be socially constructed and therefore infused with the dominant power relations in a society. Only by eliminating the capitalist wage nexus can such pernicious institutions and the exploitation associated with them be eliminated.

With others (e.g. Prychitko 2002) Burczak goes so far as to say that on purely scientific, rather than ideological, grounds, Hayek should have no objection to an economy composed of worker-managed, labour-appropriating firms 'in the context of widely held private property and market exchange' (Burczak 2006: 120). Worker-managed firms would act no differently from capitalist-managed ones; indeed, they may even perform better in terms of their ability to take a longer-term perspective and their greater willingness to use their tacit knowledge to improve the productivity and performance of the firm. Indeed, two highly respected US economists have made the argument that the former could well be more efficient than the latter because workers will have more incentive to improve productivity, less of a tendency towards workshyness, while at the same time the need for expensive monitoring and disciplining procedures will be lessened (Bowles and Gintis 1993).

These are important arguments and help to dispel many of the assumed (but largely unsubstantiated) efficiencies under hierarchical forms of capitalist management in mainstream debates. Clearly, there is considerable scope for cooperative and worker-owned forms of organization alongside the continued use of markets in particular sectors of the economy, particularly those consumer sectors (such as clothing or consumer electronics) that require more devolved decision-making in the context of dynamic and complex forms of demand and individual preference (see Chapter 7). However, the primacy attached by Burczak and others such as Hodgson to market forms and the rejection of other forms of public ownership beyond private labour-appropriating enterprises needs a little more consideration and appraisal.

The democratic limits to the post-Hayekian view of socialism

Burczak's model is appealing in engaging with Hayek's legitimate concerns while fashioning some important arguments for democratic economic management around 'appropriative justice'. However, the continuing emphasis upon markets and private (albeit collective) ownership as a solution for all economic problems seems to run counter to the more general insistence on toleration, variety and pluralism that marks out such postmodern and institutional strands of economic thought.

In the first instance, by locating the problem of exploitation under capitalism primarily within the workplace, there is a tendency to neglect the processes of power and appropriation that also work through capitalist market forces. Yet the second aspect of capitalist exploitation that has been recognized from Marx onwards is what has been referred to as 'primitive accumulation' or 'accumulation by dispossession' (Harvey 2003; De Angelis 2007). This refers to the ongoing dynamic within capitalism to bring non-capitalist spheres of economic and social relations – often held under more traditional and sometimes communal systems of rights – under conditions of accumulation and profit maximization. This is especially pertinent in the context of ownership relations, where common or public forms of ownership are appropriated for the pursuit of private wealth. Of course, such processes of appropriation also occur outside of capitalism. The point here is that the internal logic to capitalism, the competitive and dynamic impulses to expand the sphere of capitalist accumulation, both geographically and functionally, provide an important impetus to the process of privatization, marketization and commodification.

This point does not necessarily mean that all market forms lead inevitably to conditions of gross exploitation and inequality. In this regard, Hodgson makes the important point when he notes approvingly of Diane Elson's plan to refashion the labour market along more equitable grounds that 'the market can take a wide variety of forms, and some of these are much more objectionable than others' (1999: 97). As the varieties of capitalism literature highlight, markets are ultimately socially constructed institutions that vary widely in time and space and are fashioned out of existing social and cultural norms and practices, rather than having some universal set of principles. Thus Nordic capitalisms are more equitable and democratic than Anglo-Saxon ones, and East Asian forms of capitalism are more communitarian but also more hierarchical than Western forms. This is an important point to recognize. Hodgson himself notes the emergence of a particularly Anglo-Saxon form of market behaviour that came to dominate British and American capitalism from the nineteenth century onwards and emerged out of the particular historical and geographical context of a 'fractured and class-divided society, where an individualist ideology had long been established' (ibid.: 93).

But the particular point to make here is that the unleashing of the kind of deregulated market capitalism that has been pursued under neoliberalism at the global scale, and evident most notably in the privatization process described in the last chapter, has intensified the level of appropriation of common and public resources for private profit. A parallel argument to Burczak's position on private property relations might be to say that there is nothing wrong with the institution of the market per se as a solution to some problems of economic allocation – after all, markets pre-date capitalism – but there is a problem with particular forms of actively deregulated markets under capitalism which have become hegemonic under neoliberalism policy doctrine.

Even accepting a role for markets in a socialist economy, however, is a different thing to allowing the market form to become dominant. Market relations should not become the only economic relations between people. As Polanyi (1944) long ago recognized, this path leads towards societal upheaval and destruction. It is precisely the incursion and spread of 'free market values' and norms – through heightened commodification processes – into all areas of economic life which needs to be resisted and rolled back if wider social goals, such as environmental sustainability, decent and 'choiceworthy' lives and social justice, are to be achieved. Accepting that the market form should be pre-eminent ignores the diverse ethical and value systems that are required if social need and environmental sustainability are to be given priority in a more democratic and egalitarian economy. Furthermore, as O'Neill has convincingly argued, pure market economies are themselves 'amoral' and 'disembedded' from 'social custom and need' (1998: 5). Indeed, as he notes: 'because in market economies, economic decisions are not constrained directly by ethical considerations the economies are ethically indefensible' (ibid.). Indeed, it is exactly their non-normative and technocratic function that mainstream economists usually defend. Yet it is this technocratic function which needs to be challenged. Building on this point, George De Martino has recently made a spirited call for an ethical code for economists whose actions and prescriptions can have devastating consequences for the well-being of others (De Martino 2011).

Furthermore, the elevation of markets over planning oversimplifies the actual workings of economies. In a retort to the market socialist arguments advanced by Nove, the late Ernest Mandel (Mandel 1986) made the point that in advanced or 'late capitalist' economies, as he termed them, it is a fiction to believe that markets dominate economic decision-making when in fact, in an economy increasingly dominated by larger and multinational enterprises, much activity is organized and resources allocated largely independent of market mechanisms.

> Already today, in the most advanced capitalist countries, the bulk of both consumer and producer goods are not produced in any way in response to 'market signals' shifting violently from year to year, let alone month to month. The bulk of current production corresponds to established consumption patterns and predetermined production techniques that are largely if not completely independent of the market. (Ibid.: 10)

Planning continues to exist and indeed persists in the strategic decision-making of large private firms. Mandel asks why much of this could not be done democratically in collectively owned forms by what he terms the 'associated producers' (ibid.: 11). He also makes an important point about the falsely coupled binaries of markets/democracy and planning/authoritarianism when he notes that market economies exist under both democratic and authoritarian regimes, as do forms of central planning.

The central issue here is that it is possible to accept the arguments about the dangers of centralization of economic decision-making – under both monopoly or 'late' capitalist regimes or Soviet-style socialism – without rejecting the possibilities that planning and other non-market forms of organization may have important roles to play in a more democratic socialist economy. A similar point is made by Antonio Callari in his generally sympathetic critique of Burczak's proposals.

> Now, as I see it, the problem with *Socialism [After Hayek]* is not with the idea of worker ownership and surplus appropriation, nor is it with the introduction of markets into the idea of socialism. I find totally plausible a rejection of socialism as a centrally planned calculation ... The problem is, rather, with the presumption, central to the rhetorical force of *Socialism*, that these two elements (worker ownership and markets) exhaust the theoretical outline of a thickened socialism. There is no room, in this outline, for forms of ownership and appropriation other than those consonant with market processes ... and social accounting of values other than through the lever of profit. (Callari 2009: 368)

In other words, there are dangers that the socialist take-up of markets as the key coordinating mechanism for economic life leads to the narrowing of our value system to the pursuit of self-interest (even if that interest is on behalf of collectives of workers in a cooperative market economy) rather than opening up the economy to other moralities and value systems (e.g. Gibson-Graham 2006). A revolution which replaces the private and selfish rationalities of capitalist forms of organization with those of selfish collective rationalities of workers would seem to go against the basic principles being espoused. In this sense, we need to remind ourselves that capitalist exploitation rests upon three pillars: the employment relation, private property and the market; and the neglect of any one element in an alternative schema is unlikely to deal effectively with the basic problem. The danger is that we end up with another totalizing vision rather than one that promotes the institutional diversity, openness and tolerance that are essential elements of a more democratic economy.

Public ownership, pluralism and democracy

What are the implications of these debates for our thinking here on public ownership? The market socialist response seems to imply an important role for cooperative and worker-owned forms of organization, although perceived as forms of socialist 'private' ownership that transcend the exploitation of the capitalist wage relationship. Public ownership of the state ownership variety is implicitly rejected here on the grounds that it is fundamentally undemocratic; regimes that replace private ownership with state ownership replace one type of elite appropriating the product of labour with another.

Arguing in a similar vein, Hodgson criticizes traditional left thinking of the socialist rather than anarchist variety – by both revolutionary communists and the reformist wing of social democracy from Marx onwards – for its insistence on an economy where private ownership and markets have been completely abolished to be replaced by a form of common ownership of the means of production. For Hodgson, Marx and Engels's failure to take markets seriously was equated with a monolithic vision of state ownership: '... in their sparse words on the economic organization of socialism, they betrayed an overwhelming adherence to the national ownership and organization of the means of production without any space or favour for economic pluralism and a mixed economy' (Hodgson 1999: 22).

Accordingly, this failure remained the albatross around the socialist neck right up until the 1950s when the British Labour Party and the German Social Democrats, along with some eastern European regimes, began to accept the role of markets alongside planning. In other words, Hodgson reads into the Marxist rejection of markets and the commitment to common or public ownership – although by his own admission Marx and Engels were actually quite sketchy about what a future socialist or communist economy would look like and Marx could be quite contradictory on these matters (Nove 1983) – a lack of pluralism, diversity and by implication democracy in economic institutions and forms. This is something of a conceptual leap; while the state socialist regimes of the twentieth century could be criticized on these grounds, it is something else entirely to suggest that a commitment to public ownership per se need always be associated with a lack of pluralism, diversity and democracy. In this way, Hodgson seems to fall into the mistake of equating pluralism and diversity solely with some form of mixed economy in which market mechanisms, because of their price-setting and knowledge discovery advantages, must have the pivotal role.[4]

An important counter-argument in defence of socialist diversity with non-market forms comes from the work of the Manchester-based philosopher of political economy John O'Neill (O'Neill 1998, 2003, 2007). O'Neill agrees with Hodgson that the philosophical underpinnings of extreme forms of markets and planning have their limitations in their neglect of the practices through which knowledge is created and uncertainty infuses economic life. Both try to reduce economic decision-making to calculable measures (e.g. a price mechanism or accounting matrix to inform planning decisions). Drawing upon the work of the associational socialist Otto Neurath, who was involved with socialist experiments in decentralized planning in Munich and Vienna in the 1920s and 1930s, O'Neill rejects the scientific rationality of both mainstream economics and orthodox Marxism in favour of a pluralistic perspective that accepts the limitations and provisional nature of knowledge claims. This is important because it rejects both market and socialist solutions to economic problems which seek to universalize decision-making on the basis of making so-called rational choices: 'The unpredictability in science in general entails that the technocratic ideal of the discovery of an optimal solution to social decisions is untenable' (O'Neill 2003: 191).

Although O'Neill agrees with Hodgson (and Hayek) about the imprecise nature of knowledge and the importance of tacit knowledge that is not easily codified and appropriated for centralized decision-making,[5] he does not draw the same conclusions about the inevitability of market forms to deal with these problems. Indeed, at various points (e.g. O'Neill 2003, 2007), he uses the scientific and academic communities as examples of non-market orders that effectively allow the development of tacit knowledge in what elsewhere would be termed a 'global commons'. Moreover, he rightly warns that: 'The danger in the current introduction of market mechanisms into public science is that it will slow rather than increase the rate of innovation. Conflicts around the development of new intellectual property regimes center on the control of knowledge crucial to innovation' (O'Neill 2002: 147).

Again, the point here is that a rejection of centralization of economic power does not necessarily have to equate with a rejection of non-market institutions such as forms of democratic planning that are organized around public ownership.

Neurath was critical of both market economies and centrally planned ones for their attempts to impose a universal system of value to all economic decisions in the form of prices or other forms of accounting unit (e.g. labour hours worked, energy used, etc.). He used the phrase 'pseudo-rationalism' to refer to scientists and philosophers who believed that there is always the possibility of discovering one theory or solution to any problem through rational inquiry. The messiness of the real world and the impossibility of perfect knowledge in dealing with it means that our solutions are always provisional. When transferred to the realms of public policy, the logical implication of this is a scepticism about claims by either market or socialist economists that it is possible to offer 'optimal solutions' (ibid.: 191) to economic problems. As O'Neill notes, it becomes obvious that the problem of low predictability and imperfect knowledge faces all human actors tasked with making decisions about social problems. To offer up the market as the way of resolving these dilemmas – as Hayek does – is to merely repeat the mistake. Neurath effectively turns the tables on Hayek by invoking the 'intolerance of the market economy' and arguing that 'it is possible for forms of economy of various kinds to exist without being forced into competition' (Neurath 1920: 397, cited in O'Neill 2006: 71). Of course, to turn another Hayekian phrase around, it has become the 'fatal conceit' stemming from the ascendancy of neoclassical economics in the twenty-first century that all social problems (from valuing the environment, to providing healthcare, to assessing human happiness) can be calculated in monetary terms. The anti-capitalist movement that has arisen in opposition to neoliberal-driven forms of globalization has at its core both 'resistance to the spread of market norms and property rights' and the 'defence of non-market institutional and cultural forms' (O'Neill 2007: 195).

Conclusions

The paradigmatic twentieth-century models of public ownership associated with central planning and state control have been critiqued on all sides. For those socialists who are serious about learning the lessons from the past failures of 'actually existing socialisms', Hayek's intellectual arguments in particular have been compelling in seeking to get to grips with the issues of uncertainty, pluralism and democracy. One way of addressing this, as we have seen here, is to embrace the market in forms of market socialism that attempt to retain the knowledge-enhancing and open-ended dynamism of market forms alongside new forms of social organization that attempt to eliminate the exploitative social relations of capitalism within the workplace. Burzcak's insightful thesis around worker ownership and the important issue of 'appropriative justice' is an important theme to take forward from these debates. This means developing forms of public ownership where economic democracy is established as a first principle.

However, the worker management model is only a partial response to the conditions of exploitation and appropriation under capitalism. Two points are critical here in the argument laid out above. The first is that the continued emphasis upon the market as a form to promote innovation, diversity and economic tolerance has its own problems and indeed is no more likely to resolve some of the issues apparent under forms of state and public ownership. While, following the above discussion, there is clearly a role for markets in some fashion in the organization of a socialist economy, it is quite a big leap to dismiss alternative non-market institutions and mechanisms for coordinating the economy out of hand, or to put quite so much emphasis upon market forms as many of those on the left do.

We also have to go beyond market values to incorporate non-market forms and ethics in constructing a more egalitarian and solidaristic economy. Not only are the market's powers to stimulate knowledge and diversity exaggerated but the competitive and profit-driven ethos is not and should not be the only 'economic identity' that shapes economic decision-making (Gibson-Graham 2006). Market processes under capitalism designed to appropriate commonly held land and resources for private profit are themselves an important element of contemporary exploitation that needs resisting and rolling back (Harvey 2003; De Angelis 2007; O'Neill 2007). Accepting the economy as ultimately a socially and politically embedded phenomenon, the task is therefore to create institutions which both protect and encourage non-invidious decision-making in both market and non-market forms. At the core of these arguments is the need for institutional rules and organizational forms that are fundamentally grounded in democratic procedures, advance a pluralist society and are concerned with deliberative forms of decision-making. The precise nature of how this emerges will vary over time and space, and is context dependent.

The second related point, drawing upon O'Neill and Neurath (and implicitly from Hayek and Hodgson), is the importance of diversity and variety in new forms of public ownership. The key thing to avoid in this respect is that in developing new ideas about public ownership we do not fall back into the mistake of the all-encompassing model and vision: a one-size-fits-all solution. Public ownership needs to take on more variegated forms that both respect geographical variations in pre-existing economic practices and cultures and take diverse, dispersed and overlapping forms as a way of combating the centralization and concentration of economic power and decision-making. These issues are developed further in Chapter 7.

PART TWO
The return of public ownership

4 | Financial crisis and the rediscovery of the state in the neoliberal heartland

Mr Lord Mayor, we will not forget that the first and foremost duty of government is to maintain and indeed to strengthen monetary and fiscal stability that has enabled us, successively, to grow and remain free of recession over the last decade, even when facing the Asia crisis, the American downturn and now the rapidly rising oil and commodity prices of the last three years. I can assure you that through the vigilance of the Bank [of England] and our determination to ensure future public sector pay settlements are founded on our two per cent inflation target, we will maintain our anti-inflation discipline. ... So just as our monetary reforms, which brought Bank of England independence, made decision-making independent of short-term political and partisan considerations, so too do our competition reforms, which have for the first time made our competition authorities independent of government. (Excerpts from the Mansion House speech made by Gordon Brown, Chancellor of the Exchequer, to the City of London Corporation, 22 June 2006)

In practice, this celebration of pure politics entrusts the virtue of the 'political good' to governmental oligarchies enlightened by 'experts'; which is to say that the supposed purification of the political, freed from domestic and social necessity, comes down to nothing more (or less) than the reduction of the political to the state. (Rancière 2001)

In the early summer of 1992, shortly after the Labour Party's fourth successive election defeat at the hands of the Conservatives, and as part of a brief and unsuccessful career as an economic consultant, I conducted an interview with the late Joe Mills. Mills was then the regional general secretary of the Transport and General Workers Union in the north-east of England, not the most auspicious position to hold at the time. The north-east was the region of the UK most damaged by the politics of Thatcherism, deindustrialization and the emasculation of the trade union movement. In these circumstances, Mills, seen as an 'early moderniser' (see Hetherington 2003), evoked many of the themes that were to dominate Labour politics both in opposition and then in its thirteen years in government as 'New Labour'. Two parts of the conversation in particular stayed with me. The first was an interesting piece of gossip about the up-and-coming young local Labour MP, Tony Blair, who was then the shadow minister for employment. Mills told me proudly that it had been he who had 'fixed it' for Blair to become MP for Sedgefield, an old mining area to the south of Durham, by using his union influence to put Blair on the ballot at the last minute (see also ibid.).

The second thing that stuck in my mind was more profound and related to the north-east's declining fortunes and how the trade unions might deal with them. After fourteen years of Thatcherism, the miners' strike and the decimation of the region's industrial base in shipbuilding, coal, steel and heavy engineering and the social deprivation this had caused (Hudson 1989), you might have thought that the appropriate reaction would be one of anger at the perpetrators. But no, Mills was insistent that the correct approach now was 'to play down the political'. His words were not just those of a local party 'realist', coming to terms with more years of Conservative government and the need to build local coalitions with businessmen to try to inject some sort of economic life back into the region.[1] For they also epitomized the broader shift made by many social democrats in the 1990s to accommodate themselves with the 'new realities' of globalization, absorbing the politics of TINA[2] and learning to love the free market and big business. In the UK this also meant accepting the financial interests of the City of London, which, outside of the Conservative Party, had done most to destroy the manufacturing sector and regions such as the north-east that depended on it. Mills's prodigy Blair and Gordon Brown (the co-founder of the New Labour project) had absorbed these lessons well, and their wholehearted conversion to a neoliberal agenda is no longer worthy of much comment here. Three years later, as the leader of the Labour Party, Blair had what has come to be termed his 'Clause Four moment' when he persuaded the Labour Party to ditch the long-cherished commitment to public ownership in favour of a more vague aspiration to social justice and a democratic socialist politics. Although this victory for Blair and New Labour was probably more 'symbolic' than anything else, given the failure of Labour governments to deliver a democratic public ownership on behalf of the workers in the past, it did nevertheless represent an important broader trend among social democratic parties internationally to retreat from any kind of politics that challenged the rights of private business to own and control the economy.

New Labour were to become the pioneers of this rather disingenuous 'looking glass' approach to economic policy of 'playing down the politics'. As the quote from Brown at the beginning of the chapter suggests, the language of New Labour evoked the importance of an 'independent' approach to key economic decision-making issues, such as the setting of interest rates, hence its vaunted decision to make the Bank of England 'independent' of political interference. Of course, nothing was farther from the truth. Brown and Blair were doing entirely the opposite; handing over key elements of the government's macroeconomic policy to a committee of unelected mainstream and right-wing economists, primarily from the financial establishment of the City of London. A very political act but presented at the time as a mark of economic competence alongside a language of 'commercial freedom'. While this may have been a short-term strategy to secure electoral advantage, Brown and Blair were to display all the zealotry of a Pauline conversion in their subsequent embrace of neoliberalism with their commitment to privatization, deregulation and market liberalization. They also became evangelists in promoting the 'British model' of light-touch regulation and market freedoms elsewhere.

Yet, as I noted in the Introduction, this came to an abrupt halt in February 2008 when the Labour government was forced to do the unthinkable and nationalize major parts of the banking system to stem the collapse of the entire British economy. Huge amounts of state funding have been used to rescue financial institutions from the kinds of speculation and risk-taking activities that Gordon Brown had been so keen on encouraging just two years earlier. Although public ownership as nationalization has returned to the political agenda, the hoped-for shift in broader economic policy has not materialized, and almost four years on, governments throughout the world have embarked upon a series of unprecedented austerity measures to reduce the government debts run up as a consequence of bailing out the banks.

In this chapter, I chart the accommodation of New Labour and the broader centre-left with neoliberalism and the politics of global competitiveness. Focusing on the UK as a heartland of neoliberalism (Peck and Tickell 2002), I show especially how this shift has consistently been at odds with public opinion. Equally perversely, in the UK New Labour's embrace of neoliberal ideas came at exactly that point when the contradictions of privatization and the broader neoliberal agenda were becoming all too apparent (ibid.). In its bid to become electable, not only did the Labour Party (as with the centre-left globally) fully reject anything akin to an alternative socialist vision, but it also helped to rescue the neoliberal project from its own contradictions. The longer-term consequences of such political opportunism have been extremely serious, effectively removing debate about alternative strategies from economic policy-making fora. This has become particularly apparent in the aftermath of the current financial crisis when the attachment to an agenda of fiscal austerity and more privatization of public assets remains strong across the mainstream political spectrum in many European countries. Not only is this damaging for a counter-hegemonic politics of the left and dealing with important public policy concerns such as social justice and climate change, but it also weakens democracy by extinguishing pluralism and heteredox thinking around an authoritarian free market economics that is intolerant of other approaches and traditions.

The social democratic embrace of neoliberalism

Privatization and the New Labour project Following its election victory in 1997, and fuelled by public distaste at rising prices and corporate 'fat cats' in the privatized industries, the new Labour government introduced a windfall tax on all the privatized utilities as well as a price cap that had the effect of dramatically squeezing profits out of the water sector. However, in its growing accommodation with the City, the government refused to countenance the obvious solution, a return to public ownership. New Labour was to prove to be quite relaxed about privatization – in the same way that it was 'quite relaxed about people becoming filthy rich'.[3] Indeed, with the exception of the rail infrastructure company, Railtrack – of which more in a moment – Labour failed to overturn any of the privatizations introduced by the Conservatives. Moreover, the government developed and extended the privatization of public assets both through its own partial privatization of air traffic control services but also through the growing marketization of education and health services and the expansion of the private finance initiative (PFI) to fund public sector infrastructure projects. Such projects have opened up public procurement to private interests in such a way that government has underwritten most of the risk, enabling the private sector to make vast and guaranteed profits for many years hence.[4]

New Labour's conversion to neoliberalism did not stop at the English Channel but was extended into key European Union policy networks and through lobbying at the level of the World Trade Organization, the IMF and the World Bank. At EU level the Labour government continued the previous Conservative administration's policy of promoting market deregulation and liberalization while continuing to resist employment and social policy directives coming the other way which would have improved the rights of part-time workers and unions and reduce working hours (which continue to be some of the longest in Europe).[5] This was especially the case in the gas and electricity sectors, where it was keen to roll out the British model of privatization. At one European Union summit in Stockholm, for example, Prime Minister Tony Blair was reported as being exasperated by the resistance of some of Britain's partners to opening up the European energy market to greater competition (*Guardian*, 21 March 2001). As we shall see in Chapter 9, the UK played a major role in the establishment of competition directives, through its trade commissioners, Leon Brittan, from 1993 to 1999, and Peter Mandelson, from 2004 to 2008.

Labour's approach is captured well in its first review of energy strategy (DTI 1998), where it was less exercised about how energy policy might meet social objectives than with promoting markets and competition:

> The Government's central energy policy objective is to ensure secure, diverse and sustainable supplies of energy at competitive prices. ... Competitive markets and companies are the key to achieving this objective, but the Government has a contribution to make in setting the right frameworks and in dealing with issues which the market on its own may be less equipped to handle. (Ibid.: 5)

Future energy policy would increasingly be conducted in the context of global and European markets. In this context, an important item on the European agenda in recent years, and one which the UK has played a major role in promoting, has been to build the single European market in energy with a view to promoting competition and liberalization. This has been pursued not only to promote free trade in energy but more generally to improve the supply side of the European economy, to lower costs, and improve prosperity across Europe (ibid.: 55).

Despite the initial rhetoric of the 'Third Way' as a middle ground between statism and unregulated markets, the uptake of neoliberal ideology was if anything more zealous than that of the Conservatives, as anything that hinted at an 'Old Labour' style of government intervention – such as rail renationalization, which had been official Labour Party policy as late at 1996 – had to be swiftly discarded.[6] Although Blair and Brown justified their approach in terms of making Labour electable again and restoring the electorate's trust in the party, it is particularly bizarre that they accepted the politics of privatization which had arguably been one of the issues that had caused the Conservatives the most damage in the run-up to the election (Gamble 1995).

The broader social democrat embrace Tony Blair and his new-model Labour Party were not the only ones among political parties of the centre-left to shed their remaining social democratic clothes and embrace the logic of globalization and the free market in the 1990s. Bill Clinton's New Democrats – whom New Labour regarded as its inspiration – had plotted a similar pathway, albeit from a centrist and generally business-centred ethos, rather than a social democratic starting point, most notably in the introduction of punitive workfare legislation to the already minimalist US welfare state alongside tax cuts for the rich. Clinton's most notorious contribution to free market capitalism, however, was the abolition of the Glass-Steagall (1933) Act in 1999, championed by his Treasury Secretary, Larry Summers, which removed most of the remaining barriers between retail and investment banking in the United States, allowing more speculative activities into markets such as housing and real estate and extinguishing any vestiges of mutualism from the financial sector.

In other countries, as diverse as New Zealand, France, Norway, India and Mexico, centre-left, social democrat and labour parties all bowed to the pressures of neoliberalism, privatization and market deregulation during the 1990s and abandoned any attempt to use the state to constrain or regulate, let alone challenge, an increasingly rampant global capitalism. Even in statist France, Lionel Jospin's centre-left government of socialists, communists and greens embarked on a significant programme of privatization in the late 1990s. The rhetoric of globalization, the hypermobility of finance capital and the dominance of multinational corporations were all cited as reasons why the rules had changed and why national governments could not and should not intervene in, or interfere with, the running of markets. Keynesian-style market interventions were decidedly off limits, but policies of nationalization and public ownership were completely beyond the pale.

Moreover, as Table 4.1 indicates for European countries, left parties played an active role in privatization. One of the most vigorous privatizers, for example, were the Spanish socialists between 1995 and 2000, with the selling off of state assets being seen as an important stepping stone to reducing government expenditure to qualify for euro membership. Similar circumstances characterized the Italian Olive Tree Alliance, a nominally centre-left government which doubled the amount of revenue raised from privatization (compared to the previ-

TABLE 4.1 Privatization proceeds and left parties in power in European countries during the 1990s

Country	Value of privatization 1993–98 (£ billion)	Left parties in power in the 1990s
Italy	56.4	Centre-left Olive Tree Alliance, 1996–98
France	35.6	Coalition between socialists, communists and greens, 1997–2002
Spain	28.1	Socialists in power, 1990–2000
Germany	23.3	Social Democrat–Green coalition, 1998–2005
UK	22.4	Labour government, 1997–2010
Sweden	12.4	Social Democrat coalition-led, 1994–2006
Netherlands	10.9	Labour-led coalition, 1994–2002
Portugal	10.3	Socialists in power, 1995–2002
Denmark	5.7	Social Democrat-led coalition, 1994–2001
Austria	5.3	Grand coalition with Soc Dems largest party, 1990–99
Belgium	4.8	No left-majority government
Finland	3.5	Social Democrat coalition, 1995–2003
Switzerland	3.1	No left-majority government in 1990s
Greece	2.3	Socialists in power, 1993–2000
Norway	1.7	Social Democrats in power, 1989–97

Source: OECD (2003)

ous centre-right administration) between 1996 and 1998, selling off around $50 billion worth of assets during its short time in power (OECD 2003). Centre-left leaders tended to see themselves as pragmatic leaders tasked with the management of national productivity and competitiveness in the face of supposedly unstoppable global forces. The former Italian prime minister Romano Prodi was typical of the kind of technocratic politician of the era, an academic economist who had risen to national prominence in the 1980s as chairman of one of Italy's largest conglomerates, the Istituto per la Ricostruzione Industriale (IRI), which he had helped to privatize. Even the more established social democratic parties in northern Europe weren't adverse to dabbling in privatization, as we will see in the case of Norway in Chapter 8. The Social Democrats under Gerhard Schroeder in Germany between 1998 and 2005 also became enthusiastic privatizers, continuing the work started by the previous Christian Democrat coalition under Helmut Kohl.

One of the most prominent centre-left privatizers was the French prime minister Lionel Jospin. Although it was the preceding right-wing governments under Chirac and Balladur which launched the French privatization programme, the largest individual privatizations were achieved under Jospin, the sale of France Telecom with the first tranche of shares worth $7.1 billion in 1997 and the second tranche in 1998 worth $10.5 billion (Megginson and Netter 2001: 325). While it is probable that many of these governments were not fully signed-up cheerleaders for the neoliberal project in the manner of Blair and Brown, they did nevertheless prove to have no ideological objection to the prospect of privatization. Indeed, Clift (2001) makes a convincing case that privatization under Jospin fitted in with a long established policy of French dirigisme and was about making French companies competitive in the global marketplace, often through partial privatizations that allowed effective restructuring to take place. While there was still state intervention in industrial policy there was a shift from 'ownership to enduring influence' (ibid.: 173).

Common sense, convenient myths and the contested politics of privatization?

While the centre-left's uptake of neoliberalism was in large part a tactical manoeuvre, though taking varying forms across the advanced economies, it has at another level been complicit in reinforcing a certain 'common sense' of the age that persists into the present in the mainstream reaction to the financial crisis. This has penetrated deep into a received public consciousness and is associated with the depoliticization of economic questions and issues and their positioning in a separate realm of experts – primarily drawn from mainstream economics and business – where a particular technocratic discourse has emerged to justify decision-making in the interests of the elite. Not only do actions such as those of Prodi, Brown and Jospin hand over important democratic decisions regarding economic matters to unelected technocrats, who more often than not represent elite and conservative interests, but they helped to delegitimize debate around alternative and more progressive agendas.

Outside of a few left-of-centre newspapers, a broad consensus has been established around the 'economic' as a 'post-political' realm that leaves behind adversarial agendas to construct common purpose around national competitiveness and productivity strategies. Governments should not intervene in economic matters and economic decisions should not be subject to 'political interference'. 'Independence' is sacrosanct, as is the exercise of 'commercial freedom'. This state of affairs was captured neatly recently during a discussion on BBC Radio 4's flagship early morning current affairs programme *Today* when there was a more interesting discussion than usual about the economy, the role of privatized energy utilities and the soaring prices facing users of gas and electricity in the UK. At one point, the combative and avuncular journalist John Humphrys, who surely prides himself on his 'independence', and who was chairing a debate between a representative of the energy lobby and an NGO spokesperson, could be heard to say, without a trace of irony: 'Obviously we don't want to go back to a complete nationalization.' The remark went completely unchallenged and was just accepted as a piece of uncontroversial common sense. Not only was there no questioning of this easy assumption by anyone on the programme, but there was felt to be no need to even justify the comment with any rational argument. The unspoken implication was that, although privatization might have its problems, the old state bureaucracies were far worse.

For some, these developments signify a 'post-political' age in which:

> the conflict of global ideological visions embodied in different parties which compete for power is replaced by the collaboration of enlightened technocrats (economists, public opinion specialists ...) ... via the process of negotiation of interests, a compromise is reached in the guise of a more or less universal consensus. Post-politics thus emphasizes the need to leave old ideological visions behind and confront new issues, armed with the necessary expert knowledge and free deliberation that takes people's concrete needs and demands into account. (Žižek 1999: 198)

As part of this, economic policy is subjected to what Rancière (2001) in a compelling phrase has called the 'partition of the sensible (*'la partage du sensible'*), whereby an elite is charged with making decisions that are removed from, but seen as being on behalf of, the rest of us. At one level, it implies a governed consensus over what the economic situation is and what it needs, with economic scientists and experts left to work out the solutions, but at a deeper level it represents the exclusion of the majority of the population – the '99 per cent', following Naomi Klein's popularized slogan – from critical decisions regarding the economy. Moreover, as O'Neill (2007) and others note, much of the consultative and deliberative rhetoric that has accompanied this technocratic turn in the politics of economics masks the paucity of constrained choices in a market-centred universe. Real deliberation and dialogue need different politics and clashes between opposing positions (Mouffe 2005) rather than minor disagreements around trajectories that have already been chosen, as later chapters demonstrate. The effective closing down of public discourse by mainstream political parties of the centre-left has added to a growing sense of exclusion and alienation, particularly among many working-class voters, precipitating the resurgence of the far right.

While some might see this 'post-political' condition as one in which oppositional politics have been closed down (e.g. Swyngedouw 2009), this ignores the ongoing and contested nature of neoliberalism, with the recent 'Occupy Wall Street' protests being just the latest manifestation. It also fails to acknowledge how the current elite agenda around the economy is bolstered by a series of myths that are constructed in the face of robust counter-evidence. The myth-making around the failings of nationalization was particularly powerful to the neoliberal cause in both its 'roll-back' and 'roll-out' phases, developing out of a set of received wisdoms that struck a chord with a wider public, building upon political grievances and discontent in the 1970s which were then appropriated for a more sustained narrative. Of course, the discourse flew in the face of much of the available evidence about real economic performance of public versus private enterprises.

A more critical and systematic assessment of the merits of privatization versus public ownership reveals a very different picture than that portrayed in mainstream political narratives. In the first instance, there is little evidence the privatized entities have yielded better long-term performance than their nationalized predecessors. A detailed study in the late 1990s found that: 'evidence does not support any notion of the inferiority of public ownership, a conclusion reached even without regard to the wider objectives of public ownership with private ownership' (Sawyer and O'Donnell 1999: 1). In the UK, and despite the problems of underinvestment and a lack of strategic direction noted in Chapter 1, total factor productivity (which includes the productivity performance of labour and capital) in the nationalized industries of gas, electricity and water increased by 3.1 per cent between 1950 and 1985, a figure that was higher than both their US privately owned counterparts (2.6 per cent) and UK manufacturing as a whole (1.8 per cent) over the same period. With regard to the comparative experience before and after privatization they found that 'privatisation has produced mixed results. Where there have been noticeable efficiency gains, these have tended to occur mainly in the run-up to privatisation, where the industries were rationalised and prepared for sale, suggesting one-off efficiency gains' (ibid.: 27).[7]

We need in this sense to distinguish between an elite and hegemonic discourse on the one hand and a more fragmented, often suppressed, yet perhaps emergent set of counter-hegemonic discourses around the economy. Returning to the UK and New Labour, its continued refusal to consider public ownership as a policy solution wilfully flouted its own democratic structures. Successive Labour Party conferences in the 1990s voted overwhelmingly in favour of rail renationalization, for example. Given such democratic disregard, it is not surprising that a declining number of people vote in national elections. Not voting – particularly for local government but increasingly also for the emasculated Westminster Parliament – is a rational response to disenfranchisement rather than a register of apathy, as the most important decisions controlling our lives are made by unelected bankers and FTSE chief executives.

The failure by the political elite to take public ownership seriously is in stark contrast to public opinion, which, when consulted, has stubbornly and consistently posted large majorities in favour of the idea. Again, this is particularly the case in the UK, where one might have expected that mainstream media discourse would have shown a more favourable disposition towards privatization. The most recent example was a poll conducted by YouGov in January 2011[8] on the current government's proposals to sell off England's state-owned forests, which found that 84 per cent opposed the idea. In the face of a wider campaign, which drew support from many traditional Conservative voters, the government quickly dropped the idea. A more general poll conducted in 2006 found that 74 per cent opposed any increased role for private companies in running public services, while only 17 per cent were in favour.

Indeed, over the longer term there has been considerable and sustained opposition and resistance to privatization. Even at the height of its popularity as a policy in the 1980s, there continued to be a majority in opposition to it. As Clifton et al. note: 'when the public was eagerly buying privatisation shares with the aim of making a quick capital gain, public opinion polls often recorded a majority against the policy of privatisation' (Clifton et al. 2003: 91). By the end of the 1990s as the problems of privatization became increasingly self-evident, particularly with regard to the crisis in the rail industry, both before and after the fatal Hatfield crash, there was growing public support for the principle of public ownership and renationalization of many of the utilities. For example, a survey of over a thousand 'random voters' for the *Guardian* (20 March 2000) found that 66 per cent of those interviewed agreed with the proposition that public services should not be run for a profit. Another significant finding was that 61 per cent of self-professed Conservative voters agreed that public services should not be run for profit. Seventy-two per cent of those polled disapproved of government plans to privatize the national air traffic control service, while 76 per cent thought that the railways should be brought back into public ownership. A sizeable minority – 40 per cent – also thought that even British Telecom, a so-called successful privatization, should be brought back into the public sector. What is surprising is the failure of any mainstream political parties to attempt to represent this public majority view for most of the two decades before the onset of the financial crisis.

The financial crisis and the return of public ownership

In the summer of 2007 the first inklings of a serious financial crisis that was eventually to threaten the very foundations of global capitalism became apparent. This brought with it a radical, if somewhat makeshift, reversal in policy: free market fundamentalists of every political hue rediscovered the essential hidden truth of capitalism – that from time to time its over-exuberance requires the state to step in to avoid systemic collapse. The bankruptcy of Northern Rock was the first British episode in a wider global unravelling of financial markets. This had been preceded by a warning from France, where the Banque Nationale de Paris announced that some of its mortgage assets could not be valued, itself precipitating what became known as the 'credit crunch' or the seizing up of interbank lending on a global scale. As the contradictions of unfettered markets and a globally integrated regime of hyper-capitalism became more evident by the day, policy-makers were forced to do the unthinkable and intervene on a massive scale to avert the meltdown of the entire global economy. The key policy tool for doing this was massive and unprecedented nationalization of the financial sector around the world.

Bank nationalization in the UK: a brief detour from business as usual
The Northern Rock nationalization in February 2008 came on the back of months of prevarication, following the government's initial £25 billion financial rescue package in September of the previous year. In the intervening period the Labour government had done everything in its power to avert nationalization, but not surprisingly there were no serious private investors willing to take on Northern Rock at a time of tightening credit markets. The government had briefly contemplated a takeover by Sir Richard Branson's Virgin Group, although the terms being offered by Branson amounted to the appropriation of the bank's

remaining valuable assets while leaving the 'toxic' assets in the hands of the state. That the maverick entrepreneur, lacking any experience whatsoever of running a bank, was viewed as a more preferable option than public ownership by the Labour Chancellor of the Exchequer, Alistair Darling, tells us much about the prevailing mood and ideology in ruling circles. The eventual sale to Branson's group in 2011 merely confirms the continuing slavish adherence to neoliberal nostrums, despite their obvious failings and contradictions.

The nationalization of Northern Rock was followed by an even more momentous series of events, with the full or partial nationalization of hitherto proudly independent bastions of finance capital such as the Royal Bank of Scotland and HBOS, as well as smaller former building societies such as the Bradford and Bingley (Table 4.2). The subsequent acquisition of HBOS by Lloyds meant that the state now held majority stakes in two out of the four leading UK banks. In total £123.93 billion was provided in the form of loans or share purchases, with a further £332.4 million in the form of guarantees (e.g. covering pension liabilities) (NAO 2011). At its peak, the total debt to the taxpayer, once interest and fees were added, was £1.162 trillion in 2009 (ibid.).

TABLE 4.2 Government support (loans) and share purchases of nationalized banks (as of 31 March 2011)

Bank	£ billion	Value as of 31 March 2011	Govt share (%)
Royal Bank of Scotland	45.8	36.97	84
Lloyds	20.54	16.04	43
Northern Rock	21.59	21.59	100
Bradford & Bingley	8.55	8.55	100

Source: National Audit Office

Although many on the left hoped that this might all signal a new and more radical approach to tackling the financial sector, Darling was quick to reassure business interests that nationalization was a necessary evil, but a temporary measure: 'It is better for the Government to hold on to Northern Rock for a temporary period and as and when market conditions improve the value of Northern Rock will grow and therefore the taxpayer will gain. The long-term ownership of this bank *must lie* in the private sector.'[9]

Nationalization was presented as a means of dealing with extraordinary events that departed from the 'normal' functioning of markets, rather than accepting, as a growing body of opinion has, that perhaps the underlying structures of the financial sector might themselves be at fault and that endemic crisis is the new normal. A brief period of state involvement would help to get the patient back on its feet to allow business as usual to resume. As part of this discourse, there was no discussion in government circles about wider issues of ownership, social responsibility or the rationale underpinning the financial sector. It was assumed – and still is – that the benefits to the UK economy from the wealth generated by its financial sector were such that any tampering with the existing model and structures should be avoided.

In other ways, the UK's 2008 bank nationalization programme was a pretty peculiar form of public ownership. Having finally 'nationalized' the private banks that had done so much to bring the economy to the brink of collapse, the government remained insistent that 'commercial logic' would remain the order of the day. A return to profitability was the leitmotif of government policy, despite the opportunities that the crisis offered to rethink the banking sector's remit and perhaps to redesign the country's broader approach to economic and even industrial policy. There remained a deep, if not a somewhat religious, fervour for the virtues of private enterprise and a refusal to even consider that an appointee from the much-maligned public sector could make a better fist of the job. To a man (the world of finance capital remains a heavily male-dominated one), the new appointees to the nationalized companies were drawn from the same commercial banking cartel that had brought about the financial crisis in the first place (Brummer 2009).

Not only was there no real change in the constituents of banking management, but the government was equally clear that it wanted as far as possible to allow the nationalized banks to engage in business as usual. While the government's Financial Services Authority was given some new powers to intervene and regulate the sector as a whole, and various government ministers exhorted the banks to help increase lending to hard-pressed consumers and business customers, there was no attempt to intervene on behalf of the new owners of these new banks, the taxpayers. Banks were allowed to restore their depleted balances and restructure their operations with scant regard for the effects either on their customers or their employees. A report in the *Observer* newspaper in August 2009 reported that one year on, the newly nationalized banks had repossessed more than 6,700 homes from hard-pressed families.[10] At the same time, a Treasury Select Committee report noted that, as in the United States, the effects of home repossession were being felt by some of the most vulnerable in society, those in the so-called 'sub-prime' sector;[11] exactly the people effectively forced into the home ownership game by the lack of alternative publicly owned or privately rented housing and induced into taking out unsustainable loans by the credit free-for-all of the 1990s and early 2000s.

In the same month, one of the state-owned banks, Royal Bank of Scotland, announced a Lazarus-like recovery in its investment banking arm with profits rising from £1 billion to £5 billion over the previous six-month period.[12] Like the other banks it had also been given the go-ahead by the government to separate out its 'toxic assets', the high-risk speculative investments that had all but destroyed the company, from the rest of its business. Furthermore, the government's Asset Protection Scheme, whereby 90 per cent of the bank's 'toxic loans' are underwritten by the taxpayer, represented the equivalent of a massive corporate welfare system. Like other aspects of the nationalization programme, state intervention is unashamedly geared towards enhancing private profitability with scant regard for broader social values or needs.

Bank nationalization elsewhere The rediscovery of government intervention and nationalization was not restricted to the UK but was a global phenomenon. The United States government was forced to rescue investment bank Bear Stearns and the insurer AIG, as well as nationalize the mortgage companies Fanny Mae and Freddy Mac and provide financial rescue packages for some of Wall Street's biggest financial concerns (including Goldman Sachs), as another bank, Lehman Brothers, went to the wall. As well as partially nationalizing one of the largest private banks, Commerzbank, and fully nationalizing the mortgage lender Hypo Real Estate, the German government was forced to bail out many of its regional banks, *Landesbanken*, which had also become involved in speculating in the US property market. Publicly owned, under the German federal system, by regional states or *Länder*, and committed to providing patient long-term funding for the German *Mittelstand* (small and medium-sized firms), these supposedly solid and trustworthy institutions were also sucked up into the global financial bubble by gullible chief executives anxious not to be left behind in the dash to make fortunes in high-return but also high-risk and complex international markets.

One of the major casualties was West LB, the bank for the largest (in population terms) federal region of Nord-Rhein-Westfalen, which made losses of €2 billion (or $3 billion) in 2007 as a result of its exposure to the US sub-prime market.[13] The bank also laid out a plan to lay off

1,350 staff, or one quarter of its workforce, by 2010.[14] Commenting on these events without any apparent irony, the company's outgoing CEO, Alexander Stuhlmann, said the company would in future concentrate 'more on its small and middle-size company business and work more closely with savings banks'.[15] The feeling was that 'the bank's previous business model – a strong focus on lucrative but risky foreign markets – has proven dangerous and, in recent years, repeatedly led to losses that threatened the company's existence'.[16] West LB was bailed out by the taxpayers of the Rhineland with a €5 billion rescue package agreed by the regional government.

Socialism for the rich, capitalism for the poor: the state underwrites neoliberalism's contradictions

As we have seen with the example of Alistair Darling and New Labour, the recent wave of bank nationalizations and state interventions is portrayed as an aberration: an unwelcome throwback to a recidivist era of the overweening state. Yet this flies in the face of the diverse ways and means through which the state has been brought in over the period of neoliberal reforms to correct for 'market failure' (Harvey 2005). The arch-neoliberals Thatcher and Reagan both used state intervention and bailouts to rescue financial interests from speculative adventures in the 1980s: most notably the Thatcher government's nationalization of the Johnson Matthey Bank to prevent it going bankrupt and Reagan's intervention in the Savings and Loans crisis when the US Congress approved $105 billion of public money to underwrite losses made by the collapse of over seven hundred S&L companies (Curry and Shibut 2000). The early 1990s witnessed bank failures – following deregulation – across Scandinavia and led to wholesale nationalizations in Sweden and Norway. Later in the decade, the collapse of the US hedge fund Long Term Capital Management cost the US taxpayer $3.5 billion (Harvey 2005: 73). A report by the Bank for International Settlements noted that there had been nine serious financial crises (two in the USA and three in the UK) in the 1990s (BIS 2004).

For the more critical observer, the failings of the neoliberal project were evident well before the financial crisis with the period from the mid-1990s onwards already revealing the limits to market fundamentalism as numerous financial crises and corporate scandals required active state intervention at the national and transnational scales to prevent systemic failure. From the bailing out of hedge funds in the USA, to the continuing role of state enterprises and banks in underpinning rapid economic growth in China and beyond, to the renationalization of oil and gas resources by the Russian state, the profile of government interventions is increasingly visible; even if it is not necessarily consistent with progressive means and ends. Indeed, much recent intervention is tailored to circumventing the inherent systemic contradictions of 'money manager capitalism' (Crotty 2009; Palma 2009; Wray 2009). Beyond the financial sector, privatization across whole sectors of the economy has not prevented continuing and often increasing levels of state support to many privatized entities. The energy sector is perhaps the classic example here, a report for the European Union concluding that between 1995 and 2001 around €125 billion was given to energy companies with UK privatized entities being among the highest recipients (EEA 2004).

As I noted earlier in the chapter, the UK, as one of the pioneers of neoliberalism and privatization, was the place where such contradictions became most evident. New Labour's role in sustaining and resuscitating privatization needs emphasizing in this regard. Its unwillingness to interfere with the commercial running of privatized companies did not prevent it spending billions of pounds in subsidizing and re-regulating where idealized private market forms led to serious failures in the water sector in the 1990s and the rail sector in the early 2000s. The virtual collapse of the privatized rail network led to the renationalization of the track infrastructure in 2003, and in July 2009 the nationalization of one of the most important passenger routes, the east coast line between London and Scotland, as the existing operator, National Express, reneged on its franchise agreement. National Express's failure to deliver on the national network's most significant passenger rail contract was itself a reflection of the wider financial malaise and the group's failure to raise revenue to deliver promised improvements in customer services. But its decision to pull out came only three years after the previous franchisee, GNER, had withdrawn for similar reasons. British rail privatization has proved to be the embodiment of the contradictions and tensions of marketization and privatization (MacKinnon et al. 2008).

Despite all this, there is little sign that the country's political elites are willing to challenge the established and cross-party economic orthodoxy in favour of private ownership. Adherence to abstract market visions and solutions remains strong. In the case of the rail industry, the previous Labour minister of transport felt moved to underline the temporary state of nationalization as a reassurance to private investors.

It is the government's intention to tender for a new East Coast franchise operator from the end of 2010. The specification of the new franchise will reflect my concern to secure better passenger services and facilities. I intend to consult fully on the new franchise specification, including with passenger groups, parliamentarians and the Scottish Executive.[17]

This mantra was repeated again and again in Labour's approach to questions of ownership and the choice between public and private. This was also evident in government spending plans, with – up until the financial crisis – Gordon Brown vetoing various attempts to finance investment projects through public investment, preferring his PFI route in order to keep official public debt low. This led to the axing of a £30 billion government bond scheme to finance long-term rail investment projects and the financing of renewal of the London Underground through a similar public scheme.[18]

In a similar vein, behind the recent hasty wave of bank nationalizations is the clearly stated intent to return the stricken assets to private ownership as soon as 'normal market conditions' have been restored, although it is never clear what ministers regard as 'normal'. Moreover, in the UK, there is also an obvious lack of political desire for a 'hands-on management' of financial institutions; the preference being for a benign, distant and transient ownership. As many commentators have noted, nationalization has been about the public sector taking on bad debt and the costs of the financial crisis, which has been treated as an aberration from market norms with little questioning of the systemic causes behind it. This has been borne out in the Northern Rock reprivatization by the current Conservative–Liberal Democratic coalition government. As the *Guardian* succinctly put it:

> Only the 'good' bit of the Rock is going into private hands. The 'bad bank', the bit that holds the 125% mortgages, remains very firmly in public hands. The taxpayer remains on the hook for Northern Rock (Asset Management), which has about £50bn worth of mortgages, many of which were parked offshore in the perfectly misnamed 'Granite' vehicle, which turned to dust during the credit crunch. Currently, this book of mortgages is performing rather better than expected, helped by interest rates remaining at 0.5% for longer than anyone thought. But if and when the rates rise, and mortgage holders start defaulting, the losses from Northern Rock's madcap lending spree will fall squarely on the public sector, not on the buyers – Richard Branson, US billionaire partner Wilbur Ross and a fund controlled by oil-rich Abu Dhabi. (Collinson 2011)

In this respect, and despite appearances, recent government interventions have actually been consistent with New Labour's embrace of market-led solutions to almost all areas of economic and social life in the period since 1997. Although the weakness of free market thinking was self-evident by the mid-1990s with the growing criticisms of privatization and the virtual collapse of public services, subsequent government interventions in the sphere of the labour market, education and health were underpinned by the nostrums of mainstream economics, endogenous growth theory and the self-serving analytical device (from a business perspective) of 'market failure'. Recent policy interventions – such as the nationalizations outlined above – remain cloaked in the language of better regulation and management of market forms, with a continued commitment to private ownership as the more efficient form of service delivery. The appointment of bankers and private executives to run the nationalized companies and their personal relations with government officials and ministers (Brummer 2009) in question reinforce this point.

An alternative view: a brief history of mutualism and finance as a collective endeavour

The stubborn adherence to the principle of private ownership means that the UK ruling elite (including the Scottish Nationalist Party) has effectively set its face against all forms of more collective ownership that might challenge private interests. The sanctity of private property rights and the strict Hayekian connections between liberalism, markets and the 'heroic individual' (although applied in most cases to the large joint stock corporation as the recipient of these rights) must be preserved. Returning to the Northern Rock case, it is instructive to remember that the bank was only in the private sector for ten years out of its 147-year existence, having been demutualized in 1997. When the government-appointed executive chairman of Northern Rock, Ron Sandler, said, in relation to its sale to Richard Branson: 'The return of Northern Rock to the private sector has always been one of our objectives',[19] he glossed over the major part of the bank's history.

The building society movement in the UK emerged as a cooperative grassroots enterprise on behalf of industrial workers in the late eighteenth century: the 'friendly society' (Cook et al. 2001). Such societies were founded as forms of collective action to raise funds for housing workers living in poor conditions in Britain's northern industrial cities, with laws formalizing their operations in the middle of the nineteenth century. Their aim was simple: to borrow money from investors to build houses through affordable loans to the working and lower middle classes while offering investors a reasonable rate of return on savings. Up until the 1950s, they remained small-scale and relatively localized, strongly embedded in the communities from which they had emerged. Although over time there was a process of merger and acquisition so that the number reduced from 2,286 in 1900 to 130 by 1988, prior to demutualization they still retained an important status as collective democratic organizations owned by members with the principle of one member one vote being the guide to all key decision-making (ibid.). Critically, they were governed by a series of laws and acts that restricted their abilities to undertake financial activity outside their original expressed purpose or, up until the mid-1980s, to offer loans to non-members. By 1985 it was estimated that the sector had built up £16 billion of reserves in its roughly 150-year history (ibid.).

As part of Thatcher's financial deregulation, the Building Societies Act of 1986 and subsequent legislation removed most of these barriers, effectively eroding the legal distinction between building societies and banks. There followed a demutualization wave in the 1990s with the financial capital built up so assiduously and carefully over a century and a half released to the speculative frenzy of the global financial markets. Nearly all the largest building societies – the Abbey National, Alliance and Leicester, Halifax and Cheltenham & Gloucester, for example – demutualized as, under pressure from management, 'carpetbaggers' and many speculators who opened accounts in the hope of obtaining cash windfalls, members voted to become public limited companies. Deregulation created an unholy alliance that led to the severing of the ties between building societies and their local and community roots (Marshall et al. 2012).

By the time of the financial crisis, and with the demise of Northern Rock, none of the converted building societies remained as independent entities (NEF 2009). Although the demutualization wave had passed by the time the Labour government arrived in power, there was little enthusiasm to reform the banking sector or to encourage alternative forms of ownership. Although the government identified social exclusion from financial services – as a result of the disinvestment by major banks – as a key issue in many poorer urban and rural areas, it failed to engage with some of the arguments being made to support non-private mutual and cooperative forms of ownership that were being advocated by pressure groups and left-of-centre think tanks in the 2000s (e.g. Moore and Mayo 2001; NEF 2009; Compass/NEF 2010). Although it provided some support for the fledgling credit union movement, this was never on a scale to challenge the existing power of the private financial giants, and it did little to encourage existing and remaining mutuals (Marshall et al. 2003).

Moreover, Labour, Conservative and the current coalition government have all failed to engage with the role of privatization and demutualization processes in stimulating the recent financial crisis and economic recession. As one of the government's own panel of Housing Advisers noted in a recent commentary:

> the experience since the last (1990s) recession is that institutional memory is very short. The view that reckless lending would never happen again, and institutions had learned from their mistakes was widely expressed. In retrospect the seeds for the current boom/bust cycle were sown in the aftermath of the last recession – for example arising from building society demutualization creating institutions that were prepared to take greater risks in return for greater returns, and also creating a demand for sub-prime mortgages. (Stephens 2009: 9)

In other words, a contributing factor to the UK's financial crisis and housing market collapse was the demutualization process that occurred in the 1990s, when many soundly run building societies – which had evolved historically as risk-averse organizational alternatives to joint-stock public limited companies – were allowed to become profit-driven corporate banking concerns. Dividend payments and short-term shareholder interest increasingly overrode the traditional caution and long-term perspective of the mutual financial sector.

In the wake of the financial crisis, there has been much new and innovative thinking about the British banking sector and how it might be transformed to more socially useful purposes with discussions of community banks, green banks and state regional development banks, to name but a few (Compass/NEF 2010). The continuing vitality of mutual organizations such as the Co-operative and the Nationwide also testifies to the enduring popularity and role played by mutual and collective forms of financial organization, despite the ignorance and wilful neglect of successive governments. However, the vitality and appeal of alternative models of ownership seems to largely bypass the ruling classes, of whatever political hue. Prior to Northern Rock's 'return to the private sector' in May 2011, Labour MP Chuka Umunna put down an early day motion signed by 100 MPs from all parties that the bank instead be turned back into a mutual. It fell on deaf ears, despite a pledge in the Conservative–Liberal Democrats' coalition agreement to stimulate the mutual sector. In defending his decision, the Chancellor,

George Osborne, claimed that he had no choice as the original nationalization, enacted by the Labour government, had under EU rules been undertaken under the specific instructions that it be returned to the private sector as soon as possible.

Conclusions

The centre-left's embrace of market fundamentalism has encouraged it to dispense with alternative thinking about critical categories such as the market, ownership, competition and even knowledge and innovation. More serious for our purposes here is that it encourages sterility and conformity in dealing with the key problems of our time. The absorption of elite economic ideologies at the expense of more heterodox thinking has seriously eroded the possibilities of an alternative left narrative – even more from a more traditional social democratic or Keynesian perspective – percolating into the broader public consciousness. This shift towards a post-politics technocratic discourse, as noted by many left thinkers from Mouffe to Žižek, has closed down the necessary spaces of deliberation and dissent that are essential for a more democratic economics. In Veblen's terms, the approach is one in which 'ceremonial', as in elite, interests and values come to dominate over more instrumental ones which might furnish a challenge to our existing economic decision-making practices (Veblen 1990). A consequence of all this is that private ownership has become completely uncontested as a concept, even at a point when state and public resources were required to rescue the economy from the damaging actions of particular vested private interests.

Although I have focused here on New Labour's wholehearted embrace of neoliberalism and its subsequent rather diffident embrace of nationalization, many of the themes are consonant with a broader shift across the European and North American political mainstream, as the austerity politics of the Eurozone crisis, renewed privatization, the further slashing of government programmes and welfare support demonstrate. Although the situation is far from uniform and we do detect some differences in emphasis across the policy-makers of the advanced economies in dealing with the economic crisis and in their approach to issues of ownership, it nevertheless remains the case that mainstream political parties seem keener on resurrecting neoliberalism and its highly questionable assumptions and political implications than addressing the more serious structural contradictions facing the global economy. To date, the cushion of the European welfare state has probably stopped the growth of more widespread resistance to the ongoing process of neoliberalization, although this may change as the middle classes feel their living standards decline and their employment position become more precarious. Elsewhere, however, the opposition to neoliberalism has been more profound and more threatening to its hegemony. In Latin America in particular, the effects of privatization and marketization from the 1980s onwards deeply eroded the economic base of society, spurring radical opposition movements that have begun to articulate an alternative political economy framed around collective ownership, democratic participation and a renewed commitment to social justice. These are the subject of the following chapter.

5 | Public ownership and an alternative political economy in Latin America

> The Left, if that's what it wants to be, cannot define politics as the art of the possible. Realpolitik must be opposed by a notion of politics which is realistic, doesn't deny what is happening but does set about preparing the way to transform existing reality. (Harnecker 2007: 67)

In September 1999 the Bolivian government awarded a forty-year contract to a private consortium of US, Spanish and Italian interests, Aguas del Tunari (ADT), to provide water and sanitation services to the country's third city, Cochabamba. One of ADT's first acts was to put water charges up by an average of 35 per cent, although for some users the figure was closer to 200 per cent (Lobina 2000: 2). Unsurprisingly this had a brutal impact upon many low-paid workers. In a city where the minimum wage at the time was less than $100 per month, the new charges accounted for 22 per cent of the monthly pay of a self-employed man and 27 per cent that of a woman (ibid.). Mass protests ensued, which turned into street demonstrations and then at the end of January 2000 a four-day general strike, which effectively shut down the city's economy. In the days of marches and demonstrations that followed, a violent response from the state and subsequent clashes with riot police and soldiers led to the injury and imprisonment of hundreds of protesters and the death of one. By April demonstrations were spreading to other major Bolivian cities, including the capital La Paz. As the situation spiralled out of the authorities' control, the government responded by reversing the price changes and, as the protests continued, it was finally forced to cancel the contract.

The immediate local consequence of the dispute was that the city's water returned to public ownership in the shape of the municipal corporation, SEMAPA, but the events in Cochabamba were to have a much wider resonance. Nationally, they led to the cancellation of privatized water contracts and the resurrection of municipal public ownership in other cities, most notably in the capital, La Paz. They also spawned a movement that was to bring to power the government of Evo Morales in 2005. Globally, the city became a cause célèbre of the anti-capitalist movement with its 'Water War' taking on a similar iconic status to the 1998 'Battle of Seattle' against the World Trade Organization as a significant moment in the struggle against neo-liberalization and privatization. More critically for us here, it was part of a broader revolt across Latin America against the World Bank-inspired model of market-led development that had been imposed on the continent since 1980. The 1980s is often referred to as the continent's 'lost decade' because of the reversal in economic growth trends since the 1940s, but in fact the continent's performance continued to be poor on almost every economic indicator through the 1990s and 2000s (Palma 2010). The contrast is made with many East Asian countries, which have overtaken Latin America as a global centre of production for Western markets.

Cochabamba was one of many privatizations that have been reversed in the past two decades in Latin America, but it has also been part of the emergence of an alternative left discourse that, more than anywhere else in the current conjuncture, is articulating different forms of economic development around solidarity and a collective consciousness in opposition to the dominant paradigm of market competition and the selfish individual. In this chapter I consider the nature of these developments and their wider implications for rethinking public ownership.

Rolling back neoliberalism: a continental rebellion against privatization

It is not surprising that Latin America has become a beacon for the left given the wider and dismal landscape of subservience to corporate interests in much of the rest of the world. Events such as the Bolivian water and later gas wars rekindled hope in the possibilities of successfully turning back the neoliberal tide and forging a counter-hegemonic project. Although the Latin American 'pink tide' should not be overestimated, given a situation in which the resistance to neoliberalism and the evidence of a more serious left project remains limited to a minority of countries on the continent – namely Bolivia, Ecuador and Venezuela – while other recent left governments (e.g. in Brazil, Chile and Uruguay) have not fundamentally challenged the established political and economic order, we can nevertheless point to a significant counter-hegemonic politics emerging in the growth of both social movements and wider civil society mobilizations and in the articulation of an alternative agenda at the level of the state (Robinson 2008; Escobar 2010).

Some historical context is important in understanding these developments. Behind the recent uprisings against neoliberalism have been twenty years of the kind of economic austerity measures now being visited on countries in the global North. These were enacted in many cases following the return to democracy after periods of military rule in the 1960s and 1970s. These periods of dictatorship themselves represented attempts by ruling elites to quash popular uprisings and social change from below (Robinson 2008). Military dictatorship was gradually replaced by a kind of economic dictatorship or 'polyarchy' as a 'system in which a small group actually rules, on behalf of capital, and participation in decision making by the majority is confined to choosing competing elites in tightly controlled electoral processes' (ibid.: 273). Obviously there are similarities with some of the post-political processes emerging elsewhere, and we can note the manner in which the mainstream political left in Latin America signed up to the market disciplines of neoliberalism as much as the right (Palma 2010).

Clearly, the broader geo-economic dimension was critical here too, with World Bank development aid under the Washington Consensus tied increasingly to marketization and privatization. The Cochabamba water privatization was made at the behest of the World Bank, which had insisted that Bolivia privatize its water resources in return for the renewal of a $25 billion loan (Lobina 2000). Another characteristic feature was the involvement of foreign investment – supposedly to render public services more efficient by drawing upon external expertise and management – but at a considerable cost with a guaranteed return of 15 per cent for the private contractor (Bayliss 2002). There are similarities too with some of the PFI projects initiated in the UK, with the Cochabamba deal involving a related investment project, the Misicuni 'renewable energy hydro-electic project'. Privatization and the broader neoliberal policy agenda were tied to a new modernization discourse on the continent. However, instead of the investment coming directly from the state in the form of traditional loans, private (foreign) capital would provide the expertise but only with substantial incentivization that was ultimately to be paid for by the end user.

Latin America was therefore the region where the Washington Consensus was first 'crafted' and where political elites most wholeheartedly signed up to it. Escobar refers to: 'a level of callousness and brutality by the ruling regimes that reached staggering proportions' (Escobar 2010: 8). While there are similarities elsewhere – particularly in the experiences with development in parts of Africa and Asia (McDonald and Ruiters 2012) – neoliberalization in Latin America has had important local dimensions, the most important of which are the history of earlier waves of modernization and state development projects and with them experiences of colonialism and racism. From the perspective of many of the indigenous peoples of Latin America, neoliberalization did not represent a break as such with the existing power relations and marginalization from economic decision-making, but represented yet another externally imposed system of economic management of local resources, with severe effects on living standards, that at the same time persisted with the ongoing destruction of traditional cultural, economic and social practices.

In this light, the uprising across Latin America has been read by many commentators as a rebellion against 'liberal modernization' (Escobar 2010); as much a reaction to five centuries of oppression at the hands of different generations of European colonizers and to the transplantation of successive Western visions of development. In particular, an individualistic ethos, framed from a particular enlightenment tradition and reaching its apotheosis under neoliberalism, has been at odds with more communal and collective indigenous practices (ibid.). While there are differing perspectives on the precise political contours of these developments – compare Escobar (2008, 2010), for example, with Robinson (2008) or Webber (2010) – there is a general consensus that the 'pink tide' is different to previous left insurrections in the fusion of an indigenous perspective with a more traditional class politics around a shared antagonism to neoliberal capitalism and its practices of enclosure.

Significantly, the revolt against privatization did not emerge from traditional parties and movements but came from a fusion of indigenous groups with new movements representing poorer rural and urban communities as well as green groups at the sharp end of privatization. The coalition mobilized in Cochabamba, for example, La Coordinadora de Defensa del Agua y la Vida (the Coordinator for the Defence of Water and Life), involved an alliance between the trade union representing minimum-wage factory workers, peasant farmers, environmentalists and youth groups (Lobina 2000). Although the wider world's attention was attracted in the late 1990s, and slightly earlier if we include the Zapatista uprising in Mexico, there was already widespread resistance to IMF-imposed austerity policies in the 1980s with food riots a common occurrence. By the early 1990s there were serious organized grassroots resistance movements campaigning against the effects of neoliberalism in every country (Robinson 2008; Routledge and Cumbers 2009), but it was only in the latter years of the twentieth century that these began to coalesce into serious alternative political movements to challenge the neoliberal project.

Water as an 'uncooperative commodity' and the return of public ownership

As Karen Bakker has noted, water has often proved itself to be an 'uncooperative commodity' (Bakker 2003). Many of the world's leading utility MNCs have discovered this to their cost in their dealings with Latin American water privatization. In 2007, French MNC Suez, the leading private water contractor in Latin America during the 1990s, announced that it had withdrawn completely from the water sector. It was not alone. As Table 5.1 shows, in the face of public opposition, and also the failure to realize the expected profits, there has been a massive withdrawal of foreign companies associated with the reversal of privatization and return to public ownership in many parts of the continent (Lobina and Hall 2007). The problems associated with water privatization, and in particular the contradictions between providing decent water quality as a human right to all citizens[1] and the profit-seeking rationale of private capital, are becoming globally apparent in the accumulating evidence of poor performance and failure to deliver on contractual obligations (Hall et al. 2010).

TABLE 5.1 Multinationals that have withdrawn from the Latin American water sector

Multinational	Country of origin	Country withdrawn from	City/region
Suez	France	Argentina	Buenos Aires
		Argentina	Santa Fe
		Brazil	Limeira
		Bolivia	La Paz/El Alto
		Puerto Rico	
SAUR	France	Venezuela	Lara
		Argentina	Mendoza
Thames Water	UK	Chile	Essbio, Essel
Anglian Water	UK	Chile	Essval
Aguas de Bilbao	Spain	Argentina	Buenos Aires Province
		Uruguay	Maldonado
Azurix	USA	Argentina	Buenos Aires
		Argentina	Mendoza
Aguas do Portugal	Portugal	Brazil	Prolagos

Source: Derived from Lobina and Hall (2007: 5)

The retreat of foreign multinational corporations from the water sector has occurred throughout South America, although the implications for ownership have varied: in Bolivia, Venezuela and Uruguay all operations have returned to the public sector, both to forms of central and local state control, whereas in Brazil and Chile a mix of local and foreign private capital remains and elsewhere there is a more mixed pattern.

In some cases, the return of water companies to municipal control has also led to innovative attempts to construct more democratic and participatory forms of organization involving trade unions and wider civil society groups. A case in point involved the return of the Azurix-led contract (Table 5.1) to the provincial government for the Greater Buenos Aires area. A new public organization, Aguas Bonaerense SA (ABSA), was created which represented a 'public–public partnership' between the local authority and a workers' cooperative, 5 de setiembre S.A., set up by the water and sanitation workers' union (ibid.). The cooperative is key to providing the technical expertise and assistance lost by the local government following privatization. A similar initiative was established in the Peruvian city of Huancayo, which had been under pressure from potential foreign investors, including the German government and Inter-American Investment Bank, to develop a public–private partnership to implement its part of a national sanitation plan. After considerable popular resistance to these proposals, in 2007 the city developed a partnership with local civil society NGOs and with the Argentinian ABSA, which again involved the trade unions (both local and the Argentinian union) providing their own technical expertise as an alternative to a privatized solution.

'Twenty-first-century socialism' and the Bolivarian participatory process

It is not just in the water sector that foreign MNCs have had their fingers burned in recent years. In Bolivia and Venezuela in particular a more substantive challenge to global capitalism has occurred with the election of popular left governments committed to renationalization of energy resources so that they are used for the public interest rather than in the interests of foreign shareholders and companies. Elsewhere, nationalization has been threatened – as in Ecuador's threat to nationalize its oil industry unless it improves the government share of revenues – rather than actual, but nevertheless there is a sense that where a vanguard leads others may follow. The commitment of the

Venezuelan president, Hugo Chávez, to build a 'twenty-first-century socialism' (Robinson 2008: 323), with public ownership and a radical democratic approach to the economy at its core, also represents a more serious counter-hegemonic response to neoliberalism than anything yet articulated elsewhere.

The election of Chávez in 1998 and the beginning of his Bolivarian[2] Revolution were the result of a growing disaffection with Venezuela's neoliberal politics, of which the turning point was a popular uprising in the capital Caracas in 1989 against the IMF economic shock therapy being meted out by the country's president, Carlos Andrés Pérez (ibid.). In the repression that followed between 500 and 3,000 people were killed, sparking off a decade of popular protest and the emergence of a movement for change.[3] One of the most important steps following Chávez's election was the establishment of a new constitution in 1999 which enunciated the key principles of 'participative and protagonist democracy' (Escobar 2010: 14). The Constitution was a critical departure from the previous administrations in two ways: first, by reinserting the role of the state in the shaping of social and economic life, and secondly, by developing a number of mechanisms to deepen democracy and popular participation (ibid.). After surviving a coup attempt sponsored by corporate and foreign interests in 2002, two business strikes in 2003 and 2004 and a recall referendum (Robinson 2008), Chávez has enacted a series of radical reforms. Inheriting a situation in which much of the country's oil wealth – Venezuela is the fifth-largest producer in the world – was being appropriated by local and foreign elites with little 'trickle-down' to the country's broader population, the first task was to secure control of the state oil company, PDVSA. Having achieved this and stabilized the economy from 2003 onwards, including revoking the Central Bank's independence, the government has achieved some impressive economic and social reforms (ibid.; Escobar 2010; Webber 2010). A report by the US-based Center for Economic Policy and Research (Weisbrot et al. 2009a) highlighted the following achievements between 2003 and 2008: 13.5 per cent annual GDP growth; a reduction in the poverty rate from 54 per cent to 26 per cent of households; a fall in inequality as measured by the Gini index from 48.1 to 41; a fall in unemployment (over the decade to 2008) from 11.3 to 7.8 per cent; and a 33 per cent drop in infant mortality rates.

Having been given considerable independence during the neoliberal period, PDVSA was brought back under the strict supervision of the Energy and Mines Ministry and its management team replaced by one less amenable to foreign financial interests (Robinson 2008). The company has subsequently increased the amount spent on social programmes, from $48 million in the 1999–2003 period to $2.4 billion in 2005 (Escobar 2010). Additionally, a new taxation and royalty regime has been applied to the oil industry to tackle evasion. The government's macroeconomic policy has been described as 'heterodox but hardly radical' (ibid.: 329); currency controls have been put in place but there has been little in the way of deficit spending. The regime has committed itself to respecting private property rights but it has also introduced land reform and state support for worker cooperatives and renationalized the social security system.

As various authors have noted, the Chávez government started life as a reformist social democratic government but has been pushed in a more radical direction by opposition from business and elite interests, and critically by social movement mobilization (Robinson 2008; Webber 2010). As Webber notes:

> Modestly reformist at the onset of its first term, the Chávez government was slowly and partially radicalized when faced with a series of imperialist and domestic, legal and (mainly) extra-legal, right-wing destabilization campaigns. ... the government's radicalizing tendency is a result, more specifically, of counter-revolutionary pressure that spurred a dramatic effervescence of grassroots struggles amongst the working class and urban poor, a small but important minority of whom are committed socialists, beginning in April 2002 and accelerating during and after the oil lockout of 2002–2003. (Webber 2010: 13)

One of the most celebrated elements of Chávez's radical programme has been the network of Communal Councils, set up in 2006. These are local councils – consisting of 200–400 families in urban areas and twenty families in rural areas – which are at the heart of the desire for protagonist democracy and self-determination outside the state. The councils come together to develop strategies to target local issues and problems (e.g. infrastructure upgrading or utility provision) which then apply for state funding. They invoke the principles of participatory, rather than representative, democracy by being organized on a horizontal basis without leaders but by electing spokespeople of equal ranking to the rest of the collective. By 2007 around 20,000 had been created and had been awarded a total of $5 billion, which represents around 50 per cent of the state's local and regional development budget (Chodor 2009).

The most radical element of the regime – in terms of developing an alternative economic agenda – has probably been the establishment of a series of *'misiones'* (missions) since 2003, aimed at encouraging local autonomy in the form of local self-governing spaces independent of the perceived corrupt state bureaucracy. These account for 20 per cent of the state's budget (Robinson 2008: 331) and include health and education missions, among them Misión Robinson, which has greatly increased literacy rates (by 1.5 million people between 2003 and 2005 alone), Misión Sucre, which provides free university education, and Misión Barrio Adentro, providing basic healthcare, aided by 30,000 Cuban doctors and health workers operating in rural areas and urban barrios (ibid.). A critical programme for developing economic democracy and participation is Misión Vuelvan Caras ('about face'), which has been geared towards a programme of endogenous development (ibid.) involving the encouragement of small firms, urban and rural cooperatives, employee-owned enterprises and the relocalization of economies to break the dominance of transnational capital over the economy that persisted under neoliberalism. Central to these plans are Nuclei of Endogenous Sustainable Development (NUDES), local economic zones that aim to integrate the endogenous resources of their communities, especially the newly created cooperatives and *misiones*, to provide self-sustaining local forms of development (ibid.; Chodor 2009). They have received both considerable financial support from the state and technical support from the various *misiones* and aim to: 'instil new socialist values through stressing work as the development of human capacity and developing relations of production based on cooperation, solidarity, protagonism and collective property' (Chodor 2009: 6–7).

While there have been considerable problems, arising from corruption, the failure of many cooperatives to sustain themselves and in some cases the continuation of more capitalistic profit-centred practices among some forms of cooperative and employee-owned firms, there has nevertheless been an impressive level of development, with over 140,000 cooperatives operating by the end of 2006 (ibid.). Whether these local autonomous economic zones can inculcate a broader post-capitalist work ethos in what remains a competitive market economy remains to be seen.

Recovering sovereignty of natural resources: nationalization in Bolivia under Morales

In Bolivia, the water wars were followed by the 'gas wars' in 2003 and 2005 (Spronk and Webber 2007), whereby demands for the return of the privatized gas sector to public ownership became the focus of demands. The tipping point was the attempt by the transnational gas consortium Pacific LNG (involving Repsol YPF, British Gas and Pan-American Energy) to build a pipeline to the coast in Peru to export natural gas to the United States, but resentment had been brewing much earlier at the effective appropriation of the country's gas supplies by foreign interests. Bolivia has the second-largest gas reserves in Latin America and makes considerable export revenue from fulfilling growing demand from its neighbours. In this context, the privatization legislation in 1996 effectively returned the sector to the kind of rampant colonial exploitation of the country's resources by corporate and foreign interests which had existed up until the 1920s. As part of the privatization deal, for example, the royalties to the state from gas production were reduced from 50 per cent to 18 per cent for all new discoveries (ibid.). Furthermore, prior to privatization, the state-owned company YPFB (Yacimientos Petrolíferos Fiscales Bolivianos) was about to complete a pipeline connecting the Bolivian gas fields to Brazil, which would increase profits to $50 million per year for forty years (ibid.).

A palpable sense of national injustice brought together diverse social groups in the struggle to articulate collective control of gas over foreign and corporate interests. Rural indigenous communities such as the Aymara in the Altiplano and Lake Titicaca regions allied with shanty-town residents in El Alto and neighbouring La Paz, mine workers allied with coca growers, in addition to landless movements and the campaign that had mobilized around the Cochabamba water dispute (ibid.). A series of roadblocks and demonstrations were met with fierce repression from the state and a series of massacres in September 2003 that brought 500,000 people on to the streets of La Paz and El Alto, resulting in the resignation of the government of Sánchez de Lozada, who had been behind the original privatization. A demand for renationalization of gas resources quickly became the key focus for the campaign. As Alvaro García Linera, vice-president under the current Morales regime, has put it: 'There is a sort of collective intuition that the debates over hydrocarbons are gambling with the destiny of this country, a country accustomed to having a lot of natural resources but always being poor, always seeing natural resources to enrich others' (quoted in ibid.: 36).

The outcome was the renationalization of YPFB following the election of Morales and his MAS (Movimiento al Socialismo) party to the presidency in 2005, and a wider decree to nationalize the entire oil and gas sector. In practice this has meant renegotiations with many existing foreign corporations, but the assertion of the state's control of all resources prior to extraction. In May 2007 a further step towards state control was accomplished when the state renegotiated contracts with forty-four private companies and took monopoly control of the sale of gas within the country while raising the tax rates on gas production. Further nationalizations have occurred in the mining sector (Bolivia is one of the world's leading producers of a range of important minerals), telecommunications and electricity generation.

The basic economic impact of these reforms has been substantial in reorienting the country's wealth away from a rich domestic elite and foreign MNCs into the public purse. Despite falling foreign investment in response to the nationalization programme (although all the existing companies in the oil and gas sectors have remained, giving a sense of how much wealth they must have been extracting previously), declining prices for Bolivia's mineral exports following the world recession in 2008/09, and the US government's hostile revoking of trade preferences, Bolivian GDP grew at an average of over 5 per cent between 2006 and 2009, higher than at any point in the previous thirty years (Weisbrot et al. 2009b), and continued to be well above the continental average at 4.2 per cent in 2010, according to the World Bank's World Development Indicators.[4] Inequality – as measured by the Gini index – has fallen considerably in the period since 2007, although there appears to have been less success in combating poverty rates, which are still some of the highest in Latin America (ibid.).

The renationalization of the country's gas resources in particular has bolstered government revenues and allowed it to pursue an expansionary policy to cushion the domestic economy against the impact of the wider world recession. Clearly, Bolivia, like other natural-resource-rich countries, has also benefited considerably from the continuing demand for raw materials from the global South's rapidly developing economies, such as India, China and Brazil. Government revenues have been used for a number of progressive social programmes such as payments to poorer families to boost school enrolment, an expansion of the state pension system to relieve extreme poverty among the elderly, and an increase in payments to mothers for pre- and post-natal care in an effort to reduce child mortality.

Renationalization and the prospects for economic democracy

Aside from progressive macroeconomic and social policy initiatives in both countries, the precise direction of the nationalization programme and the broader commitment to an alternative political economy founded upon more democracy and public participation in Bolivia and Venezuela remains unclear. At the level of the nationalized companies, it is difficult to escape the conclusion that little has changed in the governance of companies: foreign and domestic private ownership has been replaced by state ownership with all the gains in terms of revenue distribution described, but they continue to be run largely as hierarchical organizations with little improvement in workers' rights. Additionally, in both Bolivia and Venezuela, renationalization has been achieved through buying back shares in privatized companies rather than direct expropriation, as was the case with the 1930s nationalizations (Harstad 2009).

At the most basic level, evidence from the gas nationalization programme in Bolivia, for example, suggests that there has been little improvement in working conditions or the representation of employees in corporate governance structures (ibid.). Although there have been new laws to recognize workers' rights to organize, nationalization has not helped organized labour recover its relatively strong position before the onset of neoliberalism and employment restructuring in the 1980s. Moreover, in interviews, the management of the newly renationalized company has maintained a commitment that 'the state enterprise aims to operate according to international standards of "efficiency" and maintain a lean employment profile' (ibid.: 180), while the minister of finance in Morales's government has spoken of the need to 'aggressively' (ibid.) court foreign investment with the technology and know-how to exploit the country's vast gas reserves. Indigenous communities in particular have been dismayed by the continuing marginalization of their interests in pursuit of an economic growth agenda around rapid resource extraction, with the Morales government facing increasing opposition to its current plans (as of August 2011) to build a highway through the TIPNIS national park to the north of Cochabamba.

In Venezuela, Chávez replaced the old management within the state oil company, PDVSA, but many of the broader structures of state ownership and control remain prone to bureaucracy and corruption. But, as in Bolivia, the basic structures of power within the nationalized industries have remained unchanged. As Chodor puts it:

> Moreover, the companies in these industries largely continued to be run as state-owned enterprises, and moves to turn full control over to the workers did not materialise. Thus, overall, Chávez's macroeconomic policies, while stepping outside the neoliberal mould, essentially boiled down to state intervention in the capitalist economy,

rather than any fundamental challenge to capitalist relations of production. (Chodor 2009: 6)

Although there has been a more aggressive nationalization programme than in Bolivia, of over three hundred companies in a range of strategic sectors including steel, cement, electricity and finance, in all cases the existing owners have been compensated at full market value (Wilpert 2007). Critics suggest that, behind the rhetoric, Chávez remains committed to a more social democratic or state-capitalist project than anything more radical, given Venezuela's continuing need to secure foreign markets for its oil supplies, notably the USA, its most important customer (Webber 2010).

However, such criticisms need to be placed in the context of the contingent circumstances facing the two movements. In Venezuela, they need to be set against the formidable opposition that Chávez has faced in his Bolivarian Revolution. The actions of local and transnational elites in the neoliberal period had successfully reoriented the domestic oil industry and PDVSA to global markets and interests, such that many of the profits of the oil company were invested overseas and never repatriated (Robinson 2008). Simply getting to grips with this situation and effectively securing the country's oil revenues for the broader public was an achievement in itself. Moreover, the level of technology and expertise required to develop hydrocarbons necessitates a degree of pragmatism. In the Venezuelan case, there has subsequently been a concerted attempt to build up local knowledge and skills that can counteract foreign dominance of the industry, borrowing much from Norwegian experiences (Chapter 8). In Bolivia similarly, there is now a commitment to building up local expertise by forcing foreign companies to employ local labour. Outside of the oil industry, there have been some important initiatives in Venezuela to broaden participation and economic decision-making. Direct democracy has been introduced into many areas of the public sector, as evidenced by the setting up of '*mesas técnicas*' (technical committees) in the water, gas and energy sectors, which bring together community organizations, trade unions and state agencies to address particular problems in the poorer urban neighbourhoods (Escobar 2010).

At another level again, perhaps it is too early to judge the radical potential of the changes under way in the two countries in what is a dramatically evolving political landscape where it is difficult for outsiders to fully understand the nature of changes taking place. As Escobar has noted, the higher echelons of Morales's MAS party, such as the vice-president and leading intellectual of the movement, Alvaro García Linera, remain committed to a radical programme of modernization that evinces an '"Andean-Amazonian capitalism" which articulates capitalist and non-capitalist forms and which, through virtuous state action, can generate the surplus needed to support a transition to a post-capitalist order' (ibid.: 29–30). In a slightly more top-down fashion, Chávez's administration's activities have both strengthened existing grassroots mobilization and at the same time have been re-energized by the growing radical consciousness of social movements outside the state. These led Chávez to declare a much more radical set of plans to open up the state to 'popular power from below' 'and a "social comptroller" role over the state by grassroots movements' (Robinson 2008: 335). These included the transfer of much greater power to the Community Councils established by Chávez, which could then be built up to higher scales, local, regional, national, as an alternative geometry of power (Massey 1993) that could displace existing corrupt state structures. In essence, then, there are understandable tensions in both countries between the immediate needs of securing state revenues to serve the material needs of diverse populations and retain popular support and longer-term aspirations for more participatory and revolutionary democratic change.

Conclusions

Both through local innovations and experiments, and through the national 'revolutionary' movements in Bolivia and Venezuela, the return of public ownership in Latin America has proved an inspiration to progressives elsewhere, where neoliberalism and further privatizations of the public realm continue to cast long shadows. Despite the advances made, there remain many unanswered questions and challenges concerning the future direction of political and economic change. Nevertheless, as Escobar (2010) notes in his review of Bolivia, Ecuador and Venezuela, they all hold the promise of renewing the relations between state, economy and society in a more democratic and participatory direction while also invoking a 'pluri-cultural' imaginary where the rights of local and indigenous groups over their diverse and autonomous models of development are recognized.

Not only have important sectors of the economy been brought back under public ownership and control but new forms of management and public participation are also evident, both at the local level, through initiatives by municipal governments, and at the national level in Venezuela in particular through the Chavista commitment to a protagonist democracy. Tensions remain between the desire to move beyond older forms of state-led socialist projects to more radical forms of anti-capitalism that draw upon older indigenous traditions of collective and communal ownership as well as linking in to the anti-globalization movements for local autonomy and social action beyond the state (Holloway 2010). In this regard, many in the latter remain suspicious of any engagement with the state and its forms and institutions, arguing for forms of collective commons that develop new spaces of deliberation and economic democracy beyond the state. It is to these debates that we now turn.

6 | Alternative globalizations and the discourse of the commons

Burczak's claims for appropriative justice and commonly held forms of private ownership, as a response to the Hayekian critique of centralized models of public ownership in Chapter 3, represent an important element in rethinking public ownership around issues of economic democracy and social justice. But, as the critique of Burczak in the latter part of the chapter emphasized, this remains a partial response to the problems posed by capitalist social relations in creating destructive forms of market competition that lead to inequality and the concentration of power. In other words, the underlying economic value system would not have changed. Furthermore, it makes the assumption that all industries and sectors would basically conform to a single set of market logics, thus replicating some of the existing problems with both mainstream economic perspectives and the more traditional models of market socialism and central planning.

A more radical starting point is to challenge the value system of capitalism itself and argue for forms of economy that promote solidaristic and collective forms of economic relations over narrowly individualizing and competitive ones. Such a demand brings us into the territory of the 'alter-globalization' movement that has arisen in recent years to contest processes of neoliberal forms of globalization. One of the most important and interesting aspects of this 'movement', as the focus on resistance turns towards the imagining and construction of alternative agendas, has been the emergence of a discourse around a 'global commons'. Precisely because of its emphasis upon alternative non-capitalist values and its appeals to more democratic forms of economic practice, the 'new commons' discourse is useful here both in critiquing older and more centralized forms of public ownership and helping us envisage new and more participatory forms. It is also important in invoking an older set of non-capitalist collective practices and traditions which have long been ignored or derided by those on the left.

Global resistance and the resurgence of an anti-capitalist politics

The emergence of globalized resistance to neoliberal capitalism has been one of the most important and heartening developments on the left in the post-communist era. Defying the earlier 'end of history' rhetoric of many liberal observers in the early 1990s (e.g. Fukuyama 1992), the eruption of localized, but globally networked, social movements of resistance to the spread and deepening of global accumulation and commodification processes has also marked an important stage in the renewal of attempts to theorize and practise an alternative anti-capitalist politics.

Although the global networks of resistance that have emerged are socially and culturally divided, spatially uneven and often more territorially rooted in their politics than is often acknowledged (Cumbers et al. 2008b; Routledge and Cumbers 2009), what unites them is a common opposition to the heightened commodification of economic, social and cultural life that is present under neoliberalism. Appreciating the potential for connections between the diversity of indigenous social movements, trade unions, environmentalists, peasant farmers' organizations, landless and homeless people's movements and immigrants' rights groups – to name but a few of the diverse forms of resistance that have coalesced around a 'common enemy' – is often difficult. As one of the most influential left commentators on neoliberalism, David Harvey, has observed:

> The effect of all these movements has been to shift the terrain of political organization away from traditional political parties and labour organizing into a less focused political dynamic of social action across the whole spectrum of civil society ... It drew its strength from embeddedness in the nitty-gritty of daily life and struggle, but in so doing often found it hard to extract itself from the local and the particular to understand the macro-politics of what neoliberal accumulation by dispossession was and is all about. The variety of struggles was and is simply stunning. It is hard to even imagine connections between them. (Harvey 2006: 156)

For many on the left, the upsurge of resistance was a pleasant, if somewhat unexpected, surprise, given the vanquishing of trade unions, left political agendas and alternatives in the 1980s. While these diverse forms of resistance invariably have different ideologies and perspectives, ranging from demands for a more ethical or caring capitalism alongside variant shades of green, social democratic, socialist, communist and anarchistic politics, what does connect them is a desire to

> **Box 6.1 The demands of the Bamako Appeal: a manifesto for a democratic globalism**
>
> - The cancellation of the debt of countries in the global South.
> - Implementation of the Tobin Tax on financial speculation.
> - The dismantling of tax havens.
> - The implementation of basic rights to employment, welfare and a decent pension, and equality in this regard for men and women.
> - Rejection of free trade and implementation of fair trade and environmentally sound trade principles.
> - Guarantees of national sovereignty over agricultural production, rural development and food policy.
> - Outlawing of knowledge patenting on living organisms and privatization of common goods, especially water.
> - Fight by means of public policies against all kinds of discrimination, sexism, xenophobia, anti-Semitism and racism.
> - Urgent action to address climate change, including the development of an alternative model for energy efficiency and democratic control of natural resources.
> - Dismantling of foreign military bases except those under UN supervision.
> - Freedom of information for individuals, the creation of more democratic media and controls on the operation of major conglomerates.
> - Reform and democratization of global institutions incorporating institutions such as the World Bank and the IMF under the control of the UN.

'roll back' the juggernaut of commodification processes; to create space for alternative social and ethical values and practices independent of the exploitation and alienation of economic life under capitalism.

At the centre of demands for an alternative globalization has been the World Social Forum initiative with its logo 'Another World is Possible', the first meeting of which was held in Pôrto Alegre, Brazil, in 2001. Although the forum arguably peaked in its influence in the mid-2000s, with over 155,000 participants and 6,873 organizations present at the 2005 meeting (Bramble 2006: 289–90), it has been important in giving voice to a set of alternative visions. The fusion around an anti-capitalist set of values and practices is apparent, for example, in the 2006 World Social Forum's Bamako Appeal (Box 6.1). Ten out of the twelve demands have at their core the need to tackle the increasing private appropriation and control of global economic wealth and resources and to put in place democratic forms of economic decision-making.

The emergence of an agenda around the commons

Struggles against capitalism are always in some shape or form struggles against 'enclosure' and of course are nothing new (De Angelis 2007). The history of capitalism is replete with resistance from social groups and movements 'dispossessed' by its accumulative thrust (Harvey 2003). Attempts by wealthy elites to enclose common land in England in the sixteenth and seventeenth centuries spawned resistance movements such as the Levellers and the Diggers committed to more democratic and egalitarian forms of government and economy, invoking a traditional 'commons' against privatizing accumulation processes.

David Harvey has incisively characterized contemporary privatization processes as an ongoing capitalist strategy of 'accumulation by dispossession', which, although taking different forms in different places, is about an enclosure of commons (ibid.). More broadly, neoliberalism is seen as deepening existing processes of exploitation, through the intensification of employment in globalized chains of commodity production, aided by increasingly disciplinary state processes of welfare and labour regulation in both the global North and South, alongside new forms of enclosure. These involve both processes of privatization as well as attempts to extend property rights and market rules to new jurisdictions (both functionally in terms of the penetration of capitalist logics into education, health and even prison services, and geographically in terms of the incorporation of new lands and communities inside a single global economy geared to commodity production). There are also attempts to construct new markets and property rights in other areas as 'solutions' to supposed public policy problems, notably climate change and intellectual property rights. The overall effect is a concerted attempt at a universal global regime of capitalist enclosure to the extent that all areas of social life are governed by market logics and the profit motive.

In opposition, commons are viewed as collective spaces created 'outside' of the workings of capital where different social relations and norms can be reclaimed. Caffentzis (2009) notes there are considerable ambivalences with regard to the commons, not least of which is the fact that it is perfectly compatible with capitalism itself, as the recent mainstream discourse (as articulated by the Nobel Prize winner in economics, Elinor Ostrom, and her colleagues) indicates. Responses by the World Bank and other more thoughtful capitalist policy organs to the failed utopia of neoliberalism have accepted the principle of common rights to certain kinds of resources as a way of dealing with problems of 'market failure' in terms of the husbandry of certain kinds of material and knowledge resources. Such views, of course, see commons rather narrowly in terms of issues of good governance and management, rather than recognizing the politics and social relations that underpin questions of ownership. In contrast, the more radical invocation of a global commons as an alternative politics to global capitalism represents the attempt to escape the logic of capitalist valorization processes and instead construct collective projects around mutualism and respect, social need and use value, rather than exploitation, profit and exchange value (De Angelis 2007; Hardt and Negri 2009; Holloway 2010).

The 'global' aspect of the commons is important in signifying that commons are not localized or hermetic communities, which end up with more exclusionary forms of politics in opposition to the faux liberal cosmopolitanism of capital. This broader and relational (following Massey 2005) imaginary of place is critical. Thus while the importance of 'community' is recognized in the new commons discourse, as part of 'a radical project of decommodification and a democratisation from below' (Barchesi 2003: 4), or as social networks of trust and reciprocity that can contest commodification – sites of 'learning practice' (De Angelis 2005) – this is not a return to older forms of territorially bounded community with their own hierarchical power relations based around patriarchy, nationalisms or racisms that are at the same time exclusive of 'outsiders'. Rather, community and commons are trans-local in their openness as a way of escaping other forms of non-capitalist enclosure and oppression based upon gender, race, caste or national identity.

'Commoning'[1] projects are attributed to a diverse array of struggles perceived as invoking alternatives to capitalist appropriation processes, from the open-sourcing and open-access projects of cyber-activists, to the emergence of the independent media network Indymedia, to campaigns against the patenting of seeds by multinational corporations, to the movements for an intellectual commons that promotes traditional academic freedoms against the privatization and marketization of higher education (Harvie 2000). A typical criticism of the commons invoked in this sense is that its orbit is so wide that its radical political potential becomes meaningless. Do we recognize everything that creates space outside of capitalistic logics as revolutionary, as 'cracks' in the system that point to an alternative order (Holloway 2010)? Can we talk of an equivalence – in terms of creating non-capitalist commons – between groups engaged in the illegal downloading of music from the internet and struggles of landless movements or indigenous peoples in the rainforest?

Some of the most influential theorists of the new commons focus their attention on the twin appropriative evils of 'private' capitalist processes of exploitation and alienation, and 'public' forms of economic governance, in the sense of twentieth-century state-driven processes of development and modernization (Hardt and Negri 2009; Holloway 2010). Much of the resistance that has emerged in the global South to so-called globalization processes over the past decade is directed at World Bank-sponsored and state-driven projects of modernization that involve the attack on traditional and collectively held land and natural resources for the purpose of commodity production for global markets (Caffentzis 2009). The anti-statism of the commons literature is significant, for it focuses upon the legal, regulatory and sanctioned violent means through which the state has aided and abetted capitalism since its inception, being used to appropriate common lands for the purposes of private wealth accumulation (Linebaugh 2008).

The 'commons' is thereby frequently evoked as a more democratic, participatory and horizontal model of ownership which at the same time respects local difference and diversity of ownership forms (De Angelis 2007; Linebaugh 2008) against the prescriptive one-size-fits-all models of market-driven capitalism or statist socialism/social democracy. Following on from this, a further critical aspect of the contemporary commons literature is the rejection of the classical Marxist revolutionary call for a vanguard to smash capitalism. Instead, the radical project today is to construct autonomous spaces outside capitalism in the here and now – i.e. prefigurative – rather than a once-and-for-all future revolutionary uprising to overthrow capitalism through an assault on the state (Holloway 2005, 2010).

The contemporary discourse on the commons recasts the temporal and spatial imaginary of anti-capitalist politics in important and interesting ways. The classical Marxist perspective views primitive accumulation as a early stage in the development of capitalism whereby nascent capitalist forces secure enclosures against older examples of pre-capitalist forms of collective ownership and traditional rights as a precondition for the processes of intensive and extensive accumulation (Marx 1906: ch. 24). The freeing of labour from the land and the appropriation of land for capitalist purposes are important precursors for the exploitation of labour in production as labour cannot subsist outside of capitalist processes. Struggles against enclosure are 'pre-capitalist' in the sense of defending traditional and even conservative hierarchical social relations against more progressive forms.

However, an alternative perspective is to view primitive accumulation as an ongoing element of capitalist exploitation and appropriation marked by continuing violent class struggles between commons and enclosure. As Federici puts it (2010: 3): 'commons have been the thread that has connected the history of the class struggle into our time'. The struggles going on today in the global South between indigenous peoples and their defence of traditional rights, collective lands and subsistence production against the attempted expropriation by the state and corporate interests in a wide range of countries – Nigeria, Mexico, Guatemala, Ecuador, India, to name but a few of the most celebrated – are now viewed as being at the forefront of struggles to secure a commons outside of capitalism. While it is important not to underestimate the continued non-capitalist power hierarchies (e.g. castes, race, patriarchy) that infuse such commons, what links these contemporary struggles to the earlier processes of enclosure in England that Marx documents is a determined and ongoing resistance to enclosure, the appropriation of labour and resources into capitalist practices and the subordination of economic and social life, production and social reproduction to commodification processes.

Moreover, struggles against enclosure should not be seen as merely responsive to capitalist accumulation processes but as a direct threat to the rule of capital because of their continued adherence to a form of working and living outside of capitalism. The continued existence, for example, of subsistence farming and traditional agricultural practices in large parts of the world, which would have been the targets of socialist state modernizers in the past, are now viewed more positively by many of those on the left as being at the forefront of challenges to global capitalism (Caffentzis 2004). Spatially, this does not necessarily mean that the locus of anti-capitalist struggle has shifted from the urban, the industrial and the so-called developed economies of the global North, to the rural, the agricultural and the subsistence economies of the global South, but it does signify the continuing importance of diverse and alternative local place-based traditions and practices of solidarity, knowledge construction and collective action for radical anti-capitalist politics (Escobar 2001). Indeed, one of the most interesting and productive aspects of the contemporary commons discourse is the way that it fuses post-colonial sensitivities for subaltern groups constructing their own economic practices at the local scale, independent of and in opposition to dominant top-down agendas – whether these are state socialist, neoliberal marketization or even a more state-driven capitalist modernization project – with a continuing Marxist concern for anti-capitalist class-based politics (e.g. Hardt and Negri 2009; Bohm et al. 2010).

Practising the commons

The most celebrated example of contemporary commons practice is the Zapatista movement in the state of Chiapas in southern Mexico. The Zapatista Army of National Liberation (Ejército Zapatista de Liberación Nacional, EZLN) was set up in opposition to the North American Free Trade Agreement (NAFTA) in 1994 as a group dedicated to fighting the neoliberal agenda of NAFTA and the actions of the Mexican state in pursuing that agenda. In particular, the Zapatistas opposed the threat to traditional farming practices and the rural way of life that NAFTA posed by opening the Mexican economy up to cheap agricultural imports from the USA. A particular source of opposition in the NAFTA treaty was the repeal of Article 27 Section IV of the Mexican Revolution which guaranteed the '*Ejido*' common land practices of indigenous Mexican communities in Chiapas and elsewhere (see Cunninghame 2008). Since 1994 the Zapatistas have attempted to establish their own autonomous communities in Chiapas that seek to retain indigenous control over local resources, especially land.

The Zapatistas are held up as exemplary in invoking the spirit of the global commons for a number of reasons. In the first instance, their establishment of Autonomous Communities, outside both the Mexican state and the rule of multinational capital, epitomizes the rejection of both the public (in the sense of a centralized state) and the private (processes of global accumulation) spheres that is key to contemporary commons discourses. Secondly, their insistence on the rights to self-management and self-governance of their communities independent of external control is an important element of self-realization. Thirdly, the Zapatistas insist on horizontalist forms of power and participatory, democratic engagement, rejecting more hierarchical and representative forms of mainstream governance. Fourthly, the Zapatistas practise an egalitarian politics in contradistinction to some of the problematic gender and racial power relations of older pre-capitalist forms of commons, which leads Hardt and Negri, for example, to refer to them as 'altermodernist' as opposed to 'antimodernist' (Hardt and Negri 2009: 106). Fifthly, as noted earlier, the Zapatistas combine demands for local autonomy with a trans-local politics of solidarity against neoliberalism and global capitalism. Finally, they represent a fusion between revolutionary Marxist anti-capitalist ideals and support for pre-capitalist forms of social relations – in this case Mayan and indigenous traditions of collectivization and common ownership of land.

Outside the example of the Zapatistas, there has been a flourishing of what we might in a broader sense term movements for commons throughout the world. Latin America, as we saw in the last chapter, has witnessed a particular flourishing of social movements, from Ecuador to Bolivia to Mexico, that are both propagating the rights of indigenous groups in righting colonial injustices but also evoking different social values to global capitalism (see Bohm et al. 2010). We can also recognize commons in the operation of urban and (post-)industrial communities in Argentina, in the wake of the country's financial crisis in 2001, that seek to develop alternative economic practices following the effective breakdown of the mainstream economy (ibid.). Farther afield, we can recognize similar processes of commoning in Asia and Africa, whether it is in the defence of communal land, the growing share of food production for local use or the development of mutual credit unions or associations. As Federici notes, women, through their critical role in social reproduction, are often at the forefront of these commoning processes: 'as the primary subjects of reproductive work, historically and in our time, women have depended on access to communal natural resources more than men and have been most penalized by their privatization and most committed to their defense' (Federici 2010: 5).

We can also point to a resurgence of 'commoning' in the global North in the burgeoning number of non-capitalist economic forms that have been created (Seyfang 2006), ranging from local currencies, time banks (where people volunteer their time on a reciprocal basis for activities such as dog walking, DIY, etc.), community or social enterprises, credit unions and community gardening (e.g. North 1998, 2007, 2010; Seyfang 2006; Federici 2010). There is also the persistence of longer-standing cooperative organizations as a form of common ownership. Since Robert Owen's early attempts to spawn an alternative to capitalism in the early nineteenth century, whereby workers owned and controlled their own labour, the cooperative movement has become a worldwide phenomenon. To provide a few examples, in 2010 9.8 million people in the UK were members of cooperatives, 236 million in India, 9.1 million in Argentina, one in three people in Norway and Canada and one in four in the USA,[2] while in 1994 the United Nations estimated that the livelihoods of 3 billion people had been 'made secure' by the cooperative movement (ibid.). While not all cooperatives necessarily operate differently to more conventional privately owned firms, there is nevertheless an important set of possibilities for alternative economic practice opened up by such collectively owned endeavours. Cooperatives can be powerful influences, particularly in situations where they control a large share of the market, although this does not automatically mean that cooperative actors will pursue more social, as opposed to capitalistic, ends.

The commons, the state and the limits to anti-capitalism from above

While there are considerable differences in perspective and emphasis in the anti-capitalist literature on commons and autonomy, there tends to be a commonly held distrust of the state as a vehicle for radical reform (compare Hardt and Negri 2009; Holloway 2002, 2010; De Angelis 2007). In his most recent book, for example, John Holloway talks of the state and the public realm as part of the same disciplining apparatus of power that supports the pursuit of capital accumulation and the subordination of labour:

> The state is not just any organization but a particular form of organization, and to focus the struggle for change on the state has profound implications for the movement against capital. The state is a way of doing things: the wrong way of doing them. The state is a form of organization developed over centuries as an integral part of the capitalist system. ... The state is part of [a] process of separation. It is the separation of the public from the private, of the common affairs of the community from the community itself. The state is an organization separated from society, staffed principally by full-time officials. Its languages and practices express that separation: the language of officialdom, the practices that follow set procedures and formalities. The separation of state from society is policed by rules and hierarchies that ensure the maintenance of the established forms of behaviour. (Holloway 2010: 58)

For Holloway, any left strategy aimed at the state must inevitably mimic state hierarchies and practices, reproducing in its own politics the forms 'of behaviour and thinking that are characteristic of the state' (ibid.: 59), although it is not really clear how and why this should come about automatically. It also essentializes the state and those who populate the state as somehow removed from society. In a rather overdetermined fashion, he argues that the state under capitalism becomes the form that secures the regulation and subordination of subjects, creating its own 'rules and hierarchies' through which we are governed. It therefore exists outside of and in opposition to any real democracy or attempt at self-realization. Radical attempts to engage with it are inevitably forced to play by the same rules, leading not to a radical democratic politics that is capable of freeing human subjects from oppression, but to new forms of domination.

Hardt and Negri are similarly dismissive of the state and the 'public' sphere in their arguments for a project aimed at winning back 'the common and its powers' (2009: ix) when they attack what they see as the existing left dichotomy between public and private, socialism and capitalism:

> The seemingly exclusive alternative between the private and the public corresponds to the equally pernicious political alternative between capitalism and socialism. It is often assumed that the only cure for the ills of capitalist society is public regulation; and Keynesianism and/or socialist economic management ... Socialism and capitalism, however, even though they have at times been mingled together and at others occasioned bitter conflicts, are both regimes of property that exclude the common. The political project of instituting the common, which we develop in this book, cuts diagonally across these false alternatives – neither private nor public, neither capitalist nor socialist – and opens a new space for politics. (Ibid.)

In their analysis of the contemporary global economy, they go further, suggesting that the emergence of 'biopower' as a tendency in capitalist production towards the primacy of knowledge and immaterial labour means that the 'commons' is emerging organically through the reorganization of production and work. The increasing importance of information, knowledge and human creativity, and the development of the internet in particular, constitutes a situation where new open spaces of communication, dialogue and mutualism are emerging – a new commons in effect – that is impossible for either capitalist or state actors to control. What they see as older socialist strategies of intervention – both revolutionary and parliamentary – through the state become increasingly untenable in these circumstances:

> The incompatibility of socialism and biopolitical production goes for all forms of socialism, bureaucratic planning, state regulation, and so

forth – not just the Soviet model. At the most fundamental and most abstract level, the two primary aspects of socialism, as we conceive it, public management of economic activity and a disciplinary work regime, directly conflict with biopolitical production ... [which] is increasingly autonomous from capitalist control. Autonomy is equally required from state control and government forms of discipline. (Ibid.: 270)

Furthermore, they argue that 'whenever the common is expropriated and its value corralled in private hands or public means, under capitalist command or government control, the result is the same: the cycle of biopolitical production is stunted and corrupted' (ibid.: 270–2). Intriguingly, there are clear traces of the arguments that Hayek, Hodgson and others have identified as the knowledge problems, the subsequent implications for innovation, freedom and democracy being made here against the state and what Hardt and Negri categorize as socialism or social democracy.[3] Certainly, there is no disagreement here with the criticism of over-centralized and appropriative state practices of the sort that Hardt and Negri have in mind.[4] This critique has been around a long time, as we have seen in previous chapters, and was articulated by many of the 1960s and 1970s new left in arguing for more democratic forms of public ownership.

But what autonomists also point to is the fact that the nature of the state is itself changing, becoming more repressive – which certainly in the global crackdown on civil liberties and immigrants and the upsurge in more authoritarian and violent forms of state action against insurgency and protest post-9/11 is difficult to dispute. In the epilogue to the second edition of *Changing the World without Taking Power*, Holloway notes that this takes states even farther away from 'any semblance of popular control' (Holloway 2005: 235). For him this makes the attempt to win state power as a socialist/communist strategy even more futile, although, in response to many of his critics, he does not reject outright forms of left politics that continue to engage with the state. His central point, though, is that a politics of commons is one of self-determination which cannot be achieved through the state.[5] Self-determination comes out of the everyday lived experience of the antagonisms brought about by capitalism: enclosure, exploitation and alienation of living labour. For Holloway, anti-capitalist politics therefore emerges from the 'cracks' that are evident in the workings of capitalism, both through its own contradictions and inability to completely enclose and capture our work for valorization processes, but also because we are conscious actors who both individually and collectively seek to develop our own independent practices outside of capital. An oppositional politics can only come from this lived set of practices in the everyday, rather than be imposed 'top-down' by some state project of emancipation.

Holloway argues that the emphasis in current anti-capitalist politics is not only shifting away from the idea of state capture and a 'totality' or totalizing vision of an alternative egalitarian politics but towards 'the unstructured confluence of struggles from below, the coming together of particular struggles' (Holloway 2010: 207). This has to happen through local autonomous projects recognizing their common interest but through horizontalist relations of empathy and mutual recognition, rather than through a more organized form with a traditional leadership structure. He goes on to reject those, such as supporters of Chávez's Bolivarian Revolution, who advance a dual strategy of radical change from both above and below, because he views these as fundamentally 'antagonistic' in nature (ibid.: 208). While projects from below can be self-determining, socialist projects from above – like capitalist globalization, according to Holloway – end up imposing their own 'tight weaving of social relations that left little room for determination from below: in this sense they were totalitarian' (ibid.: 210).

The implications of this analysis for a radical project are that any attempts to move from more micro or local levels of organization and common ownership towards higher scales of organization must be rejected. A key issue then becomes how we move from the micro cracks – the autonomous spaces – that are emerging in the interstices of capitalism to something that begins to join up these cracks. Like other autonomists, Holloway is characteristically vague on these issues. Rather than formal organizational and institutional structures at local, regional, national or international scales to solve critical problems like climate change, eliminate nuclear weapons and tackle global finance, we must rely on 'a much looser integration of social connections, a "world of many worlds" ... Just what this might look like can only be the result of struggle, but it would presumably have at its base smaller and more autonomous units' (ibid.: 210). While we might agree that certain 'global' problems need global solutions or at least some form of 'global co-ordination' (ibid.), these cannot be resolved through international top-down agencies such as the United Nations or more grandiloquently some kind of world eco-socialist state. This is because existing forms of global coordination are 'so bound up with capital and the pursuit of profit that they offer little hope of a solution' (ibid.).

Another autonomous writer, De Angelis, takes a softer line, recognizing the advances for working-class and oppressed groups from forms of state-led intervention in the twentieth century, notably the post-war western European welfare state in providing relief for certain groups from capitalist appropriation processes. Nevertheless, in *The Beginning of History*, he argues that there is a need to move beyond a focus on the state which is, in his words, a 'nuisance we inherit from another era' when we thought that 'power was up there' (2007: 6). Recentring a radical politics around 'commons' and 'community' is considered a more productive way forward. However, unlike Holloway and Hardt and Negri, De Angelis does at least hint at a more nuanced understanding of how a radical anti-capitalist politics must confront capital and the state through a range of strategies and scales when he talks of how:

> our struggle must seek to push back our degree of dependence on capitalist markets, reclaim resources at whatever scale of social action, and on the basis of these invent and practice new forms of exchanges across the social body, new types of local and translocal communities. In all these cases, what is required is an emphasis on relational and communicational processes, as well as on the conditions within which we access resources. Competition is replaced by communication and enclosures by commons. (De Angelis 2005: 204)

However, even for De Angelis, engagement with the state and the attempt to forge new sets of social relations around state institutions is ultimately a dead end, again reflecting the failures of past forms of socialist strategy and the over-centralizing tendencies of previous anti-capitalisms.

The '(im)possibility of autonomy' and the limits to commons thinking

Although there is much to be said for the new commons discourse in recasting an anti-capitalist imaginary around a more egalitarian and horizontalist politics, there are some clear problems, particularly with the rather rarefied position in dealing with the capitalist state (McCarthy 2005). While the critiques of past forms of socialism – both the revolutionary variants and the more social democratic tendencies – in their focus around state capture as the chief means for delivering left agendas have their merits, and chime with other perspectives that have been developed in this book, it is a whole different matter to write off the state as a sphere of political engagement for an anti-capitalist politics.

On one level even many who are sympathetic to autonomous ideas recognize that social movements, if they are serious about developing a broader anti-capitalist politics on a wider terrain that goes beyond a residual localism, or a minimalist grassroots anarchism, will have to engage with the social forces and processes of the capitalist mainstream. Bohm et al. (2010), for example, argue persuasively for an autonomous politics that recognizes the impossibility of being completely independent of the state, capital and the broader developmental discourse around economic growth. Concern about autonomous social movements or commons discourse being incorporated or captured by other social actors to promote and sustain existing hegemonic agendas misses the point. Invoking Laclau and Mouffe's 'agonism':

> We have argued that autonomy cannot be completely fulfilled. This is because capital, the state and discourses of development continuously seek to 'recuperate' autonomy and make it work for their own purposes. However, autonomous practices are rarely completely captured by existing institutions. This means they continue to produce the possibility of resistance and change. (Ibid.: 27)

A related point is that many of the forms of autonomy that are celebrated by the commons discourse, such as credit unions, cooperatives and LETS schemes, are often quite compatible with neoliberal capitalism. As critiques of the social economy discourse have pointed out (e.g. Amin et al. 2002), autonomous self-valorization activity often fills the gaps in social and public provision that are evacuated by capitalism and the state. Only when such activities show signs of economic success or vitality do capitalist actors begin to attempt to appropriate them back into capitalist practices (Harvey 2003; De Angelis 2007).

The broader point, however, is that the pursuit of autonomy and a commons requires ongoing struggle with state and capitalist actors rather than the evacuation to some kind of purified outside space. This requires both self-valorization projects and strategies that reclaim a 'commons' from capital and the state:

> because autonomy never completely reveals itself and always remains as a possible promise, it can be appealed to in many different ways. This can create the possibility of antagonism and struggle around what autonomy itself might mean and how it might be actualized. This means autonomy becomes a site of political struggle over what it could possibly mean in practice. For instance, the introduction of autonomous practices into the corporate workplace does not involve

a complete capture of notions of autonomy by capitalist interests. Rather, it opens up autonomy as a potential site of struggle in the workplace. This opens up new possibilities both in terms of how work is done and how this is resisted. (Bohm et al. 2010: 27-8)

At another level, the commons discourse represents one among many globalization narratives and is equally suspect for the same reasons as more elite cosmopolitanisms. It over-celebrates the possibilities afforded by the increasingly networked nature of global society[6] and the horizontalist social relations that are able to bypass the more sedimented and hierarchical structures of the state and national-scale institutional structures.

With the failure of the alter-globalization movement to dent the power of traditional state structures and corporate hierarchies, it is clear that the appeal to more networked, decentred and democratic forms of politics remains a lofty aspiration rather than a more sober assessment of realities. Autonomous movements cannot avoid engagement with the state and its institutional structures. Moreover, the appeal to a flatter horizontalist politics inherent in the global commons discourse erects a somewhat false set of oppositions between state and society, horizontalism versus verticalism, institutional structures versus transient liberated spaces. The rejection of established social movements such as trade unions and traditional political party structures associated with the state is part of the rhetoric that is deployed here, but it rests upon a false set of distinctions between a 'them' up there who exercise power in traditional ways and seek to dominate and 'us' who seek escape into an idealized set of non-hierarchical, fluid and participatory social relations.[7]

Returning to the example of the Zaptistas here, their refusal to engage with what they see as the corrupt and verticalist practices of the Mexican state (however much we might agree with this analysis!) and existing left parties such as the PRD means that their movement has stagnated in recent years, unable to broaden its base to appeal to the masses of Mexican society while global capitalism continues to make inroads in Chiapas (Robinson 2008). Similarly, the autonomous movements of the Argentinazo[8] have come no closer to challenging the old clientalist structures of Peronism which seem to have reasserted themselves as the economy recovered in the second half of the 2000s (ibid.). In contrast, the indigenous movements in Bolivia and Ecuador have both made considerable strides in recent years because of their abilities to fuse powerful autonomous mass social movements with action both in and against the state. In Bolivia, the autonomous movements have neither been incorporated into the state nor remained outside it, but rather are able still to 'mobilise in an autonomous manner, both against the elite and the right, and to pressure the Morales government' (ibid.: 344).

Practising the commons in, against and outside the state

Much of the anti-state discourse in the radical commons literature is curiously lacking in concrete analysis of the relations between something called the state, civil society and radical social movements When real-world cases are invoked they tend to be rather simplistic in their analysis. The Zapatista struggle, for example, sees the Mexican state as a negative totalizing apparatus of domination and enclosure. Yet things are more complicated than this. The *Ejido* laws, repealed under the Salinas government in the run-up to the NAFTA agreement, were themselves the creation of the 1917 revolutionary state in response to the original communal movement (led by Zapata) to reinsert traditional collective rights to land. While the Mexican revolution, like many in the twentieth century, failed to live up to the more radical expectations, the state's role in promoting collectivism versus appropriation was certainly more ambiguous. The relations between state and civil society are surely more complicated, historically contingent and fluid than some of the commons discourse allows for.

While we can agree once again on the way a state legislature under capitalism will have strong tendencies to protect the dominant class interest – as evidenced by the disproportionate attention and punishment given to property-related crime as opposed to violent sexual crimes – it must be acknowledged that the state has been an important terrain of struggle for certain basic rights and freedoms, whether these are the promotion of gender equality, sexual freedoms, racial equality, indigenous rights, etc. As Erik Olin Wright notes:

> struggles for social emancipation should not simply ignore the state as envisaged by evolutionary interstitial strategies, nor can they realistically smash the state, as envisaged by ruptural strategies. Social emancipation must involve, in one way or another, engaging the state, using it to further processes of emancipatory social empowerment. (Wright 2010: 336)

Although the outcomes of such struggles are often partial, uneven between places and in some instances highly flawed and problematic, because of hierarchical and dominant capitalistic rationales within state bureaucracies, this does not detract from the importance of the state as a site of struggle. For example, in many northern European countries (Norway and Sweden being particular exemplars) the successful campaign for maternity and paternity rights, both through the political process and social movement campaigning, involves a challenging of dominant capitalist priorities through the state. The creation of a public discourse in this way is an important example of re-establishing certain rights and commitment in the realms of social reproduction, and the rights to basic income outside of capitalist production processes, but also challenges dominant social and gender relations in society more broadly.

The same can also be said for the critique of state forms of ownership. Too easily do autonomous perspectives write off the progressive potential of state or public ownership (e.g. Hardt and Negri 2009). Yet, as the overview of state ownership post-1945 shows, the experience was mixed. While the criticism of bureaucratic, centralized forms of public ownership, shorn of democracy and participation and disrespectful of localist and commons traditions, holds in many cases, does that mean that we write off state ownership as a potential space for anti-capitalist forms of collective ownership? For me, the answer is clearly no. Projects of state ownership were rarely reducible to capitalist values of profit accumulation and were often part of more alternative programmes of reform and development that pursued different values such as national development and the provision of universal services (such as electricity, water supplies, telephone communications, transport infrastructures, etc.) which did dramatically improve and enhance the quality of life for the vast majority of working-class people.

In keeping with other state forms, these organizations were also the sites of struggle of competing narratives and visions. Where over-centralized and concentrated forms of ownership were enacted, these were more easily captured by dominant interests, whether these were of the state development and modernizing tendencies (between 1950 and 1980) or of the neoliberal agenda from 1980 onwards. This does not, however, detract from the need for forms of public ownership at higher scales beyond the local – whatever shape and content these take and whether we call these 'state' owned or not – which are necessary in advanced societies to grapple with the problems (such as climate change, transport and communications, supply of electricity) that cannot always be dealt with at lower scales. As our earlier discussion in Chapter 2 demonstrated, there was continual contestation of the forms of nationalization taken by Western states such as the United Kingdom in the post-1945 period from the left, culminating in quite serious proposals for more radical and democratic forms of governance. Indeed, the neoliberal project – a successful reclaiming of the state by business interests – was a reaction to the threatened democratization of the economy through the state in various guises.

Conclusions

The arguments around a new global commons are very insightful in identifying the need for new and more democratic structures of public ownership that are anti-capitalist in their emphasis upon mutualism and collective spaces outside in opposition to enclosure and appropriation. However, as theorists as diverse as David Harvey, Chantal Mouffe and Erik Olin Wright have observed (Harvey 2010; Mouffe 2005; Wright 2010), the failure to engage with the state leaves the most important questions about left political strategies in forging alternatives unanswered. The standard response is that these are not matters that can be easily conceived of in advance, and that even to conceive is to begin to plan, which is to begin to totalize. While most left theorists can agree on the problems of past forms of socialism in putting top-down models before radical democratic practice, the autonomous perspective that things will somehow emerge organically from the bottom up and bypass the spaces of state and capital to embrace broader trans-local networks of solidarity looks disempowering and unhelpful in this respect.

While we can retain the commons aspiration of anti-capitalist and democratic practices and acknowledge the pitfalls in state-driven projects for social emancipation, a more valuable approach is to see the state–economy–society nexus in terms of more dynamic relations that are an ongoing terrain of struggle (Mathers and Taylor 2005). Above all, the state is not some sort of homogeneous entity, 'out there' or 'above us'. Gramsci's overarching perspective here remains important with his insistence on the importance of counter-hegemonic projects and discourses which can develop out of small-scale autonomous practices and become expanded into broader projects in a 'war of position' (Gramsci 1971). In this respect, there is a need both for forms of public ownership that develop a commons 'outside of' capital through self-valorization processes – typified by cooperative and mutual forms – but also strategies that seek to expand and upscale these practices and values to higher levels through engagement with reconstituted forms of state ownership. A genuine anti-capitalist politics is one that seeks to take back public ownership from capital rather than the false prospectus of exodus offered by some branches of autonomism.

PART THREE
Remaking public ownership

7 | Remaking and rescaling public ownership

Introduction

The previous chapters in the book have addressed the shortcomings in older and existing forms of public ownership while also seeking to puncture some of the 'commonsense' nostrums and misconceptions that have been formulated by its critics from both the left and the right of the political spectrum. A central theme of the argument so far is that the forms of public ownership (particularly through the state) pursued in very different political and economic circumstances in the twentieth century have in the main been over-centralized and undemocratic in practice, while at the same time being ineffective in dealing with the problems of knowledge, diversity and innovation that are critical to the functioning of all economies. Nevertheless, I have also cautioned against writing off forms of state ownership as a means to secure progressive ends.

In this chapter, I argue for a reconstituted and pluralistic approach to public ownership that prioritizes economic democracy and public participation in dealing with the deep problems facing society in the twenty-first century. In particular, I integrate some of these earlier arguments to set out a preliminary sketch of what this reconstituted form of public ownership might look like. The chapter sets out some key principles for reconfiguring public ownership before dealing with issues of space and scale – a traditional blind spot for many on the left – with what I term here a left geographical imaginary and the need for a more nuanced and fluid perspective on space, democracy and economic governance issues. The penultimate section goes farther in setting out the diverse forms of ownership that could be operationalized under the broad frame of public ownership with an indicative set of proposals that might apply in practice across different economic sectors.

Principles for a democratized and deliberative public ownership

Five key principles can be identified for the pursuit of a more democratized model of public ownership. The first relates to taking seriously the importance of class justice in the pursuit of social justice;

in other words the appropriative practices of enclosure, exploitation and alienation that have animated discussions around the commons and which characterize capitalist accumulation processes. The second concerns the importance of distributed power in economic relations as opposed to the over-concentration of power among elite groups, institutions and places. A third principle concerns the need for tolerance, respect and engagement with different traditions of collective and public ownership; the fourth develops out of this to emphasize the importance of institutions that promote knowledge, innovation and deliberation, while the final principle espouses the importance of diversity and pluralism to the practice of economic democracy. I now deal with each of these in turn.

Tackling social justice as class justice The most important underlying principle and rationale for public ownership is that it remains critical to delivering social justice, but only if forms of ownership are developed that tackle the fundamental issues of class justice that animated Marx and his followers – the exploitation and alienation of the vast majority of the population from both their labour and the fruits of their labour under capitalism. Many well-intentioned liberals and social democrats – including Keynes and post-war Swedish social democrats[1] – who have been committed to tackling the vast inequalities produced by unfettered capitalism have tended to prioritize distributive justice as the main route to social justice. This is a politics that focuses attention on dealing with the redistribution of income outside the realm of paid work and productive economic activities, typically through progressive taxation and welfare policies, education, health and public transport and other essential services. Even policies that promote minimum- or living-wage legislation are essentially about the redistribution of the surplus – or profit – that comes out of the labour process, rather than challenging the way the owners of capital control that process or the wider decisions that make and shape economies. Addressing class justice, therefore, is about giving people participation in the economic decisions that affect their lives.

As we have seen in previous chapters, there has been a generalized retreat among many mainstream left political parties and trade unions in the advanced capitalist economies from issues of ownership and control, in stark contrast to the situation in Latin America, where they are at the heart of revitalized radical agendas. But in North America and western Europe in particular, the lack of commitment to a class justice agenda (as opposed to a more narrowly conceived class politics) has been a fundamental error of centre-left and social democratic thinking that goes back much farther than the accommodation with neoliberalism set out in Chapter 4. Even in the post-1945 period – the high watermark of social democratic politics – where there were programmes of nationalization and improvements in worker representation in corporate governance structures, the fundamentals of private ownership and the rights of a capitalist class to control, manage and plan the fundamentals of economic life have remained sacrosanct.

The extent of this retreat has varied, from the co-determination and corporatist practices of social democrats in northern Europe and Scandinavia to the complete absence of any meaningful attempt to establish workplace or economic democracy under British Labour governments throughout the post-1945 period. Additionally, as we will see in subsequent chapters, there remain strong non-socialist alternative traditions of economic democracy and collective governance, many with religious roots, and many pre-dating industrialization and capitalism, which continue to shape the institutional frameworks of many economies and account for the persistence of variations within capitalism. Nevertheless, we can detect a general tendency to downplay class justice issues in the era of globalization and competitiveness in the interests of maintaining the integrity of 'commercial freedom'.

Of course, those social democrats who remain true to a politics of redistribution might question whether this really matters if we can tackle inequality through distributive policies.[2] Others might justifiably make the argument (which has also been made in previous chapters) that the performance of public ownership so far has not been great in delivering either distributional or class justice. Yet another argument, advanced to some extent by non-mainstream leftist economists such as Geoffrey Hodgson (and partly paralleled by the arguments of Hardt and Negri with their thesis on the growing immaterial economy), is that the changing nature of the economy from productive to knowledge-based activities, the fragmentation of the organization of work, the increasing autonomy of much work and the increased difficulties of traditional capitalist forms of command and control are making traditional left concerns about class justice increasingly irrelevant.

One counter-argument to the latter point, put by those working in the labour process tradition, is to question the empirical evidence for a knowledge economy, given that the vast majority of people continue to be employed in relatively low-level and often highly coercive and exploitative work (e.g. Thompson 2004; Warhurst and Thompson 2006). But the most compelling case for the resurrection of a left politics around public ownership remains the original Marxist desire for an economy geared towards collective community concerns and social need in opposition to its appropriation by elite interests. A useful way forward here is to return to the concept of appropriative justice discussed in brief in Chapter 3 in relation to Theodore Burczak's work. In its original formulation under George de Martino (De Martino 2000, 2003), appropriative justice is part of a threefold composition underpinning notions of class justice, which includes distributive justice and productive justice; the latter referring to 'the distribution of the labor effort that generates the social surplus' (De Martino 2003: 8), in other words the division of labour within the workplace. A key concern here is with how the social surplus in society – the Marxist term for the total profits arising from economic activities – is constructed, controlled and distributed. The three elements of class justice here refer to who contributes to the production of the surplus, who directly appropriates the surplus, and who determines at a broader level how the surplus is distributed.

A critical point for us here is that those who are able to appropriate the surplus, in the first instance by virtue of their ownership and control of the economy, are also in a strong position to affect the distribution of benefits from the surplus. The mainstream orthodoxy accepts the rights of the owners of firms to extract profits in return for entrepreneurial risk-bearing and organizing the factors of production, while failing to recognize that this process occurs at least in large part through the appropriation of the fruits of the labour of others. Traditional social democratic policies around progressive taxation and welfarist redistribution can of course partly address this. But what they don't allow for – in the absence of strategies directed at productive and appropriative justice – are the equally important questions of how an economy is organized, but more critically who controls the key decisions about what is produced and to what purpose.

> We have already considered the distribution of that share of the surplus that is destined for consumption goods, this being the domain of distributive class justice. One of the distinguishing features of Marxian class justice is that it reaches beyond this limited (though important) domain, and highlights the normative significance of the processes by which a society allocates its social wealth across all uses and purposes. Authority over surplus allocation comprises decisions over investment in productive enterprises, housing, and other private institutions – something that is treated today in most societies as a right that

attaches to the ownership of capital – as well as over the nature and quality of public services, and so forth. ... Allocating surplus is therefore fundamental to the processes of social (and personal) construction, expression, and experimentation. To be 'cut off' from this process is therefore tantamount to disenfranchisement in a most fundamental sense. It is to be denied not one's rightful property but one's rightful participation in a process that defines one's community and even oneself. Clearly there is far more at stake here than the level of wages workers receive for their labors. (De Martino 2003: 16–17)

The threefold conception of class justice enunciated here is important for us – not just because, following Burczak, it recognizes the exploitation and alienation of labour by capital through the latter's ownership of the means of production, but also because it asks questions about the rights of all citizens to participate in the decisions shaping both the way the economy is organized and the direction that it is taking. Ownership based solely around private property forms, whether these are employee-owned firms in Burczak's account (Burczak 2006) or conventional capitalist firms, is exclusionary and undemocratic in its negation of some groups' rights to participate in economic life. As De Martino notes: '... it is not difficult to imagine a society in which the producers of surplus with full and exclusive rights of appropriation live lavish lifestyles at the expense of those who do not (or cannot) participate in its creation' (De Martino 2000: 105–6). The role of the state and institutional mechanisms beyond the market is critical here, therefore, in allowing all groups and citizens in society to participate at some level in economic decision-making.

To be clear, this is not an argument that all citizens must have democratic representation in all economic decision-making; the kinds of argument that were the subject of critique in Chapter 3. But it does lay emphasis upon economic decision-making as a collective undertaking that should be exposed to broader scrutiny and participation than we have at present. Addressing the economic problems facing society – whether it is specific concerns such as a strategy for dealing with climate change, questions over housing needs and allocation, or more general macroeconomic questions such as what goods and service should be produced to serve whose needs, or how to achieve full employment and tackle poverty – needs collective and diverse forms of ownership and decision-making, framed around a democratic negotiation of a general interest rather than private interests capturing economic decision-making institutions. The old phrase 'commanding heights of the economy' is actually apposite here. Emphasizing the importance of the critical 'big decisions' about an economy being subject to democratic control and scrutiny, while taking all three elements of class justice together also take us beyond a narrow productivist (or workerist) discourse that recognizes the importance of economic rights in the different spheres of the economy: production, social reproduction and distribution.

A commitment to distributed economic power, but not necessarily in decentralized forms Following Hayek, Hodgson and Nove, I argued in Chapter 3 that it is unrealistic to imagine that all economic decisions can be subject to collective democratic planning. Nevertheless, this does not detract from the need to try to find, within the limits posed by efficiency considerations, solutions that open up the economy to more collective and participatory decision-making processes as a general philosophy. An important way of achieving this will be through diverse forms of public ownership that allow different groups of citizens to have some level of participation and stake in the economy, compared to the situation at present, where a small minority globally (the 1 per cent!) hold most of the key decision-making power. To furnish these ends, alongside the pursuit of class justice, a reconstituted public ownership requires institutional arrangements that foster distributed and dispersed powers of economic decision-making against tendencies towards hierarchy and centralization.

As we have seen in previous chapters, the most compelling critiques of nationalization and public ownership in the twentieth century, from writers as diverse as Hayek, Hodgson and Holloway, were those that focused on the strong tendency to centralize and concentrate powers in party and state bureaucracies far removed from the everyday lives of workers and consumers, creating both knowledge problems and alienation; the fusing of Marxist and Hayekian concerns. However, addressing this defect should not be interpreted automatically as a commitment to localism and decentralization per se. As I note below, there will remain the need for planning and ownership at higher geographical scales, but these in turn need not necessarily be overwhelmingly concentrated within particular places, organizations or social groups. What it does require is a commitment to the decentring of knowledge and decision-making power wherever possible, both in geographical and functional terms. Within any territorial form of political governance, the key decision-making functions for different economic activities can and should be dispersed. We might here contrast the decentralized and federalized polity of post-1945 Germany favourably with the growing concentration of political and economic power in the UK (despite recent devolution) around London and the south-east of England. In relation to the latter, for example, Amin talks of the need to 'decentre the nation' through a

> multi-polar polity in which the regions can run discrete areas of national life (rather than just a limited set of their own affairs) as well as count on action by the state to redirect opportunities towards them, bolster their bottom-up strategies, and regulate inter-regional competition. This is not an argument for a 'hand-out' approach to local regeneration, but recognition of the principle of spatial mutuality and connectivity. (Amin 2005: 625)

An economy organized around public ownership should therefore be one that also disperses administrative units, knowledge production and competence and has a plurality and diversity of organizations (e.g. mutual bodies, trade union research networks, small business associations, government and autonomously funded think tanks) to offer alternative and competing interpretations of economic problems. Of course, there are no guarantees in any economic system that elite or special interests cannot capture policy agendas to the detriment of the social body as a whole, but dispersing functions, knowledge and institutional capacity does at least provide important countervailing tendencies, as we shall see with the example of Norway in the next chapter.

Tolerance, tradition and heterodox thinking Socialists need to recognize and respect different traditions and perspectives on public ownership if broader support for anti-capitalist values is to be generated. Forms of common ownership have been around a long time and pre-date capitalism (Megginson and Netter 2001). Early Greek philosophers from the sixth century BC onwards, such as Phaleas of Chalcedon, and even Plato, were concerned about the distribution of wealth and power and the need for some forms of state and community-centred decision-making. There have also been strong supporters of public ownership from diverse Christian traditions, including the Franciscans in the Middle Ages, and the Taborites and Anabaptists in Germany and central Europe in the fifteenth and sixteenth centuries (Macfarlane 1996). Even the 'Diggers' of seventeenth-century England based part of their appeal on religious grounds. Their leader, Gerrard Winstanley, in his appeal to Cromwell to turn more land over to the commons, urged the latter to 'follow the path of community and mutual aid laid down by God and the Christ and to forsake the covetousness and self-seeking which were the province of the Devil' (ibid.: 25).

One of the few early socialist theorists to recognize the importance of older traditions of public and common ownership was Eduard Bernstein, who acknowledged the New Testament appeal to the common good over private greed (Bernstein 1993 [1899]). He was in a small minority, however, and this recognition was somewhat opportunist, in the sense of broadening the socialist appeal to the still-religious working classes in the early twentieth century. Most socialist or communist projects of public ownership in the twentieth century disregarded or, worse, sought to destroy older traditions rather than recognizing potentially important allies in building a discourse around the common good. As Neurath, a rare heterodox thinker in the Marxist tradition, noted in the 1920s:

> If socialism should bring liberation, it must be joined by tolerance, it must do justice to the differences in civilisations and fit each one into the economic plan and the administrative economy in its own way. Such a world programme of socialism does not exist today. The Germans, the Russians, each believe that their own brand of socialism is the only one that brings salvation. (Neurath 2003 [1920]: 402)

In contrast to most other socialists, Neurath's early career researching the economies of ancient societies gave him a broader and more diverse canvas to articulate his own perspectives on public ownership. His recognition and respect of older traditions of mutualism and cooperation was in stark contrast, of course, to many of his contemporaries, who regarded older forms of social relations as inevitably conservative and antiquated.

Whatever their many differences, the revolutionary and the reformist wing of the socialist project in the twentieth century by and large shared a modernist theoretical monism when it came to ideas about alternatives to capitalism. Neurath was also critical of the Manchester market liberals in terms reminiscent of Polanyi for destroying older institutional forms, such as the guilds and forms of community ownership, with contempt in their aggressive doctrine of laissez-faire. While Neurath still held to the vision of an overall grand plan – at least at this point in his career – he did advocate a tolerance of older forms and traditions of collectivism that could be an important element in strengthening broader social support for public ownership: 'Today's socialism has many intolerant traits ... Why could the peaceful movements for community-oriented economy not be united? Community economy, guild economy, social economy characterise certain periods, but they also exist side by side and give satisfaction to different types of human being' (ibid.).

Ultimately, public ownership needs to be forged in a manner that respects differences in economic identity and practice (Gibson-Graham 2006). What unified the different traditions of state ownership in the twentieth century from Soviet communism to a French statist technocracy to East Asia developmentalism was a radical modernist centralism that deliberately sought to destroy older and more localist economic cultures and traditions. Ironically, such examples are used by capitalist apologists to justify private enterprise, eliding over the collective learning practices through which many peasant agricultural systems evolved successfully over time. Drawing upon the commons critique of twentieth-century statist forms of governance in the previous chapter, we need to recognize that such traditional forms of collective ownership are important in articulating alternative practices, values and ways of doing the 'economic' that provide resources for constructing new forms of public ownership in the current conjuncture.

Promoting knowledge, innovation and deliberation in economic practice I have already discussed at length the knowledge problems associated with forms of public ownership organized around centralized or even decentralized collective planning, so I will briefly restate the main point here. Recognizing the realities of incomplete and divergent knowledge and information about the world outside and the attendant dangers of capturing or appropriating knowledge (Chapter 3), there is a need for institutional forms that can promote dispersed forms of knowledge creation and economic action linked to localized innovation (Hodgson 1999). This is important when considering what forms of public ownership are most appropriate for delivering economic democracy and participation. Eliding over the social context through which knowledge develops in practice – as both mainstream economists and some Marxists do (ibid.) – not only demonstrates a flawed understanding of how innovation and social creativity operate (Cumbers and McMaster 2010), but is fundamentally undemocratic, because it will create closed information hierarchies, rather than allowing new forms of knowledge to emerge and develop in a more horizontalist fashion. While one does not have to sign up to Hodgson's more market-centred perspective, the importance of an approach that recognizes the open-ended and evolutionary nature of economic life and the incremental yet collective development of knowledge and decision-making in particular is critical.

The importance of dialogue, pluralism and diversity in creating genuine economic democracy Recognition of the limitations of centralized ownership for innovation and knowledge production leads in turn to an appreciation of the importance of diversity and variety in institutional arrangements and organizational forms. One of the few socialists to recognize this in the period of classical Marxism at the turn of the nineteenth century was Karl Kautsky, who argued that 'the greatest diversity and possibility of change will rule ... The manifold forms of property in the means of production – national, municipal, cooperatives of consumption and production, and private – can exist beside each other in a socialist society' (Kautsky 1902: 166).

The implications of this are critical, for it implies that there should not be any one dominant model of ownership or governance. Returning to the work of John O'Neill and Otto Neurath is instructive here. While we might agree on a common or shared set of rules and principles for public ownership, such as a commitment to production for social needs rather than exchange values, the pursuit of social equality and economic democracy, environmental sustainability and as far as possible renewable forms of production and resources, the principle of organizational diversity should also be enshrined in a new approach to public ownership (Cumbers and McMaster 2012). Diverse forms of collective social relations would act as a further brake in preventing the emergence of totalitarian power structures. Open dialogue and democracy in this sense require a degree of diversity and variation in economic practice. In this respect, and in the defence of decentralized forms of democratic planning, O'Neill convincingly argues that markets – with their propensity towards commodification and alienation at the expense of all else – are no more a guarantor of individual freedoms or choice than planning committees, a fact also recognized by Keynes (Keynes 1936).

This commitment to diversity implies that there is no one definitive form of public ownership but a range of collective forms can and should coexist. Neurath clearly shares some of the autonomous concerns with an overweening and centralizing state insofar as he is distrustful of the militarism of nation-states and prefers self-governing associations (O'Neill 2003). This did not mean that there could not be an overall coordinating body charged with a 'general plan': in effect this is what elected governments do at present. But, underneath this, and enacted in his proposals for the socialization of the Bavarian economy following the brief post-1918 revolutionary period, was a commitment to organizational diversity:

> The programme of socialization here discussed makes an attempt at a simultaneous realization of socialism, solidarism and communism ... It provides for cooperatives for peasants and craftsmen, for collectivist settlements on a communist basis and for large-scale socialist production in agriculture and industry to exist side by side, in order to do justice to their different aspirations to realize a collective economy in their own way. (Neurath 2003 [1920], cited in ibid.: 196)

The diversity and pluralism celebrated by Neurath would decisively shift people's identities and allegiances away from what he saw as the 'intolerance' of the market economy or nationalisms towards a set of more dispersed identities and loyalties. A system of associational planning whereby people would be members of many different associations at overlapping scales and spheres of life would advance genuine solidarity and mutualism between peoples and social groups by developing a 'multiplicity of ways of life' and 'non-conformism' (Neurath 1945) which would guard against the totalitarian demand for one loyalty to 'devour' all others.

While there are clearly some problems with Neurath's account, most notably how this diversity of forms can work and coexist in practice, there are important insights here that help to take the debate beyond the standard critiques of socialist planning and public ownership. The Hodgson critique of democratic planning is not entirely overcome here. How much of his schema could practically be put in place today, given globalization and the increasingly complex nature of the capitalist economy, is another matter. Nevertheless, one does not have to sign up to Neurath's vision of a market-free decentralized socialism to recognize the importance of his arguments in overcoming the totalitarianisms of free market thinking or centralizing state projects. Reclaiming the diverse heritage of public ownership as an important element of creating democratic and pluralistic forms of economic relations is very much in the spirit of the arguments advanced here.

Making space for public ownership

Socialist thinkers more often than not have a blind spot when it comes to geography and lack what we might term a 'spatial imaginary' in conceiving of their alternative economic strategies. Yet all past attempts to create collectively owned economic institutions as alternatives to capitalism are always, whether or not this is explicitly stated, space-making projects (Lefebvre 1991). Many existing socialist and social democratic perspectives tend to take state boundaries as sacrosanct and given, focusing on the nation-state as the site of struggle and often, for example, rejecting any demands for devolution and local autonomy as reactionary or automatically opposing attempts to construct supranational structures of governance such as the European Union. In contrast, other shades of left thinking are avowedly localist, ranging from anarchism, guild socialism (Cole 1920), associational socialism (Hirst 1994, 1997), to the more recent autonomous thinking discussed in Chapter 6 and much radical green economics (e.g. Hines 2000). All share a somewhat romanticized view of the local level as the key scale for forging radical democracy and social justice against the behemoth of corporate-owned and state-directed globalization.

From a left perspective, I have already argued in Chapter 6 against forms of autonomy and localism that fail to take the state seriously as an institutional form that can both constrain but also potentially enable a more democratic agenda. While it is in the spirit of the argument of the book to applaud decentralization and the distributed power of economic decision-making, it is both naive and simplistic to argue for an alternative politics rooted purely in local organizational forms, or espouse vague notions of a horizontal trans-localism between otherwise self-governing autonomous communities. This is not to say that progressive initiatives cannot be instigated at the local scale or indeed that important connections cannot be made horizontally between 'locals' that bypass central state structures. One of the most interesting new departures in public ownership, as noted in Chapter 5, is the growing network of cities that are linking up globally to exchange knowledge and support around new forms of public management and against the dominant neoliberal agenda.

Nevertheless, there needs to be a more nuanced appreciation of the dynamic nature of spatial organization and governance under advanced capitalism and the possibilities this may afford for rethinking public ownership. Rather than reifying particular geographical scales (e.g. the nation, region, city) it is important to understand that space, place and scale are refashioned through economic and political agency, whether by political or corporate elites or by social and labour movements (Harvey 1982; Herod 2001). While there is usually an acknowledgement of the spatial connections between places and the importance of some forms of scalar governance that links activity at the local or national level to higher scales, this is usually woefully underdeveloped as a guide to political practice.

One appeal to a spatial imaginary is to highlight the geographical variety of actually existing economies, both at the national level and the subnational scales in what is usefully termed 'variegated capitalism', rather than a set of different models of national capitalism (e.g. Peck and Theodore 2007). The implications of the path-dependent and evolutionary nature of economic institutions (Hodgson 1999, 2006), the different ways in which economic actors and practices are regulated, interact and reproduce themselves, leads to the obvious conclusion that public ownership should be both variegated and multi-scalar.

Capitalism does not make space in a logical ordered fashion but creates new geographical orders in line with the needs of accumulation, the contradictions that are thrown up resulting from this and the crises these provoke (Harvey 1982, 2003). One of the fundamental strengths of capitalism to date has been this spatial dexterity in adapting itself to changing conditions by creating, destroying and re-creating the economic landscape. Conversely, one of the overriding failings of many past and existing forms of socialism and public ownership is the attempt to too tightly manage, design and control economic relations within a particular spatial container – usually the nation-state or the Keynesian National Welfare State (Jessop 2002) – rather than recognizing the complex spatial mosaic of actually existing economies.

Intellectually, many of the state-centred projects of the last century suffered from 'a Cartesian rationalism and the technocratic conception of planning' (O'Neill 2006: 67); centrally imposed schemes that try to fit neat, ordered geometries of economic governance on to a messy, disordered and decentred economic reality. One problem the centralized Soviet system and the decentralized Yugoslav systems of public ownership never got to grips with was how to resolve the tensions between the strategic planning of sectors on a national scale and developing local and regional plans to create coherent functioning spatial agglomerations and clusters. Spatial uneven development was worse in many centrally planned economies than in many Western unplanned ones.

Neurath's recognition of the spatial complexity of economic life led him to the adoption of an unusual flexibility regarding the scale at which socialist organizations and associations should operate. Reflecting a distrust of the nation-state as an operating unit, Neurath believed that the geographies of ownership should be variable and driven as much by functional rationalities as any political geographical administrative remit. As O'Neill notes, partly in response to an otherwise sympathetic assessment of G. D. H. Cole's guild socialism, Neurath was critical of Cole's 'state fetishism', and instead advocated overlapping associations:

> In a world socialist society the fields of life could be linked to each other in the most varied ways, without having to be detachable national units. We might for instance reach a stage ... where areas along navigable rivers would form one administrative unit for building, transportation and production, whereas the educational units might depend on language ... The national areas might for instance have different boundaries from those of the health areas ... (Neurath 1928, cited in O'Neill 2003: 193)

At a more basic level, disastrous consequences all too often flowed from grand centralizing designs imposed uniformly across diverse human landscapes. Once again, Neurath was one of the few early left thinkers to recognize these problems, critical of a 'pseudo-rationalist' perspective which was wilfully ignorant of actually existing economic conditions on the ground (see O'Neill 2006). In his writings, Neurath is clear that there is no one organizational model that can be imposed everywhere but that historical and cultural diversity need to be respected. Anticipating the kinds of arguments constructed by the alter-globalization movement today against the cultural imperialism of free market economics, Neurath asks: 'Should China, India, Central Africa really get one and the same socialism?' His response, in the negative, emphasizes the recognition of difference and tolerance that would chime with many subsequent post-colonial critiques of both capitalist and socialist modernization projects.

The spatial relationships between capital (or business actors), the state and other social actors are constantly evolving through time, reflecting both the changing needs of the economy but also the ongoing conflicts, tensions and struggles between social groups, a fact recognized by David Harvey and captured superbly in his concept of the 'spatial fix' (Harvey 1982, 2003) and also the idea of a 'scalar fix' (see Brenner 1998, 2004). In very brief terms, the spatial fix refers to the way in which capital and the state need a stable geographical arrangement of material and labour resources to allow production and accumulation to take place. A good example would be the post-war Keynesian Welfare State, founded upon a Fordist compromise between the state, trade unions and business at the national scale, which produced a period of economic growth and stable employment relations in western Europe and North America by sharing the gains from improvements in technology and production methods (Jessop 2002). On a smaller scale, this takes the forms of the local landscapes of cities and local production complexes, whereby local elites or coalitions of different social groups are to secure the conditions for sustainable profit accumulation. The spatial fix is also manifested in particular relationships between places or even countries captured in terms such as the spatial divisions of labour (Massey 1984).

With each new round of capital accumulation, the nature of this fix will change and in turn produces a 'scalar fix' in the changing set of relations between economic activities and actors from different scales, from the local, through the national to the global. Couched in these terms, a critical understanding of globalization is not about the withering away of the national state per se, but rather a changing set of relations between economic and social actors across geographical scales. Thus, an increasingly integrated global economy has brought new forms of supranational government and economic governance (such as the EU, NAFTA, MERCOSUR, etc.) as well as an increased visibility and policy-making (or increasingly disciplining) role for global governance institutions such as the IMF, the World Bank and the WTO. But it has also brought some political decentralization and devolution, particularly across European states, representing new attempts to manage space and the contradictions emerging from capitalism and uneven development. As part of this rescaling, neoliberal ideology has produced a new sub-national competitiveness agenda whereby national states have been shifting away from Keynesian redistributive regional policy between places to encourage increasingly boosterish and competitive local politics at city and regional scales. Such state 'rescaling' processes reflect the contingent and dynamic nature of the state itself, which can be seen as a set of institutional structures and practices through which particular social groups attempt to develop their own strategies and politics. Although the literature tends to be rather 'top-down' in its orientation, reflecting its origins in regulation school concerns with modes of social regulation, it is useful for us here in emphasizing the more fluid relations that exist between geographical scales and their implications for left strategy.

The scale literature has tended to emphasize the state and capital over other actors, with the increasing importance of development and regeneration strategies to service the needs of business, rather than providing a more social or welfarist politics. However, from a left perspective these new state spaces need to be critically interrogated and appreciated if alternative and counter-hegemonic discourses are to develop. Political devolution, for example, can open up new spaces for progressive alternative agendas (Mackinnon and Shaw 2010), given the right circumstances and effective social mobilization around key social and environmental justice issues. The re-establishment of the Scottish parliament in 1999, for example, which brought to an end almost three hundred years of rule from London, did not initially lead to a great difference in public policy (as the same party, Labour, was the dominant party in government in both Edinburgh and London) but it did create space for an alternative discourse around economic and social issues and lead to policy divergence over time, particularly with regard to devolved areas such as health and education, where the Scottish parliament remained committed to non-marketized forms of service delivery compared to its New Labour-led counterpart. For our interests here, the highly politicized issue of landownership in Scotland, and in particular its ownership and control by a minority of wealthy individuals and corporations, did become the subject of intense debate and legislation that gave local communities limited rights to buy out landlords (Callaghan et al. 2011).

Beyond this, left thinking must develop its own spatial architecture and scalar politics around public ownership. New scalar fixes are required that construct institutions at and across scales in support of projects for economic democracy. One response to all this from the autonomous camp would be to say that these are spaces constructed for capital and that an alternative politics should start from the bottom, in self-valorization projects that can then be rolled out and emulated elsewhere. While there is nothing wrong with the motivation and vision here, the politics, as I argued at greater length in the previous chapter, is flawed, for it lacks the sense of how the more significant 'projects for social emancipation', to use Wright's term (Wright 2010), are almost always those that link up local experiments with broader and higher-level initiatives. A brief example from the UK will illustrate the point here.

The most important and enduring publicly owned institution in the UK – though under fierce privatization pressures for some time now – is the National Health Service, which, from its inception in 1947, has provided a system of socialized medicine for the entire country. The idea for the NHS drew upon the experiences of local schemes of cooperative and mutual aid among working-class groups. The NHS was modelled on the Tredegar Medical Aid Society, a mutual organization established in the South Wales valleys town in 1890 by miners and their families. At the height of the Great Depression of the 1930s it was providing free medical services to many of the local population. Aneurin Bevan famously declared on the setting up of the NHS: 'All I am doing is extending to the entire population of Britain the benefits we had in Tredegar for a generation or more. We are going to Tredegarise you.' Perhaps what has been lost from the narrative of the NHS is the extent to which its foundation involved the scaling up – or perhaps scaling out – of a local mutualist self-valorization project to the national scale. Similar cases can be found in the housing sector of many western European countries, with local municipal public housing schemes in the 1920s and 1930s becoming the model for state-led projects in the post-1945 era. Whatever the subsequent problems and criticisms of these national-level projects – suffering from many of the problems of centralization, bureaucratization and alienation discussed in previous pages – they did represent major challenges to capitalist social relations, while articulating important alternative visions around social justice that dramatically improved the lives of many working-class people.

In the current period it seems to me too that the most hopeful radical prospects are to be found in projects that emerge in particular places as incidences of working-class 'self-valorization' (Cleaver 1979), which at the same time seek to contest existing structures of power in the formal capitalist economy at higher scales by making claims on the institutional and legal apparatus of the state. Examples such as the right to the city movement in the United States and the living-wage campaigns in the USA and the UK are good examples of social movements that have both a broader social vision and autonomous agency on behalf of subaltern and working-class groups, but at the same time are concerned with making claims on and through the state which challenge the hegemony of capital over economic decision-making.

Socialist projects always involve their own spatial imaginary, even if this is not recognized by the protagonists. Whereas past left projects have tended to be linked to national state agendas, centralizing and totalizing grand narratives to tackle issues of equality and social justice, the kind of solutions required in the contemporary era need to navigate between a spatial politics that is sensitive to local variation and autonomy, and an imperative to decentre decision-making. They must at the same time recognize the limits to localism in promoting a broader agenda of economic rights and social justice. Thus they require a complex and ongoing set of negotiations between different scales rather than essentializing or rejecting one over another.

A preliminary sketch of a publicly owned economy in the twenty-first century

Any proposals for an economics centred around public ownership will necessarily be rather embryonic in form. Given the concerns raised above with regard to the importance of tolerance, pluralism, historical and geographical contingency, and the necessary variegated geography of public ownership that follows from all this, there can clearly be no one-size-fits-all model that can be applied. To be effective, and consistent with the arguments advanced here, strategies for economic democracy will need to evolve out of particular circumstances, and work with the grain of existing collective practices and institutions in different places. Nevertheless, I do provide here some preliminary thoughts around what forms of ownership might work best for different economic activities, what the boundaries might be between market and non-market forms, and how organizational responsibilities will be organized at and across different geographical scales.

While democracy is best served by attempting to disperse rather than centralize economic decision-making power, and in many cases this can be achieved through spatial decentralization, the realities of globalization and the complexities of advanced economies mean that there will always in practice be a trade-off between higher-level coordination and local autonomy and participation. At the same time, following Hayek and Hodgson, the complex division of labour in advanced capitalism and the impossibility of centrally codifying local tacit knowledge mean that for efficiency reasons decentralized economic decision-making is preferable to centrally planned economic systems in many cases (Nove 1983; Gorz 1982). However, there will always be some economic activities that require central coordination and some element of strategic planning and cannot be left to a more spontaneous order (e.g. dealing with global climate change, managing communication, transportation and power supply networks).

A further issue regards the old thorny problem of adjudicating between different forms of social justice – in particular, how do we reconcile appeals for appropriative and productive justice – which seem to lead us in the direction of more localized autonomy and difference – with the broader pursuit of distributive justice. This means that even where it is economically efficient to organize decision-making on more localized lines, we would still require some forms of centralized coordination and regulation to safeguard the basic economic, social and cultural rights of each citizen. Moreover, even if we accept the basic principles of decentred decision-making, there will still need to be some democratically elected way of dealing with the broader macroeconomic decisions at higher scales, at national, supranational (e.g. EU) and even global scales in the case of a tax on financial speculation, for example.

Still more critical issues concern the economic mechanisms and institutions that would most suit different circumstances. What would be the balance between market and non-market forms, public and private forms of ownership? What areas of economic life would benefit from market signals and values – though still regulated by broader concerns about social justice and economic rights? As I have noted in earlier pages, inevitably a socialist economy will have elements of both market and non-market exchange. Market forms will also require competition and forms of commodity production both to provide alternatives to consumers and to provide a remedy for failure, in the sense of a product or service not delivering what the end user requires – whether we are talking about shoes or a café latte (Nove 1983). These, of course, are controversial and complex issues and need a much greater discussion than is possible here.[3] Although competition is anathema to many socialists, it is important to recognize it as an essential human trait, which cannot be wished away.[4] In the Soviet system, market-based competition may have been eliminated but, as Nove notes, avaricious competition remained within society but took dangerous and even deadly forms; political competition within the party hierarchy could lead to the execution of political rivals (ibid.).

In a socialist economy, rules and institutions could be fashioned to support the more cooperative aspects of human behaviour, but some forms of competition should also be encouraged, particularly if they are linked to innovation and excellence in performance. Although the economy would be primarily organized into forms of public ownership, some limited forms of private ownership should continue to exist. The self-employed would remain as a category, and even small firms up to a certain size (perhaps fifteen to twenty employees), after which conversion into forms of cooperative or mutual ownership would be required by law. As Burczak has argued, market competition centred around cooperative or worker-owned enterprises is entirely compatible with Hayek's well-known critique of market socialism.[5] Some economic activities, because of minimum efficient scales of production, marketing, distribution, etc., are better organized at higher scales (e.g.

electricity grids), whereas others can be organized at the more localized community level (e.g. renewable energy production through wind or wave power). But even in the case of industries that lend themselves to localized forms of ownership, there will still be the need for higher-level deliberation and strategies to secure particular social objectives, such as dealing with climate change, securing distributive justice, etc. (see the example of Denmark in Chapter 9).

Outside particular sectors, there are also key economic and social policy goals (for example, tackling poverty) that require higher-level coordination, strategy and target setting, whether at the level of large sub-national regions (e.g. Scotland, Catalonia, California, Rio Grande do Sul) or the national or supranational (e.g. the European Union), or which may even require global forms of economic governance (such as the United Nations or a reformed World Trade Organization). It has become something of a mantra for many on the left to deride such forms of organization as always inevitably acting in the interests of capital or elite state actors, but, as with our arguments about national state forms, this is too reductionist and evacuates alternative discourses from critical spaces of governance (Mouffe 2005). While it is possible to be against neoliberal-inspired visions of the European Union such as the Single Market Project or monetary union (on the current fiscally conservative terms), it is perverse if one is an internationalist to set one's face against any European-level (or indeed global) solutions.

Overall, we should aspire towards examples of democratically controlled forms of public ownership that are technically necessary at higher levels while relinquishing control of other activities as far as possible to the local level. Additionally, there should be experimentation with different forms of public ownership in line with local needs and aspirations. This will also encourage innovation in management and organizational forms, which can be shared and transferred across different localities. However, whatever form of ownership is chosen – and it should be recognized that in practice there are a myriad of combinations rather than a simple dichotomy between public and private – the aspiration should be towards democratic decision-making in which employees and user groups have a voice.

How would all this look in practice? Table 7.1 provides an illustrative sketch of the various forms of public ownership with a preliminary assessment of how each might deliver particular goals that an eco-socialist government might aspire to.

Following Nove (1983) and Sawyer and O'Donnell (1999), we can iden-

TABLE 7.1 An evaluation of the effectiveness of different forms of public ownership in achieving desired objectives

Objective	Form of ownership	Rating
Commanding heights	FSO	++
	PSO	+
	LMO	+
	PC	=
	CC	−
	EO	−
Local community control	FSO	−
	PSO	−
	LMO	++
	PC	+
	CC	+
	EO	+
Distributional justice	FSO	++
	PSO	+
	LMO	+
	PC	−
	CC	+
	EO	−
Environmental sustainability and justice	FSO	++
	PSO	+
	LMO	++
	PC	=
	CC	=
	EO	=
Enhance participation/class justice	FSO	=
	PSO	=
	LMO	+
	PC	++
	CC	++
	EO	++

Key: + positive effect; − negative; = neutral

tify six broad types of public ownership that are already present in the contemporary economy: full state ownership (FSO), partial state ownership (PSO), local or municipal ownership (LMO), employee-owned firms (EO), producer cooperatives (PC) and consumer cooperatives (CC). The following aspirations would be secured through public ownership:

- promoting greater participation by workers, consumers and citizens in general in economic decision-making;
- regaining the commanding heights of the economy (i.e. taking into public ownership industries too important to be left in private hands, such as banking, energy, other utilities);
- facilitating greater community control over resources, especially in the context of globalization and increasingly destructive forms of ownership such as private equity firms and other asset-stripping forms of capital;
- redistributing income and wealth through cross-subsidization of different social groups;
- securing key environmental and social goals, such as combating climate change and addressing growing inequalities.

Clearly, some forms of public ownership will be better at meeting certain objectives than others (Table 7.1). For example, taking an industry into full state ownership (FSO) – akin to the 'Morrisonian' model of nationalization preferred in the post-war period in the UK – will in theory secure the objectives of being able to influence key sectors and undertake longer-term strategic planning to secure important goals, such as dealing with climate change, building and maintaining modern electricity or transport systems, etc. Partial state ownership (PSO) is perhaps the most common form of state ownership in the contemporary economy, largely resulting from partial privatization processes, and is a feature in many European countries. While these forms can be used to secure wider public policy goals or to provide some public influence in different parts of the economy, the trend in recent years – as with many fully owned state companies – has been to allow such firms complete commercial freedom with the state effectively a sleeping partner that benefits from profit and dividends alone. LMOs which are vertically integrated and operate at the scale of city regions or devolved regions may also score high on these measures while having the advantage over FSOs of being more closely connected to local democratic structures. FSOs are less likely to secure greater participation on the part of the ordinary citizen and there is a danger that, over time, they become captured by elite groups and subject to the kinds of principal agent problems that have occurred with earlier nationalizations. These issues are considered further, together with how they may be avoided through broader institutional structures, in the analysis of Norwegian oil nationalization in the next chapter. While LMOs are spatially closer to local communities and citizens, they also run the risk of capture by elite groups, particularly at the level of city governance, for the development of boosterish projects (e.g. gentrification) that may benefit particular groups over the more general interest. The cooperative and employee-owned firms (EO, PC, CC) clearly score highest in terms of democratic participation and involvement but arguably will do less well in securing broader policy objectives. While an economy composed of decentralized cooperative firms will more than likely shift the overall nature of economic values towards more socially progressive ends, without countervailing forms of ownership it could also create new hierarchies in providing rights over appropriation of the social surplus to particular groups (De Martino 2000).

All forms of public ownership have their advantages and disadvantages and there will inevitably be trade-offs between the different objectives. If it is assumed that some form of compensation is to be given to existing owners, FSOs are obviously the most expensive and logistically the most difficult to achieve, though not prohibitively so, depending upon existing economic conditions and the value of private share capital. By contrast it is relatively easy to take a partial stake (PSO) or take over one key section of an industry, for example rail track infrastructure or national electricity grids, while still running private services on a contractual basis.

In reality the form of ownership chosen will vary according to the needs of particular industries and conditions in a particular time and place. In their recommendations, Sawyer and O'Donnell (1999) advocate very different forms across the various utilities. They do make three general points, however, with which I would concur:

- that whatever form is chosen should be accountable to a layer of government;
- that public enterprises operate according to a clearly defined public interest with set targets and objectives;
- that best employment practice should be adhered to. This should include trade union recognition, a commitment to worker participation in decision-making, and strong regulations concerning skills training and upgrading.

Table 7.2 provides an illustrative sketch of how these different forms of public ownership might be applied in practice across the range of economic sectors. The list is far from exhaustive but is indicative of how the principles articulated in this chapter might play out in different contexts. In the first instance, we can identify a

TABLE 7.2 Schematic depiction of public ownership types by economic activity

Type of activity	Spatial organization	Forms of ownership	Institutional and regulatory arrangements
Finance	Local, national, transnational	Global FSOs for international development and lending; national FSOs for monetary policy; FSOs and LMOs for funding industrial/economic development; COs for housing finance; PO/EOs for housing, pensions	Tight regulation and demarcation of separate spheres; outlawing of speculation and derivatives trading, tax havens; restrictions on 'usury'
Utility industries (e.g. electricity, water, gas)	Local, national, macro-regional	Combination of LMOs and FSOs	
Public transportation	Local, national, macro-regional	Combination of LMOs and FSOs	Public subsidy for public transport; high taxes on private motoring
Public services (e.g. health, education)	Local and national	Combination of LMOs and FSOs	Strong national regulatory structure to ensure equal standards between regions; high taxation of private forms and redistribution of income to state-run areas
Consumer products (e.g. clothing, food, electronic equipment)	Global production networks; local/regionalized food networks	Consumer + producer cooperatives; small and family-owned firms	Ethical trade rules; living wage standards; rights of collective association; tax and other subsidies to stimulate local and carbon-neutral production systems
Private services (e.g. hairdressing, car repair, plumbing)	Local	Private firms below 20; POs, EOs above 20; self-employed	Freely operating markets but subject to high minimum standards in terms of wages, conditions, health + safety, training
Consumer services (e.g. restaurants, hotels)	Local, national, international	Private firms below 20; POs above 20; self-employed	Freely operating markets but subject to high minimum standards in terms of wages, conditions, health + safety, training

category of activities that is strategically critical to the functioning of the economy and which should be owned and controlled on behalf of the community or 'general interest' rather than being dominated and exploited on behalf of elite groups. Finance and land are the two most obvious here, as examples of what Polanyi called 'fictitious commodities' which should be owned and managed in the general interest. Profiteering and speculation in the realms of finance and land in particular have created massive inequalities and wreaked considerable social havoc in the past three decades without adding to the general common wealth.

Taking financial activities first, a mix of ownership forms here would be consonant with the different needs and uses of money. State ownership at a range of scales could be used to secure broader macroeconomic objectives, relating to stabilizing the economy – in the manner currently undertaken by central banks but requiring the redemocratization of these institutions away from 'post-political' technocratic control. We should push for much greater political interference in central bank decision-making, but this should be of the deliberative kind that opens institutions up to broader scrutiny. National and regional development banks, also under state ownership, could be tasked with investing in key sectors and initiatives, and promotion of training, research and development, for example in renewable energy, medical research, etc. There could also be publicly owned and accountable international banks replacing the neoliberal institutions such as the World Bank, whose task would be to tackle global inequalities and poverty reduction but through democratic procedures that allow poorer countries and regions a say in decision-making. In contrast to finance, land should where possible be owned and controlled at the local, community level, although there may be certain activities that require national governments to override local land claims in the more general interest (e.g. in the construction of transport or communications infrastructure).

Housing would involve a mix of public, private and mutual forms of ownership, but mortgages and credit should be strictly regulated to avoid the twin evils of usury and speculation. Greater provision of public and social housing should be a key goal to provide real choice and prevent sub-prime housing speculation developing.

The utilities are another example of a set of strategic activities that require management by and for the community as a whole. Many are of course natural monopolies – such as public transport, electricity and water supplies – and also require higher levels of coordination to deliver economies of scale, but these can also in some instances be combined with more local and decentralized forms. Water supplies, for example, can be organized effectively at the municipal or regional scales. In the case of electricity and power supplies, while national or even supranational-level grid systems are important in setting broader public priorities (e.g. dealing with climate change), delivering scale economies and allowing cross-subsidization of poorer groups and access to those living in remote and peripheral regions, once again there are possibilities for more localized forms of organization (see Chapter 9), particularly in terms of renewable energy generation.

Public transportation and public services such as health and education should be broadly organized in the public sector, but these could take a range of different forms, from local community cooperatives to more national forms (such as educational authorities and basic healthcare services), where the demands of distributive justice, efficiency and cross-subsidization of poorer groups warrant higher scales of organization. These are sectors where private ownership and market-based forms of delivery should be kept to a minimum because they deal with basic social rights that require different forms of valuation around care and nurturing and for which monetized values and commodification are deleterious.

More diverse forms of ownership, including private firms – though according to the size limitations identified earlier – could inhabit consumer goods sectors, where competitive markets would function akin to Burczak's market socialism model. Clearly, in these industries in particular the problems of dealing with globally organized sectors obviously raise issues of feasibility. For now, I will assume that we are dealing with a socialism in one country experiment, in which case there would continue to exist foreign corporations trading and operating locally. These could be subject to strict ethical and regulatory rules that could even apply to their supply chains outwith the country in question if a country had sufficient market power – for example, to impose fair trade rules on all products being sold in domestic markets. For those domestic firms operating in these sectors, beyond a certain size the owners would have the choice of which type of public ownership to transfer to: there are plenty of examples of retail chains in western Europe that are already cooperatively or employee-owned and which provide a high level of service and quality of product (the John Lewis chain in the UK being a prominent example). Clearly, many other customer service activities would remain in private hands, though subject to regulation of labour practices and wages. In many sectors the small size of the average firm means that there would continue to be plenty of scope for private enterprise and genuine Schumpeterian entrepreneurialism.

Conclusions

In his book *The Economics of Feasible Socialism*, Alex Nove put forward a set of proposals for a socialist economics based around public ownership and a mixed economy, drawing upon his vast experience as a researcher on Soviet and centrally planned economic systems. Central to his concerns was a socialism that might be possible in the lifetime of a child born in the year the book was written (1983) rather than an unrealizable utopian scheme. Similarly, here, although I would not necessarily share his denigration of the principle of utopian thinking and revolutionary politics, my proposals are offered in the spirit of developing practical socialist proposals that are relevant in the context of contemporary processes of global capitalism. The continuing obstacles to the vision laid out here are immense – both in the entrenched and powerful interests that need to be overcome and in the shift it would require in public opinion – and the book has not engaged with the political mobilization required to achieve it. Nevertheless, the solutions proposed here all exist in some form in the current economy, and public ownership is once again an issue of real live debate.

At the time of writing, and as noted in earlier chapters, much of the financial system across the world is effectively nationalized and in state hands, though run not in the 'general interest' but to benefit a small handful of very rich individuals in the financial sectors. At the same time, as I note in Chapter 6, there remains a considerable amount of cooperative and mutual ownership in the economy on which to build and stimulate more decentralized forms of collective action. If we add to this the ownership of many private companies by pension funds, it is clear that the economy has considerable degrees of public ownership already. The imperative is to make these diverse forms more accountable to democratic processes, and given the current crisis within capitalism there is clearly more of a public mood for more radical alternatives now than hitherto. The possibilities for shifting the economy towards more democratic forms seems less 'utopian' than it would have a decade ago.

In the next two chapters I consider two existing experiences of different forms of public ownership, focused upon the energy sector in Norway and Denmark. They exemplify the ways in which different forms of public ownership can be constructed that shift the economy in a more democratic direction, opening it up to broader forces and stimulating more deliberative and decentred processes of economic decision-making. Although, as I show, they are not without their contradictions, they do demonstrate the concrete forms that democratic public ownership might take in practice.

8 | State ownership, deliberative democracy and elite interests in Norway's oil bonanza

Introduction

For many on the left, Norway offers itself up as a role model for progressive and egalitarian development. On most economic and social measures, Norway is usually near the top of the United Nation's Human Development Index league table (number one again in 2011), and is particularly celebrated for its income and gender equality, absence of social hierarchy and participatory forms of economic governance, with workers' representatives, at least in theory, having a role on the boards of large companies in both public and private sectors. The 'Norwegian model' is also celebrated around the world for its approach to North Sea oil and gas development, rightly acclaimed for dispersing the benefits throughout the country's economy and society. It is compared particularly favourably to both the parallel developments across the North Sea in the United Kingdom, and to the experience of oil and mineral extraction in many developing countries, where natural resources have often proved to be more of a curse than a blessing (McNeish and Logan 2012).

Norway's experience is particularly interesting for us here because of the nature of state intervention and public ownership in the development of its oil and gas resources. When the first discoveries were made in the 1960s the approach adopted had much in common with Third World countries in dealing with the power of the international oil cartel; setting up a nationalized entity that could enter into joint ventures and over time develop indigenous expertise. This involved a 'top-down' model of state ownership led initially by elite groups within the central state apparatus. However, over time, as the magnitude of oil resources became apparent, a much more wide-ranging debate over the impact of oil on Norwegian society and culture developed that went beyond narrow economic considerations. In the process, some interesting institutions and mechanisms emerged that have attempted on the one hand to embed oil development within a more deliberative and agonistic frame in which alternative and more progressive agendas could be enunciated (Mouffe 2005; Cumbers and McMaster 2010), and on the other to facilitate forms of democratic participation and engagement by a broad range of groups in the decision-making process.

Since the mid-1980s a powerful oil lobby – around the national oil company Statoil – has emerged to develop a much narrower economistic perspective whereby democratic participation in and discussion about Norway's continuing resource wealth have been marginalized for a more 'commercially driven' agenda. Despite this, I argue in this chapter that Norway's experience demonstrates the importance of a decentred and deliberative set of institutional arrangements for economic governance, which have nurtured a vibrant and continuingly active civil society lacking in many other contemporary advanced societies. Rather than holding up the Norwegian model as an example that can be easily emulated elsewhere, my purpose here is to highlight both the possibilities for constructing a more 'traditional top-down' model of public ownership subject to democratic and dispersed forms of economic governance, and the tensions that can arise when such organizations are captured by elite interests.

The Norwegian 'model' of oil development

It is easy to understand why the 'Norwegian model' of oil development is held in such esteem by outsiders. Given the alternatives, the Norwegian experience, in the words of the leader of the radical oil workers' union SAFE, Terje Nustad, 'appeared to be the only successful example of a country which has been able to secure a national governance and control of oil activities and to ensure that the profits were channeled towards the majority of the population' (cited in Ryggvik 2010: 5). As Nustad went on to emphasize, this perception was rather simplistic and glossed over the tensions, conflicts and social divisions that have characterized Norwegian oil developments. Rather than some static and romanticized model of cross-class consensus and harmony, the Norwegian experience has been constructed out of and indeed continues to be shaped by often intense struggles and tensions between competing social groups. Nevertheless, Norway's transition in the twentieth century from a relatively poor country on Europe's 'agrarian fringe' (Mjoset et al. 1994: 55) to one of the world's most prosperous and egalitarian societies is by any standards a significant achievement for a country of just under five million people; even more remarkable when its late industrialization and relatively recent independence (1907) are taken into account.

A brief comparison with the UK usefully illuminates Norway's social democratic oil trajectory. To begin with, after three decades of oil development, the UK is a far more unequal society than Norway as measured by the OECD's Gini index of inequality.[1] Historical trends suggest that while this situation has worsened considerably in the UK since the 1970s,[2] in Norway there has been a much smaller increase in inequality, far lower than the OECD average (OECD 2008: Figure 1.2). While taxes in Norway are lower than in the rest of Scandinavia, they remain higher than in the UK as a proportion of GDP when income, sales and other taxes are included. In the UK, oil revenues in the mid-1980s were critical in allowing the Conservative government to cut business and income tax rates for the very richest in society. In the 1988 Budget, the top rate of income tax was cut from 63 to 40 per cent.

The continued commitment to social equality has been matched by an impressive level of state-driven industrial development and economic modernization. Again, in marked contrast to the UK, where there has been a distinct absence of any cohesive industrial strategy towards North Sea resources (Cumbers 2000, 2012), the Norwegian government has played a role more akin to that of the East Asian developmental state (Weiss 1998). Of most significance for us here was the establishment of a state oil company, Statoil, in 1972, to protect domestic interests (Anderson 1992), as well as the creation of the state's direct financial interest (SDFI) in 1985. The latter was established because of fears that Statoil was becoming too powerful, as I discuss later in the chapter; the SDFI was valued at 834.8 billion Norwegian krone (NOK) (about £80 billion) in 2008 (NPD 2009). Another point of comparison, marking out Norwegian oil operations from those of the UK, has been the establishment of a state oil fund – known as the 'Government Pension Fund – Global' – in 1990, which is currently worth around £214 billion (Scottish Government 2009). Foreign oil companies were also required to cooperate with Statoil in the transfer of industry-specific knowledge, skills and expertise – known as Goodwill Agreements – so that by the early 1980s Statoil was able to pursue its own oil and gas field developments independent of any foreign involvement.

In common with the wider approach to distribute the benefits of oil as broadly as possible, the state fostered a geographically balanced pattern of growth with a strong regional development dimension to oil exploitation. This happened in a number of ways. First, Statoil and the government's Petroleum Directorate were located in Stavanger to create an alternative decision-making nexus to the capital, Oslo. Secondly, there was a strategy of building up separate service bases for each new field development in an effort to spread the benefits of oil-related employment to more peripheral areas (Cumbers 2000).

Thirdly, during the 1970s a number of smaller shipyards in the north of Norway received significant subsidies to help them diversify into the offshore industry. Finally, there has also been an effect through the regional dimension of national technology policy, whereby Trondheim, as the location for the country's main technical university (NTNU), has become an important centre for energy-related research.

In short, the Norwegian experience demonstrates an impressive commitment to spreading the benefits of oil throughout society, while also building up considerable industrial capacity and expertise as a means of modernizing the country's economic base. The conditions that produced this outcome were neither intrinsic to some idealized Norwegian model, nor necessarily unproblematic. As Helge Ryggvik in his authoritative account of the relations between the Norwegian state and the oil complex puts it:

> There is no single Norwegian oil experience. [It] has come about through the constant conflict between interest groups. Norwegian oil experiences, therefore, are the product of an active democracy – a democracy which has not only expressed itself through formal parliamentary representation, but equally through direct popular mobilization. (2010: 113)

Ownership and control of resources for 'the whole of society'

To understand the achievements made here, therefore, we need to dig deeper to reveal the key influences and underlying processes. In particular, three critical elements can be identified: a long-established Norwegianization strategy, an active set of democratic engagements and deliberations around the role of oil in wider society, and a strong tradition of trade union organization and mobilization.

Although the development of oil policy in the North Sea has given rise to discussions of a Norwegian model, the overriding approach to dealing with foreign corporations was constructed earlier in the century through the exploitation of the country's water, mineral and timber resources. Norway's relatively late industrialization meant that there was no indigenous business class of any size (Mjoset et al. 1994). Up until the middle of the twentieth century, the economy remained organized around small-scale and localized businesses which grew out of an economy based around agriculture and fishing (Wicken 2007). This itself was a legacy of the fragmented landownership structure with a large number of small independent farmers. This rural constituency was the key influence on Norwegian politics up to and including the first quarter of the twentieth century.[3] Wicken goes so far as to talk of the small farmer as the 'hero of the Norwegian nation during the period of nation-building' (ibid.: 11). Another Norwegian commentator has referred to this period as one of 'democratic capitalism' (Sejersted 1993).

The influence of a peasant agrarian social structure was important in terms of shaping Norwegian society well into the second half of the twentieth century, evident through institutions and laws to maintain the equitable distribution of resources, particularly in relation to landholdings, the main regulation being the '*odelsov*', which did not permit the transfer of agricultural land outside the family (ibid.). A further pillar was the emergence of local savings banks that provided finance for small-scale industrialization projects and which were to continue to dominate the Norwegian financial system up until the 1990s (ibid.). A deeply rooted commitment to localism and decentralization on the one hand went hand in hand with the persistence of strong mutualist traditions to provide protection against fluctuating commodity markets, a good example being the establishment of a single marketing cooperative for milk production in the 1930s with a law passed in parliament to prevent price competition (ibid.). This system remains largely intact, and indeed cooperatives continue to constitute an important element of Norwegian society, with one in three of the population belonging to a cooperative organization (MacKinnon and Cumbers 2011: ch. 12).

The key economic development issues for Norwegian society in the early twentieth century were negotiating with foreign MNCs over the country's rich abundance of natural resources. In this regard, the state tended to play the role of entrepreneur to stimulate industrial development, with a concern to increase the nation's skill base and technical capacity. This was done through negotiating joint venture deals and technology transfer agreements with the foreign companies concerned, with the aim of establishing Norwegian firms in strategic sectors. A strong thread of 'Norwegianization', defined as the principle that resource wealth should be evenly distributed to the benefit of the nation's people as a whole rather than appropriated by private interests, either foreign or domestic, has subsequently underpinned the state's economic development strategy in recognition of the perceived vulnerability of the country's decentralized economy to foreign control.

The response to what became known as the 'Waterfall Law Controversy' in 1905 (Ryggvik 2010: 14) created the legal and institutional basis for the state's negotiations with foreign corporations. The fear that its lack of indigenous engineering knowledge would render the country's resources vulnerable to capture by foreign interests underpinned a desire to develop appropriate legislation to retain national control. The government therefore passed what were known as the '*hjemfallsrett*' laws (literally meaning land falling back or returning), which enabled foreign companies (which were mainly German and French) to exploit water resources in the first instance but under the premise that the resource would return to the state without compensation after a given time period (ibid.). Such laws allowed the state to develop its own technical capability and knowledge over the long term, with policies put in place to increase the number of technologists and engineers in key sectors (Wicken 2007). More pertinently for us here, they also inscribed an important set of moral and institutional norms regarding the relationship between natural resources and economic interests. Influenced by the American progressive journalist Henry George, the Norwegian justice minister, Johan Carlsberg, believed firmly that the economic rent emanating from natural resources should not be captured by any private individual or group of private interests but should be the 'common property of the people' (Ryggvik 2010).

Carlsberg's Concession Law in 1909 set an important precedent for dealings with foreign companies with additional laws up to 1917 which framed a powerful obligation to use the state apparatus to ensure that the country's rich mineral and resource wealth yielded common benefits, rather than being appropriated by vested interests (Wicken 2007). This became the foundation for negotiating terms and conditions with the US oil companies following the discovery of North Sea oil and gas in the 1960s.

Oil development in an active and deliberative democracy

The emergence of Labour as the dominant party in government after 1945 resulted in an ambitious industrialization and modernization strategy, which, reflecting the broader spirit of the times, was concerned with national productivity issues and achieving scale economies. A key tension developed within Norwegian politics between the previous regime's concern with localism and community economic development and the emergence of a Labour-led national economic planning agenda concerned with creating large-scale national champions in key sectors. One interesting example concerned the development of the electricity sector after the Second World War (ibid.). While the traditionalist element of the political class (in the farming and small business parties) favoured smaller-scale electricity projects that were geared towards serving local communities and small business in a decentralized system, the leading Labour politicians, engineers and technocrats within the state bureaucracy favoured much larger-scale developments, if necessary financed through foreign investment and expertise (ibid.). In contrast to the situation in Denmark (see the following chapter), the latter interests prevailed.

Subsequently, conflict between a grander macro-level economic modernization agenda and an alternative tradition of localism has been an important recurring theme in Norwegian politics and was certainly present in the 1960s following the discovery of oil and gas. Although the early concessions were quite favourable to the oil companies, made largely by a group of elite civil servants who developed close ties to the foreign MNCs, once the magnitude of oil reserves became known, the political elite determined to take a more active role. This involved questions of ownership and control but put very much within a broadly conceived but small-'c' conservative national economic interest in opposition to foreign corporate interests. The principal aim for Statoil was to 'give the Norwegian nation as much governance and control of oil as possible' (Ryggvik 2010: 25), and it was established relatively quickly with broader political support from pro-business parties as well as those on the left. As Ryggvik puts it: 'To the degree that it established independent technological know-how, Norway could not be blackmailed by dominant foreign companies. Thus it would also be easier to push for better financial conditions' (ibid.: 34). From the outset, the concern was therefore more about ensuring that Norwegian firms and workers were able to reap the economic benefits from oil development rather than anything more revolutionary or socialist. By the mid-1980s these economic objectives were largely secured.[4]

Statoil was never envisaged as a democratic model of public ownership in the sense discussed in the preceding chapter, but it does nevertheless present some interesting and positive features in the way democratic institutions were constructed in relation to its operation. The purpose of Statoil, initially established in 1972, was to safeguard a rather vague and generally constituted 'public interest'.[5] Arve Johnsen, the first chief executive of the new company, came from a business background, having been the chief sales director at Norsk Hydro's aluminium division, while the main politicians in charge of energy policy were firmly on the right wing of the Labour Party (ibid.). Statoil was to be a commercial undertaking, at arm's length from government, although with directors appointed by the newly founded oil ministry as the body which held all the company shares. Although the constituency of its managing board, under its Articles of Association, required at least six elected representatives from the workforce among its corporate assembly of eighteen and at least three elected employer directors out of the nine on the board of directors,[6] this was broadly in keeping with the corporate governance structure in many Nordic private corporations.

While an impressive level of economic democracy by international standards, this was hardly exceptional for a Norwegian company. From the outset the intention was that Statoil should be a successful Norwegian capitalist enterprise, to counterbalance foreign dominance of oil, albeit under the close scrutiny of the government in the initial years. There was one important caveat here, however, which proved critical to subsequent developments. In the setting up of Statoil, there was an important clause, known as Paragraph 10, which required that the company provide an annual report to parliament on 'significant issues relating to principles and policy' (ibid.: 100). The effect of this was to make the company a continuing subject of scrutiny and democratic debate, which lasted into the early 1990s. As Ryggvik puts it:

> the so-called paragraph 10 plan was a by-word for wide-ranging oil debates in the Norwegian parliament well into the 1980s. ... the parliamentary debates represented important democratic control mechanisms. The insight which they enabled into the company's strategic choices contributed to raising the level of knowledge about oil questions among politicians and other interested parties. Thus in many cases the debates became an expression of genuine popular democratic involvement in questions of oil policy. (Ibid.: 100)

The growing public awareness of the scale of the resources being discovered on Norway's doorstep sparked a broader debate about the relationship between oil and wider society, which went well beyond the developmentalist and modernizing agendas of the political and bureaucratic elites. In the early 1970s, various committees within the Storting (parliament) commissioned their own reports, White Papers and consultation exercises on the impact of oil.

The Social Affairs, Finance, Foreign Affairs and Local Government committees all set up their own consultation exercises, which drew upon a diverse range of knowledge, expertise and opinions from the Norwegian professional classes as well as the various elements of civil society, from fishing and farming interests to religious associations and the trade unions. The concerns surrounding oil and its prospective impact on all areas of national life led to an impressive and wide-ranging process of deliberation and collective learning across Norwegian civil society. As Ryggvik puts it in describing the work of the various committees that formed:

> These committees drew on the general expertise which was available in Norwegian professional institutions. At the start this was not very much but both the committees themselves and the comprehensive discussions which followed their reports were part of a steep learning curve. All the reports, white papers and proposals were followed by extensive debates in parliament. Many parliamentarians later developed a considerable understanding of oil-related issues. This was expressed in parliamentary recommendations, the final outcome of white papers, which were sometimes as important as the reports they responded to. (Ibid.: 32)

The oil issue shaped, and in turn was shaped by, a wider set of debates about the country's future development path and in particular a heated set of arguments about entry into the European Economic Community, or 'Common Market' as the European integration project was known at the time. To the chagrin of economic modernizers, this resulted in a 'no' vote, in contrast to the UK and Denmark, which both voted to join in the 1970s. Twenty years later, in the 1990s, Norwegian civil society was again mobilized successfully against the drive by business and political elites for EU membership. As with the 1970s debates on North Sea oil, concerns over the autonomy of natural resources in the face of 'foreign' interference were very much to the fore.

It is easy to characterize such moments as signalling a retrograde politics within Norwegian society against inevitable processes of globalization and economic, political and cultural integration, but this is too simplistic. There are clearly darker sides to Norwegian nationalism, as evident in the emergence of an anti-immigrant populist party that has secured 20 per cent of the vote in recent national elections, and the recent massacre of seventy-seven people (mostly under the age of twenty-five) attending a Labour Party summer camp by a far-right extremist. However, the rejection of EU membership also reflects a much more positive element of Norwegian civil society; an active and continuing radical democracy where questions of national economic and social development are subject to rigorous deliberative debate and argumentation. The political debates around North Sea oil reflected a longer tradition of public participation and engagement, enhanced by a more proportional electoral system that encourages considerable political diversity and interest-group representation. Rather than two dominant parties whose rationale is to stake out a middle ground, appealing to middle-class and middle-aged conservative voters, as is the case in many less proportionate democratic systems (such as the USA, the UK, Spain and France), Norwegian politics reflects the more pluralistic range of interest groups, including a farmers' party – which has consistently campaigned against EU membership and has been a counterweight to private corporate interests among more socially conservative voters – and a party to the left of the main Labour Party, the Socialist Left, that split from the former in the 1960s.

A further important point in understanding Norwegian political economy is its electoral geography, which allocates a disproportionate share of parliamentary seats to rural areas compared to urban ones. The rules under which seats are allocated gives a weighting for both size of population and geographical area. To give an example of how this works: Oslo, with a population for the wider metropolitan area of 1.4 million, currently has seventeen seats while Nordland – a predominantly rural area but with some state-backed local industrial complexes in resource-based industries with around 12 per cent of the country's land mass but a population of around 235,000 – has ten seats. The even more remote region Finnmark, the country's northernmost region in the Arctic Circle, has a population of just over 70,000 and five seats.

These political and geographical dimensions to Norwegian social relations were important in the 1970s in exposing oil developments to a broader range of interests and resulted in some genuinely radical policy proposals. These were (ibid.) that:

- the state should extract the greatest possible economic rent from North Sea resources;
- a national state oil company, Statoil, should be established to look after the national interest in opposition to foreign multinationals;
- a separate entity, the Petroleum Directorate, should be created to develop a professional staff capable of overseeing the state's management of oil and gas resources and as an important counterweight to Statoil;
- there should be strong support for the development of an endogenous local industrial capacity supplying the North Sea;
- legislation should be introduced to guarantee a slow and controlled rate of oil extraction with a maximum output of 90 million tonnes per annum;
- (importantly and, for the time, remarkably) emphasis should be

placed upon extracting and developing oil in the most environmentally friendly manner.

The third, fifth and sixth principles in particular reflect the outcome of the broader public debates and the desire for a more 'socialized' model of oil development which would also take account of the country's broader moral responsibilities as an oil-rich state, evident in Norway's long-standing and increased commitment from the 1970s onwards to foreign development funding for Third World countries. The report that captures most the mood of the time was the Finance Ministry's 1973/74 White Paper (St Meld 1973/74), 'The role of petroleum activities in Norwegian society', which called for a 'qualitatively better society' and 'a moderate pace of extraction' (Ryggvik 2010: 34, 35). Of particular importance was a national determination not to be swayed by pressures from the wider international business and political elites for a rapid depletion from the North Sea to offset the growing power of the OPEC nations during the 1970s, but to use the resource in a mature and reflective manner driven by the sovereign will of parliament. In all these respects Norwegian political debate was informed by a much wider 'geographical responsibility' (Massey 2004) than parallel debates about North Sea oil in the UK.

As we have seen, an important democratic and deliberative ethos was enshrined in the governance framework around Statoil. While the company had operational independence it was subject to considerable democratic scrutiny. However, a second important element of this philosophy was the establishment of the Petroleum Directorate (hereafter PD) as a separate organizational actor to Statoil, charged with being the 'state's professional body for resource administration' (Ryggvik 2010: 33) with the responsibility for overall regulation and control of North Sea oil and gas resources. The PD's responsibilities were also further divided, with its resources division reporting to the Ministry of Petroleum and Energy while the health and safety function reported to the Ministry of Local Government and Regional Development (ibid.). Particularly critical was the PD's role in overseeing the health and safety, and work environment in the North Sea. Unlike the UK, where the oil companies were able to persuade the government to allow a lightly regulated and largely self-policing regime – with disastrous longer-term implications for worker safety and employment conditions (Woolfson et al. 1993) – the PD imposed a tough external monitoring regime that was independent both of the foreign oil sector[7] and of Statoil. Although it took time to build its own independent know-how, by the early 1980s it had developed an impressive level of competence and authority in oil matters. This, allied to the role played by the trade unions, meant the emergence of a far more progressive employment relations system than anywhere else in the international oil industry (Ryggvik 2010).

The final pillar of the distinctive Norwegian approach to oil was the existence of a strong and active trade union movement. Even today, trade union density and collective bargaining in Norway remain far higher than the average in most advanced economies,[8] while the tripartite model of employment relations that developed from the 1930s onwards has given the trade unions a strong institutional base. This strength did not come about because of some natural Norwegian predisposition towards social democracy or egalitarianism but through active class struggle. The period between 1927 and 1937 was a particularly formative one when the country had one of the highest levels of strike activity in the industrialized world (Cumbers 2007: 7). This strong trade union presence and grassroots base provided the ruling Labour Party with its power source after 1945 and enshrined a strong tripartite culture within Norwegian employment relations.

The arrival of North Sea oil activities precipitated an upsurge in collective labour action and militancy, in response to the strong anti-union culture imported by the US multinationals. A series of accidents offshore in the late 1970s led to a mobilization of the workforce that was to have profound and lasting effects. Before the PD had found its feet, the harsh and deregulated labour regime had resulted in an appalling health and safety regime – with eighty-two workers losing their lives between 1965 and 1978. Most of these incidents were not down to extreme weather events or other major catastrophes but instead were small-scale ongoing incidences of abuse and neglect (Ryggvik 2010).[9]

The official trade union establishment did little to challenge the existing employment relations environment; although it did set up its own specialist oil union, NOPEF, it was largely staffed by middle-class professionals with little direct experience of working offshore.[10] However, by the late 1970s growing worker resentment led to a series of wildcat strikes on drilling rigs and production platforms, described by Ryggvik as 'the widest-ranging strike wave in Norwegian industry since the Second World War' (ibid.: 74). One of the outcomes of this was the Working Environment Act, devised in 1977 but adapted and strengthened by the PD in a series of additional measures up to 1985. Its significance was to give workers a stronger voice in the operation of Norway's oil and gas resources by providing for elected worker representatives to play a role in the development of health and safety procedures. This effectively gave the workforce a veto over employers' rights to manage. With the independent regulatory position maintained by the PD, the impact was that technology was increasingly designed around the safety needs of the workforce, rather than the workforce having to accept new technology-driven standards. Erik Olin Wright has referred to this kind of institutional change as 'enhancing social power over economic power' (Wright 2010: 139). The effect was a massive decline in industrial injuries and deaths,[11] but it also signified the establishment of a strong grassroots trade unionism independent of the LO (the main trade union confederation) and its close ties to the governing social democrats. The new union, the OFS, later to become SAFE, was to become a critical independent voice with the development of a layer of experienced and knowledgeable shop stewards who had cut their teeth in the harsh working environment of the 1970s. At the level of Norwegian civil society it acted as another important counterweight to centralizing tendencies in the political economy of Norwegian oil development (Cumbers 2004, 2007; Routledge and Cumbers 2009).

The oil-industrial complex, a national competitiveness agenda and the neoliberal turn

Norway's more socialized and deliberative approach to oil development came under increasing pressure in the 1980s with the first sign of changing times being the election of a Conservative coalition government in 1981. Elements within the new administration were soon falling in with the new neoliberal *zeitgeist* by challenging the 90 million tonnes ceiling as an example of over-regulation by the state (Ryggvik 2010). Although it remained in place for the rest of the 1980s, it did represent the first crack in the established approach to oil development and signalled the growing power of a corporatized group of indigenous oil interests.

The collapse in the oil price in 1986 resulted in the first significant economic downturn in Norway since the 1930s and provided further ammunition for those who wanted a more 'commercially driven' approach to oil development. Among the demands were a more self-confident and aggressive set of economic arguments concerning the unsustainability of the more socialized approach, the need for greater rationalization, including the closure of some local operations, and a more competitive domestic oil sector to compete internationally. The very success of Statoil – which by the mid-1980s was a fully fledged oil company in its own right – and the coming ashore of the first revenues from the wholly state-owned Statfjord field further bolstered the position of the company in the wider economy. By the early 1990s the emergence of an indigenous oil supply industry meant that a national 'oil-industrial complex' had arrived on the scene (ibid.; Cumbers 2000).

A coalition that included significant elements of the political establishment within the Labour Party and the trade unions in the LO gradually coalesced around a new modernizing agenda of national competitiveness in the face of globalization. Although it was the Conservative Party that began the opening up of the economy to greater trade and the free flow of capital in the early 1980s, one effect being the increased relaxation of currency and financial controls and the collapse of the banking system, ironically requiring wholesale nationalization to rescue the sector in the early 1990s (Mjoset et al. 1994), it was the Labour Party, returned to power in 1986, which began to push forward a more serious neoliberal agenda, which included the ill-fated second EU referendum.

One of the first signs of this changing political mood was the gradual relaxation of the policy on oil production; a decision taken without much public debate (Ryggvik 2010). Falling oil prices after 1986 were used as the pretext for relaxing production controls to secure foreign investment. A new ceiling based on the level of investment (at NOK25 billion) was agreed in 1988, but within a few years the Storting had agreed to a series of massive increases so that by 1993 the figure had reached NOK53 billion (ibid.: 89). By 2008, the figure had reached NOK122.7 billion or, adjusted for inflation, three times the initially agreed level of NOK25 billion (ibid.: 89).

A key element of government policy during the 1990s was to provide Statoil with greater commercial freedom to act as a multinational oil corporation in its own right, rather than as a national company charged with securing a broader public interest. A growing complaint from the leadership of Statoil was that there was too much political interference in its strategic affairs, setting it at a disadvantage with its competitors (ibid.). Of course, as I have argued earlier in the book, the terms 'commercial freedom' and 'political interference' are regularly deployed as subterfuge by political elites, corporate groups and the business press when the real opponent is democracy itself, in the forms of public scrutiny and participation in economic decision-making.

Although there was public opposition – from the OFS trade union, some grassroots elements of the Labour Party and left-wing groups – a broad consensus among the main political parties and trade union establishment had by the late 1990s emerged around partially privatizing Statoil and giving it more autonomy from state structures and public scrutiny. This included the quiet repeal of Paragraph 10. In 2001 30 per cent of its shares were sold on the New York and Oslo stock exchanges (ibid.). While the state retained a strong controlling stake, the company was to be run entirely as a profit-seeking entity, having the freedom to pursue its commercial interests as and where required. This aim has largely been achieved as in recent years Statoil has behaved in much the same way as other oil multinationals. In 2004 the chief executive of Statoil, Olav Fjell, chairman Leif Terje and director for international operations Richard John Hubbard were all forced to resign and the company had to pay a NOK20 million fine for the alleged bribery and corruption of officials to gain oil concessions in Iran. Additionally, Statoil is leading the lobby to repeal legislation to permit offshore drilling in the beautiful but environmentally sensitive waters around the Lofoten and Vesterålen Islands.

Contesting neoliberalism and the renewal of democratic engagement

The repeal of Paragraph 10 was the most notable element of the closing down of public debate around oil developments, but during the 1990s the oil-industrial complex had already been largely successful in framing the oil discourse and persuading the political classes of the 'vulnerability' of Norway's oil-based economy in the face of broader global forces. The shift in the governing discourse is exemplified by the changing tone of policy statements. The careful control of oil developments in the interests of the 'whole of society' that characterized 1970s policy was replaced by statements such as one in a 1993 White Paper that 'Activity levels in the petroleum industry are to a considerable extent dependent on conditions we cannot control' (cited in ibid.: 89). While such statements accorded with the wider accommodation of the centre-left to 1990s arguments about the inevitability of globalization and the inability of states to influence economic agendas beyond supply-side competitiveness agendas, they flew in the face of the 'on the ground' evidence that the Norwegian economy was relatively strong by international standards in the early 1990s. The public finances were much more balanced than in the late 1970s, when the government had allowed the public sector to expand considerably before oil revenues had started to come in. Given its low levels of unemployment by international standards – unemployment peaked at a post-war high of 5.6 per cent in 1993 and has been at or below 4 per cent for the last two decades[12] – and generally secure economic foundations, Norway was better placed than most to control its own destiny. However, an accelerated rate of oil development domestically and the freedom of its fledgling multinational sector to pursue investment internationally were clearly to the benefit of the increasingly powerful oil-industrial complex. The healthy position of the nation's finances also made it possible to continue high levels of public spending and ensure that the mass of the population had rising living standards, thus neutering public opinion and dissent. Provided oil revenues could continue to support welfare spending and distributional goals, a more radical class politics around ownership and control of oil development could be successfully marginalized.

The main political arguments within Norwegian politics and society have become more about how the continuing largesse of oil resources is to be distributed rather than in continually challenging the actual nature, pace and even rationale for oil development itself. In De Martino's terms, questions of 'appropriative justice' have disappeared from the political agenda. Ryggvik suggests that even the PD's critical independent stance has diminished in recent years, as its interests are now much more firmly aligned with those of the wider oil industry in accelerating new field development. In the current conjuncture, what is particularly worrying is the failure of Norway's political elite – as representatives of one of the richest countries on the planet – to take seriously the country's broader responsibilities as an oil producer for dealing with climate change. There continues to be broad cross-party consensus around the rapid development of oil and gas resources. Governments seem content to offset continued oil production through climate change measures in other areas – in particular through their commitment to the REDD (Reduced Emissions on Degradation and Deforestation) mechanism. This market-based model effectively allows Norway to export its responsibility as a major hydrocarbon producer for dealing with climate change. Statoil and the rest of the Norwegian oil industry are currently putting considerable resources and political pressure into extending offshore developments into the Arctic with a new series of cooperation agreements with Russia opening the way for exploitation. Overall, a business-as-usual attitude of extracting oil and gas when and wherever possible, to contribute to state and corporate revenues, seems to be prevalent, with climate change policy happening somewhere else in the government jurisdiction.

Whether the continuing and even growing resistance by local fishing and farming groups can be mobilized into a much broader and more reflective debate about the country's wider geography of responsibility

(Massey 2005) remains to be seen. A possible cause for optimism has been the emergence of a grassroots alliance against neoliberalism within Norway (Wahl 2010), and in particular the introduction of market mechanisms into the health service and competitive tendering in local government (ibid.). With the election of an even more neoliberal-charged Conservative coalition government in 2001, resistance began to coalesce around a campaign to preserve Norway's welfare state, resist further marketization and privatization, and to roll out an alternative agenda for public services. What became known as the Campaign for the Welfare State (CWS)[13] emerged from an alliance of trade unions and other civil society groups. Led by the largest public sector trade union, the Norwegian Union of Municipal and General Employees, and including the national farmers' union, student and pensioners' groups and women's rights campaigners, the alliance accounted for twenty-nine organizations and 1 million members in total (about 25 per cent of the population). The campaign was important because, while emerging from the trade union movement, it staked out an independent position around a campaign of resistance to neoliberal reforms that sought to advance an alternative set of social values around community, citizen participation and democracy (ibid.).

Focusing initially on the local scale, the campaign launched an alternative to marketized reform known as the Model Municipality project, which was launched in 2002 (ibid.). Using sympathetic local municipalities – a key one being Norway's third city, Trondheim, in the north-west – the project sought to reconnect workers in the public sector with user groups. Three-year deals between the public services union and local municipalities to improve services without job cuts were agreed, which led to improved user satisfaction with services, greater involvement of the workforce in organizational change and no contracting out of work. The success of these local schemes led to the demands for national uptake of the scheme, which was achieved with the election in 2005 of a coalition government, for the first time involving a coalition between the Labour Party, the Socialist Left and the Centre Party, which is a rural party representing small farmers' interests (ibid.). The government introduced the Quality Municipality Project in 2006, which effectively halted the privatization of local government services and adopted the ethos of the local projects. Overall, the CWS has played an important role in shifting public opinion against privatization, although there remains a strong strand of neoliberal thinking within both the leadership of the Labour Party and the centre-right parties. The coalition government was re-elected in

2009 on a reduced majority, and there continues to be a battle between business interests and the wider community over the country's future direction.

Conclusions

The Norwegian experience demonstrates the importance of a state-owned model (SOE) of public ownership in the development of a country's energy resources. Given the complexities of the oil industry, the creation of Statoil was critical to securing the 'commanding heights' of the sector in order to construct local expertise and knowledge that could challenge the entrenched power of the multinationals. State intervention both through Statoil and broader economic and regional policies was also crucial in distributing the benefits of oil development to wider society, effectively managing resources on behalf of a wider collective set of interests rather than allowing their appropriation by foreign or domestic elites (Cumbers 2000, 2012).

The Norwegian case also illustrates the importance of developing democratic and participatory governance structures around state-owned corporations. In the 1970s a number of institutional checks and balances were put in place that were able to regulate the activities of Statoil and subject it to wider public debate. The establishment of a separate Petroleum Directorate to develop its own expertise in oil matters, elected worker representatives on Statoil's main governing boards, the growth of strong trade unions and effective parliamentary scrutiny resulted in a situation where the company had operational independence in day-to-day matters but was firmly embedded in wider democratic structures. For a while this worked to 'decentre' economic power, knowledge construction and decision-making in Norway's emerging oil complex to ensure that social and environmental considerations were given equal weighting to economic growth.

However, the Norwegian example also demonstrates the ease with which power asymmetries can develop in publicly owned corporations if they are not held in check by countervailing forces. By the early 1990s an oil-industrial complex had emerged both within and outside Statoil that was successful in decisively shifting the policy discourse in the 1990s to a more narrowly focused competitiveness agenda. In turn Statoil was able to develop its own rationale as a budding multinational oil entity to the extent that its priorities are now geared to capital accumulation and delivering shareholder value rather than a commitment to a more broadly defined set of 'national' interests.

The chapter also demonstrates the limits to a social democratic model of public ownership that fails to take economic democracy seriously. In the 1990s, in common with social democrats elsewhere, the Norwegian Labour Party and most of the trade union movement bought into the discourse of national competitiveness and the argument that, in the context of globalization, an efficient oil industry was key to national economic success and the continuation of the country's generous welfare state. The problem with this analysis was that, while ownership of the country's oil and gas resources remained in public hands, strategic decision-making was appropriated by an elite set of corporate interests. As a result, all other considerations were marginalized in the interests of commercial freedom and an agenda focused on accelerating oil and gas extraction from the North Sea. Perhaps the final bitter irony of all this was that it was under the premiership of Gro Harlem Brundtland that Norway turned its back on its environmental responsibilities for a pro-growth strategy. While preaching environmental restraint overseas, Brundtland's government lifted the shackles on oil production at home.

Despite all these problems, on another level the Norwegian case also shows how an 'active and agonistic democracy' (Mouffe 2005), with strong traditions of parliamentary debate, alongside a dispersed and decentralized politics, can produce an oppositional consciousness and a set of alternative policies to confront powerful interest groups, both externally and internally. Oil developments in the 1970s were subject to and shaped by such powerful democratic impulses concerned both with the distribution of the benefits from oil but also with the control and ownership of resources. Although the oil-industrial complex has managed to capture the economic agenda in recent years, the continued opposition to elite projects such as EU entry and the recent impressive grassroots campaign to safeguard the welfare state suggest the possibilities of articulating an alternative and more sustainable vision for Norway's energy resources.

9 | Decentred public ownership and the Danish wind power revolution

Introduction

In the field of energy policy Denmark has been held up as a model for other countries to follow in forging a progressive and far-sighted approach to tackling climate change. The country went from a complete dependence on imported oil in the 1970s to being self-sufficient in energy by the year 2000. Although, like the UK and Norway, Denmark benefited from the discovery of its own oil and gas reserves in the North Sea, the remarkable success story was the growth of its renewable energy sector over this period from virtually nothing to almost 20 per cent of total energy consumption (DEA 2010). As the International Energy Agency, an offshoot of the Paris-based influential international think tank the Organisation for Economic Co-operation and Development (OECD), put it approvingly in a recent report:

> Denmark's emergence as a leader in the renewable energy sector represents a remarkable transformation. Despite lacking almost entirely in hydroelectric resources and without the strong biomass tradition of its Scandinavian neighbours, the government has used policies to build up one of the biggest renewable energy sectors in the world. (IEA 2006: 9)

The cornerstone of this renewable success was the emergence of a wind power industry which has not only been at the forefront of Denmark's strategy to increase self-reliance and reduce CO_2 emissions but has also created 20,000 jobs and given the country's firms 50 per cent of the world market for wind turbine manufacture (DEA 2010). Moreover, as the IEA report noted: 'Renewable energy shares have consistently outpaced the targets established by the government' (IEA 2006: 97).

Although it has received international plaudits for its pioneering role in renewable energy generation, there has been rather less recognition of the organizational, institutional and ownership structures behind this shift, largely because they fly in the face of neoliberal orthodoxy and the attachment to market-based solutions and private ownership. Denmark's wind power revolution is neither a story of market-led growth, nor of top-down, state-driven planned development, but instead reflects a grassroots, community-based initiative, underpinned by decentralized, cooperative and municipal ownership alongside small-scale private ownership. However, the state has not been absent in the sense that this has been a spontaneous set of autonomous grassroots developments. Instead it has played an enabling role in establishing targets and the construction of particular institutional arrangements, through rules around ownership and the setting of prices outside pure market forms, commensurate with the kinds of arguments made in earlier chapters.

This 'model' of decentralized public ownership also needs to be rooted within the particular social and institutional frameworks that have emerged through the historical evolution of the Danish economy, which has been referred to variously as a negotiated or associational economy (Amin and Thomas 1996; Pedersen 2006). Compared to many of its European neighbours, Denmark has a tradition of associational governance between a small-firm-dominated economy, a system of strong collective decision-making through business associations, and a well-organized trade union movement (with 80 per cent membership) (Amin and Thomas 1996). There have also been high levels of cooperative and mutualist forms of ownership across all economic sectors. This more associational approach to economic decision-making (Hirst 1997) holds important lessons for the arguments being made here. As with Norway and other Nordic countries, there is a tendency by some commentators to stress the consensual and collaborative nature of the Danish experience, but I would stress here the deliberative and contested terrain of the debate around energy policy from which a victory was secured to support renewable energy.

From oil dependence to renewables role model

As it did with many advanced industrial economies, the decade of the 1970s exposed Denmark's increased vulnerability to imported oil as a by-product of the emergence of an affluent carbon-based and consumer society in the post-1945 era. Among the OECD countries Denmark had become one of the most dependent on foreign oil, accounting for around 90 per cent of the country's energy demand by 1973 (DEA 2010). Rising oil prices, resulting from the geopolitical crises in the Middle East during 1973/74 and 1979/80, prompted a rethink of Danish energy policy. While the country lacked the vast oil and gas resources of the UK and Norway, there were still important discoveries in the Danish North Sea that enabled it to reduce its dependence on imports during the 1980s. However, it still faced significant problems and some hard choices in achieving long-term security of energy supply.

In this context, and in common with many other European countries, there was an intense political struggle over the direction of energy policy during the late 1970s. Much of the country's political and business establishment, including the electricity distribution companies, the right-wing parties and right-wing social democrats, had been promoting nuclear power as the solution to growing oil dependence. The oil price rises of the 1970s brought the nuclear option to the centre of the national agenda, and in 1976 the first National Energy Plan advocated construction of five plants that would have accounted for 23 per cent of total primary demand (Hadjilambrinos 2000), but it was met by growing resistance from a vibrant 'movement from below' (Kruse and Maegard 2008: 134), coalescing around an alternative vision of a more localized and decentred non-nuclear future based on renewables.

The opposition represented a diverse coalition from radical leftists and greens to more conservative interests from rural areas that were suspicious of the growing centralization of the welfare state (Andersen and Drejer 2008; Jensen 2003).[1] What united them was a distrust of centralization and the fusing of green and radical demands for decentralization and radical democratic practices with a long-standing localist tradition in Danish society. An important factor that probably helped to tip the balance away from nuclear was the continuing tradition of interest in wind power as an alternative, and the existence of engineering and scientific communities that were able to showcase the viability of non-nuclear technologies in a populist way. In a Foucauldian sense, we can recognize the emergence of an alternative epistemic community that was successfully able to challenge the dominant international energy narratives of the time around oil and nuclear energy, and was part of a broader transnational environmental movement focused around the limits to economic growth while advocating smaller-scale forms of economic organization (Meadows et al. 1972; Schumacher 1973).[2] Effective use of the media to promote wind power experiments such as the Tvind school's giant windmill (Kruse and Maegard 2008) (see below) helped to articulate an alternative discourse around 'clean' and pure energy forms while also appealing to older rural practices of generating power. Additionally, wider international events such as the nuclear accident at Three Mile Island in Pennsylvania in 1978 further damaged the pro-nuclear lobby in the eyes of the public.

By 1979 there had been a decisive shift in Danish society against the nuclear option – in contrast to the experience elsewhere in western Europe – and the social democratic government introduced an 'Energy Package' followed by new energy legislation in 1981 which aimed at diversifying away from imported energy. There then followed almost two decades of concerted policy which, with the help of North Sea oil and gas, delivered self-sufficiency in energy by 1997 (DEA 2010). An important element of this strategy was a focus on developing the renewables sector to such an extent that, by 2009, renewable energy (primarily wind but also some combined heat and power generation and biomass) accounted for 28 per cent of all electricity generation (ibid.). Alongside these achievements, there have also been impressive developments in energy efficiency through new strategies to promote home insulation and investment in more efficient electricity supply techniques, such as 'district heating' from combined heat and power plants, which now supply over 60 per cent of Danish homes (ibid.). While economic growth has increased by 78 per cent over the period 1980–2009, energy consumption has remained unchanged (ibid.). Although the country continues to be reliant on coal and gas-fired power stations for much of its electricity, it has rightly been acclaimed as a pioneer in shifting towards renewable forms of energy through its wind power revolution.

Decentred public ownership and institutional supports in the emergence of the Danish wind energy sector

Although the first modern commercial turbine was built in 1977 (Moller 2010), Denmark did have an earlier history of experimenting with windmills for electricity generation. Its relatively flat landscape and exposure to the harsh winds of the North Sea and Baltic coasts give the country an ideal location for wind generation and, as such, there has been a long-standing interest in the possibilities of the technology. A high-school teacher, Poul la Cour, undertook a series of experiments using wind power for electricity purposes as early as 1891, while there was considerable small-scale electricity production from wind power in the 1920s and 1930s.[3] However, the availability of cheap imported oil and gas after the Second World War led to a decline in interest.

Nevertheless, some public support for alternative energy options remained. In the late 1950s, Johannes Juhl, a retired engineer and one of La Cour's pupils, designed the world's first alternating-current wind turbine at Gedser in southern Denmark. Although it had fallen into disrepair by the 1970s, NASA requested its recommissioning in 1975 to obtain some measurements of its effectiveness for the nascent US wind energy programme. Another important centre was established at Tvind in the district of Ulfborg in western Denmark, where what has been described as 'a left-wing school community' (Andersen and Drejer 2008: 25) set out to build the world's largest wind turbine, 'Tvindkraft', in 1975. This was also the year when the Danish Organization for Renewable Energy (OVE) was created, destined to become an important lobbying and educational association for the promotion of the technology both nationally and at the international scale. Overall, the early development of the technology was largely in the hands of what have been termed 'enthusiastic amateurs' (ibid.), although this is to underplay the specialist technical and engineering knowledge of many of the individuals involved and the formation of a coherent and determined community of interest around renewable technologies.

As the potential of the technology became apparent, state support grew, and by the early 1980s there was a concerted national strategy to encourage wind power, of which three elements were decisive. First, government funding for 30 per cent of all investment in new wind turbines over the period to 1990, before being reduced to 10 per cent and then being scrapped in 2000. This gave an important lead to Danish producers and is an excellent example of an 'infant industry' strategy in a fledgling sector. The second element, through what has been referred to as the 'Energy Package' or '*Energipakken*', was the legal requirement that electricity distribution companies purchase a certain quota of energy supply every year from renewable producers as part of nationally set targets to increase their share of electricity generation (Meyer and Koefoed 2003). This was strengthened in 1993 through an amendment to the Renewable Energy Act to set up a 'feed-in' fixed-price tariff for 'green energies' of 84 per cent of the utility's production and distribution costs. This produced stability for investment in the sector and allowed its continued growth and development. It also encouraged a more positive attitude from the Danish electricity distribution companies, which began to invest in their own larger-scale wind turbine developments. The growth in the market for domestic wind power, allied to a growing demand internationally (ibid.),[4] has subsequently resulted in the expansion of a wind turbine manufacturing industry which is now a world leader with 20,000 employees, capturing 50 per cent of the world market and accounting for 10 per cent of total Danish exports (DEA 2010).

The third pillar of the Danish wind power success story has been the encouragement of local and collective ownership of turbines. This has occurred largely through a series of laws that limit ownership of wind turbines to those residing in the municipality where the turbine is built, known as 'residency criteria' or distance regulation laws. Since the mid-1980s, the 'consumption criteria' laws have also constrained the shareholding of individuals based on consumption levels (Trannæs 2001). Although both sets of laws have been relaxed over time so that by the early 2000s it was possible to buy up land for larger-scale wind developments, they have meant that wind turbine ownership remains dominated by either small-scale forms of private ownership (typically partnerships between local neighbours) or cooperative forms. The first Danish onshore 'wind farms', in the sense of larger-scale activities that supplied more than a local neighbourhood, were cooperatively owned. At the movement's height in the late 1990s, it was estimated that around 150,000 families were involved, and cooperatives or families still accounted for around 80 per cent of wind farm ownership.[5] This 'movement' has been described as reviving 'the cooperative ownership model used in Denmark around 1900, when local dairies and Poul la Cour's "rural power stations" were established. Cooperative members all over the country were the grass roots activists with DV's support, working hard to get permission to have their turbines erected.'[6]

Assuming a conservative definition of the Western nuclear family here of 2.2 children (4.2 family members), the total number of people participating in wind farm ownership would have been at least 630,000 or around 12 per cent of the population. Alongside mass participation, another important development was the setting up of the Danish Wind Turbine Owners Association – a democratically elected membership association representing this new constituency and providing an important counterweight to state, corporate and municipal energy organizations in the policy-making process. The association has around five thousand members, and represents both private and cooperative turbine owners, providing a strong voice in energy policy for local communities and actors and an independent source of knowledge, learning and experience to inform policy deliberation processes.

In contrast to experiences elsewhere, there has been little public opposition (to date) to the location of wind farms, with the participation of communities in the ownership and development of the technology being a critical factor in their success. Surveys suggest that around 70 per cent of the population are in favour of wind farms, with only around 5 per cent against (Soerensen et al. 2003). As Moller has put it:

> Wind energy in Denmark generally enjoys a high public acceptance. One of the cornerstones for maintaining public acceptance on a

national scale as well as in local areas with dense wind turbine development was ownership. Public regulation granted a proportion of the wind capacity to be erected by publicly owned utilities and more importantly, legislation stimulated the formation of local wind energy cooperatives with limited ownership of shares in wind turbine projects within residents' municipalities. (2010: 234)

Together, the 'distance regulation' laws, state support for renewables, and the localist and collectivist traditions of Danish society have been important in both dispersing economic power and creating the conditions for greater public participation, deliberation and economic democracy in the energy sector. At this point it is also worth emphasizing the decentralized and cooperative nature of the electricity distribution system, in contrast with the more centralized and technocratic networks that were put in place in European countries such as France and the UK after 1945. The electricity utility industry in Denmark emerged at the local level in the first decades of the twentieth century and was operated by cooperative and municipal enterprises on a not-for-profit basis to provide for local needs rather than by private or state-run firms (Hadjilambrinos 2000). Although economies of scale were realized in power generation by the coming together of cooperatives to form associations and build plants – coal in the early twentieth century followed by oil after 1945 – the national state was not directly involved in such developments (ibid.).

Today the system is still heavily decentralized with around one hundred local distribution companies (primarily cooperative and municipally owned) and ten regional transmission networks (which are amalgamations of the 100 local cooperatives) (DEA 2007). This means that local cooperative and mutual forms of ownership dominate the electricity distribution system (Table 9.1). The oil and coal-fired power stations are owned by the Danish state oil company DONG (Dansk Olie og Naturgas A/S) and Vattenfall, a subsidiary of the Swedish state-owned corporation. Gas distribution is also in the hands of either state-owned or municipal companies. Although there has been a growing amalgamation of decision-making in the electricity sector through the setting up of regional associations – ELKRAFT for the main island Zealand (which includes the capital Copenhagen) and ELSAM (for Jutland and the island of Funen) (Hadjilambrinos 2000: 1119) – and these bodies wield considerable power in national energy policy debates, it is important to emphasize the continuing democratic constitution of these organizations with the two associations' main boards subject to elections. Boards of municipal authorities (which tend to be the main urban centres) are appointed by the municipal government, whereas the cooperatives (which tend to be rural) are democratically elected by meetings of consumers. The regional companies are in turn elected by the representatives of the local boards. While it has to be recognized that this doesn't militate against the capture of organizations or policy-making by elite or special interests, it does necessarily add important public participation to economic decision-making.

TABLE 9.1 Structure of the electricity power generation and distribution network in Denmark

	% share	Nature of ownership
Power generation		
Central generation plants	61	State: DONG, Swedish state subsidiary
Wind turbines	19	Co-ops, state, municipal and private
CHP/industrial/auto-producers	20	Mix of private and public
Electricity distribution		
Joint stock companies	26	State-owned under DONG Energy
Co-operative companies	55	Co-ops owned by consumers
Municipal companies	12	Co-ops or joint-stock state-owned
Other	7	

Source: Derived from DEA (2007: 17)

As we have already seen, there are inevitable conflicts between social groups, most notably in the 1970s between a 'consumer' interest committed to mass production of energy, low prices and nuclear power, which aligned itself with corporate interests around the centralization of energy generation, and an alternative vision around renewable energies, subsidizing innovative new technologies and smaller-scale development. However, the decentred nature of this political economy permitted experimentation and pluralism in the politics of energy supply to the extent that the local distribution companies held differing views on wind power, with rural cooperatives often more supportive of the nascent technology than the more municipally based utilities (Heymann 1999).

Relatedly, the depth of cooperative relations and associational culture in Danish civil society has also been important to the extent that most citizens will be involved in a range of different associations, thereby constructing complex and overlapping relations of identity formation. In these conditions, there is less of a danger that vested interests or 'principal agents' can fully capture economic agendas because economic communities and groups remain less bounded or framed by a 'silo mentality' and are more open and fluid in their constitution. Clearly there are strong echoes here of Neurath and O'Neill's emphasis on pluralism in associational governance as an alternative to market forms for promoting tolerance and democratic procedures. The thick civic and participatory culture within which Danish energy politics is embedded works against what Neurath refers to as the 'tendency for one, and one loyalty to "devour" all the others, and various loyalties are now permitted to grow side by side' (Neurath 1945: 429). It also means that a diverse range of perspectives are represented in policy formation. Although wind power producers and cooperatives have been very scornful of the position taken by the electricity utilities in the 1980s in their opposition to the new technology, the cooperative and essentially democratic nature of utility ownership cannot be reduced just to the perspective of powerful vested corporate interests (e.g. Tranaes n.d.). Concerns about the cost of supporting new technologies through subsidies also represent legitimate consumer interests about rising prices, particularly for poorer urban communities that to date have not shared in the ownership of wind cooperatives, which have largely been the preserve of rural communities. The strength of the Danish decentred model of public ownership means that different interests are represented, though of course this may not always lead to the policy outcomes favoured by left and progressive opinion.

Emergent tensions, scalar politics and the broader geographies of renewable energy discourse

The initial success of the Danish wind energy sector posed a number of critical public policy issues from the early 1990s onwards which became entangled within a broader spatial politics of climate change, fusing national political tensions with the broader European Single Market project. Within Denmark, a broad consensus emerged around expanding wind production to meet environmental goals, deliver benefits to producers and consumers, and further advance the long-term security of supply. However, the means of achieving this were contested and were laced with various forms of conflict between competing social groups and forces. At a general level, there remained a conflict between large utility distribution companies (particularly the urban municipally owned ones), much of the business lobby and centrist and right-wing politicians, who favoured larger-scale developments (private or state-owned) and reducing the cost of electricity to consumers; and the locally owned wind cooperatives, rural interests, turbine producers, and green and left groups, who remained committed to more decentralized forms of organization and continued widespread participation.

These tensions were played out in the planning process around renewables and wind power development, particularly between the spontaneous local development of small-scale turbines and the need for more effective higher-level planning at national and regional scales. By the mid-1990s, the limits of the 'localized' model were becoming apparent (Moller 2010). The original spread of wind development was often chaotic and poorly organized, often in environmentally sensitive areas (ibid.) with little overall coordination or regulation. At the same time, many older turbines were (by 2000) reaching the end of their productive lives and needed replacing. Improvements in turbine technology and the growth of much larger turbines – from on average 30 metres in height in 1980 to around 150 metres by 2000 (ibid.) – enabled the construction of more powerful and efficient machines, while the more ambitious national policy goals being articulated in the 1990s required larger-scale projects. Set against this however, as we have seen, local ownership and smaller-scale development had been important in the public acceptance of wind power, while the greater visibility and scale of turbine development being proposed raised growing fears about environmental impact. The political fallout from this was a new wave of legislation from the early 1990s onwards requiring environmental impact assessments and also greater planning restrictions alongside the creation of national and regional planning zones to regulate projects. Subsequently, there has been a steep decline in new onshore projects and greater public resistance as the size of mooted developments has increased while the extent of public participation and ownership has lessened. As a result, there has been a greater emphasis upon offshore or larger, more concentrated onshore projects in less environmentally sensitive areas (ibid.).

Danish politics in the 1990s was also shaped by the broader European context and in particular by the spread of neoliberal ideas around Single Market integration, leading to dominant narratives regarding markets and competition becoming increasingly important in national economic decision-making. In contrast to other Scandinavian countries, Denmark had a strong tradition of liberalism and decentralization, even undergoing its own period of economic deregulation and proto-neoliberalism under a new right government in the 1970s.[7] Given that it is a small open economy on the periphery of Europe, Denmark's political elites have historically tended to support lower trade barriers and greater European integration as a way of expanding markets for the country's manufacturers. Consequently, from the early 1990s onwards, governments of the centre-left and centre-right have been prepared to embrace large elements of the European Single Market agenda, although not membership of the euro.[8]

Very much in the spirit of the times, an OECD report in 2000 had taken Denmark to task for its general unwillingness to embrace market-led reforms (OECD 2000). The OECD complained that public expenditure was too high at 55 per cent of GDP, while the 'threshold of the top income tax rate is too low' (ibid.: 12), with around one third of workers facing a marginal tax rate of 62 per cent. Regarding energy, the report noted rather pointedly that 'The ownership structure in the energy sector is dominated by municipalities and consumer owned co-operatives ...' (ibid.: 98). This led it to complain that 'experience suggests that consumers have had very limited influence in practice' (ibid.), although it provided no evidence to back up this claim. The best criticism that it could muster was that 'the dominance of municipalities tends to make warranted changes a political issue at the local level' without further clarifying its point. Indeed, it seems to be the exercise of local democratic control rather than private capital over resources which irked the OECD.

Regarding energy, the European Commission's agenda in the 1990s and 2000s to liberalize electricity markets, break up and 'unbundle' what were seen as inefficient and anti-competitive state monopolies had a strong influence on Danish national government policy, particularly under the new Conservative–Liberal coalition after 2001. Even before this, however, a new Energy Act in 1999 effectively implemented EU rules and abolished the feed-in tariff (FIT), replacing it with the EU Commission's preferred alternative of tradable green certificates (TGCs), which are based on electricity companies having to source a certain quota of total production from renewables.

While at first glance the battle between the FIT system and the TGCs may seem an arcane affair for energy sector anoraks, a more in-depth appraisal reveals it to mark a critical fault-line for both Danish and European Union policy in the battle between neoliberal market-driven reforms and a more planned approach to renewables and the broader politics of climate change. Critically, the support for the TGC system in Denmark came from the Confederation of Danish Industry (DI), the main electricity utilities (with their desire to escape the cost implications of the FIT) and the increasingly powerful wind energy manufacturers, who, as the global market leaders, clearly had an interest in a liberalized European energy market with a dedicated quota for renewables (Lauber and Schenner 2011). However, the Act worked against the interests of turbine owners and those interested in investing in new technologies and products. Like many other 'open and fair market' solutions, it favoured established companies, those that are able to take advantage of scale economies and 'tried and tested' technologies rather than more innovative solutions. As Meyer and Koefoed note: 'One of the problems of green certificate markets concerns the fairness of competition between renewable technologies at different stages of development. If an open market with free competition between different renewable technologies were created today, wind power would probably sweep most of the market' (2003: 601).

This would be to the detriment of alternative forms of renewables such as solar energy, biomass or combined heat and power that would need greater investment and research and development. Additionally, allowing markets to operate in an unrestricted fashion means that green energy prices can fluctuate considerably with the demand for electricity, thereby providing little assurance for those seeking to invest in new technologies. This represents a classic example not just of market failure but of the inappropriate use of markets for public policy solutions. Although minimum and maximum prices have been established – 0.10 Danish krone (DKK)/kWh (1.3 euro cents/kWh) and 0.27 DKK/kWh (3.6 euro cents/kWh) for 'green certificates' (ibid.) – this will still not prevent fluctuations and uncertainty for investors. Various solutions can be suggested that tinker with the system under the trade liberalization and competition framework, but none will overcome the underlying problem outlined in Chapter 7 that such idealized market-based solutions are inappropriate for areas of public policy that require longer-term strategic planning (Nove 1983).

In Denmark, the evidence to date seems to bear out this prognosis. As Figure 9.1 shows, following a strong growth in the installation of wind capacity up until 2003, particularly in the 1990s, the phasing out of the FIT after this period saw a dramatic drop in wind turbine construction. Moreover, the integration of the Danish electricity sector into the common Nordic market, NORDPOOL, has meant the replacement of price regulation with an unregulated spot market that creates further uncertainty and lower returns for smaller and more innovative

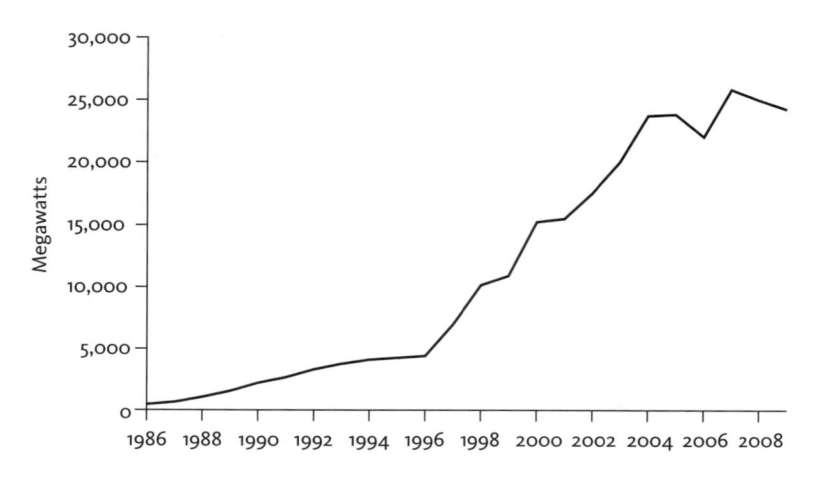

9.1 Wind power electricity generation (MW) in Denmark, 1986–2008
(*source*: Danish Energy Agency, www.ens.dk, accessed 15 November 2011)

investors. There has as a result been almost no increase in the supply of Danish wind power to the national electricity grid in the past decade (Ryland 2010). Ten years of rule by a centre-right coalition with an anti-environmentalist premier, Anders Fogh Rasmussen, who was also a big supporter of the warmongering foreign policies of George Bush and Tony Blair,[9] have also clearly taken their toll. Rasmussen's government not only cancelled three new offshore projects on coming to office in 2001 but also cut government support for the previously successful policy of domestic energy conservation (ibid.). Although the growing threat of increased foreign energy dependence (from Russian gas supplies) and Denmark's reputation abroad as a sustainable development champion caused the government to change tack in 2006, the cause of renewable energy has largely stalled as a result.

Beyond Danish national politics, there has been a dramatic battle between different interests over the direction of European Union policy towards renewables in recent years (Lauber and Schenner 2011). Backing for the TGCs came from the European Commission with its increasingly neoliberal worldview, shaped by key trade and competition comissioners such as the Thatcherite former UK minister Leon Brittan. From this perspective, the FIT was viewed as a 'market distortion' (ibid.: 514). During the 1990s such neoliberals within European institutions – with the fair wind of free market triumphalism following the collapse of the Soviet Union at their backs – were successful in branding any attempt at government regulation of industry as instances of 'command and control' in contrast to the preferred 'market-based' instruments (ibid.: 515). This discursive victory in tarring interventionist government action with the brush of a discredited Stalinist politics, while at the same time promoting an abstract, utopian vision of the market as delivering freedom of action, and the universal benefits of competition, was clearly not insignificant. Such arguments, as we have seen, were all too readily accepted the world over with devastating consequences. However, in the case of EU energy policy, there has been a more interesting set of outcomes.

An Anglo-Saxon-driven 'pure market' discourse was challenged by the more regulatory and interventionist stance of the German Social Democrat-led government, which, while neoliberal in much of its labour market and welfare policy, pursued a more strategic approach to the development of national capacity with regard to renewable energy. After a European Court case in 2001, which successfully challenged the Commission's TGC model on the grounds that existing German policy to introduce a FIT scheme did not contravene EU competition law, other countries have also pursued FIT schemes over TGCs, and the Commission has been forced to allow national subsidiarity to hold sway over attempts at harmonization. Among the larger countries in Europe, France and Spain have both introduced FIT schemes to bolster renewables. As one group of energy experts has noted, the Danish decision was 'based on wrong assumptions' (Meyer and Koefoed 2003: 600). Subsequently, both the European Parliament and the Council of Ministers have rejected the attempt to impose the TGC scheme on the basis that it infringes principles of national subsidiary and flexibility (Lauber and Schenner 2011).

What is also interesting for us here is that, like Denmark's, the growth of the German renewable sector has similarly been achieved through localized and 'distributed' forms of ownership rather than large private or state-owned corporations. The politics of energy have been similar, with green and local interests (particularly farmers and small businesses but also private households) favouring renewables in the form of wind and solar power often confronting established large energy utilities with a stake in the status quo of nuclear and conventional forms of power generation (Heymann 1999; Toke 2011). Victory for the renewables lobby came in 1991 when, after a decade of lobbying and environmental activism – including green and farming groups illegally connecting turbines to the electricity grid – the German parliament, the Bundestag, set up a FIT scheme for wind and small hydro schemes with a guaranteed twenty-year payment scheme (Toke 2011). Despite continuing pressure from both the big four German utility companies (RWE, EoN, EnBW and Vattenfall, the subsidiary of the Swedish state-owned company) and the European Commission, this scheme was extended to solar and biomass producers in the 2000s. While cooperative forms have played a smaller role than in Denmark, the dominance of ownership by small-scale private interests has been critical in spreading the benefits from renewable generation and inculcating a more participatory and deliberative process of energy management. As Toke (ibid.) notes, wind power in both Germany and Denmark has emerged as a 'grassroots technology' predicated on cooperative learning and knowledge exchange at the local level.

Alternative futures, deliberative decision-making and the cooperative ethos

In October 2011 a new centre-left government was elected in Denmark with the intention of kick-starting the country's leadership in renewable energy promotion and growth. One of its first acts was to commit the country to raising its share of renewables in energy consumption to 50 per cent of domestic electricity consumption by 2020. Whether this policy will continue to be underpinned by the dominant neoliberal market-centred perspective or instead by a rediscovery of the merits of national planning and institutional supports, around the previously successful model of decentred and diversified forms of public ownership, remains to be seen. Interestingly, the major offshore wind projects that have been developed in the past decade have been largely pursued either by the municipal and publicly owned utility companies or by partnerships between the latter and forms of cooperative. These might well prove to be an important new form of public ownership, combining civic participation with control and strategic direction from the state – at the local scale.

Perhaps the best example is the massive Mittlegrunden Wind Farm, which was constructed off the coast of Copenhagen and provides 40 megawatts of electricity, equivalent to 3 per cent of the capital's electricity needs. The farm was opened in 2001 after an eight-year planning and consultation process. Acceptance of the project by the local population was facilitated by the ownership structure, which was divided fifty/fifty between the local utility company, Copenhagen Energy (itself owned by the city council), and a bespoke cooperative, created with the aid of the city council's energy department and the support of local residents' groups, in which individuals were able to buy shares, with over ten thousand residents taking up the option (Soerensen et al. 2003). Significantly, around the same time, two other proposals were submitted for new offshore wind parks; one at Grenaa, a private proposal, was the subject of considerable local resistance that stalled the planning process, and a second at Samsoe, which has been successful in also developing the public–public partnership model of cooperative–local utility ownership (ibid.). Such examples suggest that the associational and collective ethos of Danish society runs deep and provides a cautionary tale for those of a neoliberal disposition.

As part of this associational culture, the long-standing commitment to collective learning and cooperative action over private profiteering and appropriation of national resources has also been important. A remarkable feature of the growth of the wind turbine industry was the absence of patenting of prototypes; indeed, no patents were developed in the industry until the mid-1990s, which in part was due to an 1885 law that banned rural technology patents (Toke 2011). While neoliberal encroachment has threatened some of these institutional features of the Danish system, the evidence suggests that there remain deeply entrenched historical commitments to local participation, the decentralization of economic power and meaningful deliberative decision-making.

A continuing culture of mutualization and localism is expressed in the willingness to challenge the appropriation of the economic development process by elite interests, as the continuing resistance to the private and corporate development of offshore wind power suggests. Even the earlier opposition among cooperative utility groups to the fledgling wind power industry can be seen in this light: the protection of lower-income consumer groups from rising electricity prices is a legitimate cause of popular concern and probably was reflected in the support given to centre-right groups in the late 1990s and 2000s. Issues of appropriative justice are also dynamic ones, in the sense that changing economic conditions can unsettle the balance between social groups in their appropriative relations. Wind power and renewable energy more generally provide a good example here. In its infancy, wind generation costs were far greater than those of established sources of power, hence public support for wider social and environmental interests was justifiable, but over time, as the technology and productivity improve, the danger that wind power groups can effectively earn high profits at the expense of consumer groups must be considered in any policy analysis of state support. One way of dealing with this is through the adjustment in feed-in tariffs over time, which the German government seems to have done effectively in gradually reducing the subsidy for solar energy.[10]

Overall, the Danish experience demonstrates the importance of a more equitable approach to resource development that also builds popular participation in combating climate change. It also deals with appropriative justice by spreading ownership and decision-making rights beyond a small group of interests to the community as a whole but in complex ways that allow diverse perspectives and positions to be articulated, represented and deliberated in the formation of economic policy.

Conclusions

Despite recent setbacks, several themes inherent in the Danish case are relevant for our broader argument here. While there is much in the Danish case that is historically and context-specific to its particular associative economy traditions (Amin and Thomas 1996), there are nevertheless important broader lessons, particularly in the way that supportive institutions at higher spatial scales (i.e. national) can promote and foster more localized and participatory forms of public ownership. Critically, institutional and regulatory mechanisms – such as the 'distance regulation' law and state support for renewables through taxation, investment subsidies and the use of price controls and support for nascent technologies – have been important in both dispersing economic power and creating the conditions for greater public participation, deliberation and economic democracy in the sector. Furthermore, a commitment to local participation in the ownership of wind turbines, and the restrictions upon private or special interests' abilities to profit from collectively owned resources, has been critical in mediating the kinds of conflict over such developments in environmentally sensitive areas elsewhere and offers important lessons in the battle to take decisive action against the threat of dramatic climate change.

Denmark also illuminates the growing conflict in the battle of ideas over economic development between an elite discourse that seeks to manage change from above in a way that is to the benefit of established interests, and which, in its latest neoliberal form, attempts to construct markets, maintain a sacrosanct commitment to private property rights and an idealized notion of competition (which at the same time masks the continued pursuit of powerful corporate vested interests), against an alternative vision of a deliberative and democratic policy formation. However, the argument here is that we need to go beyond a recent tendency in much critical left thinking (e.g. Hardt and Negri 2009; Holloway 2010) that tends to juxtapose a 'top-down' and undemocratic model of economic decision-making, whether of a statist or neoliberal kind, against a more virtuous bottom-up process of participatory economic democracy. Certainly the Danish case demonstrates the possibilities for a more decentred form of public ownership that contains important community-based and localized elements. It also shows the need to draw upon non-state forms of collective organization, particularly more traditional cooperative and mutualist forms that can play an important role in engaging a broader public in economic decision-making. But Denmark also highlights the importance of higher-level state coordination and planning mechanisms in achieving progressive policy goals in tackling climate change. Moreover, the limits to localism also suggest the continued need for state forms of ownership – such as the state energy company DONG, which has played a leading role in the extraction of the country's oil and gas resources and may be well placed to coordinate a more ambitious national programme of renewables development in the years ahead.

Conclusion

The twentieth century was marked by two competing dogmas: a centralized and planned vision of socialism and a free market unregulated capitalism. Both are unrealizable utopias (Hodgson 1999) which, when put into practice, will over time produce socially and environmentally destructive dystopias. Both projects were exposed by the harsh and everyday realities of economic practice and actually existing conditions on the ground, leading to extreme concentrations of power and decision-making, whether in the apparatus of party machines or in the boardrooms of multinational corporations and on the floors of financial exchanges. Both sets of ideas stem from the best of eighteenth-century Enlightenment thinking, but neither can deliver on that movement's aspirations to place human development on a better common path.

Neither of these utopian visions pushed to their extremes is able to deliver on the progressive aspiration for a world that marries social justice with individual freedom, or economic efficiency with a proper participatory democracy. Finding a way out of the current impasse requires that we develop new thinking on the best paths to embark on in delivering the French Revolution's still relevant triumvirate of *liberté*, *égalité* and *fraternité* (or solidarity). As I have argued in this book, an important element of this will be new forms of public or common ownership. While many horrors were visited in his name during the twentieth century, Karl Marx's nineteenth-century analysis of the underlying exploitation and alienation in a system of unbridled and deregulated market exchange based upon the private appropriation of resources remains as pertinent today as when he wrote it. Following Aristotle, the pursuit of the good life as the common good requires that we develop collective solutions, not the narrow individual rationality of neoclassical economics.

However, those on the left also need to come to terms with the limits to Marxist thinking, its agoraphobia and its neglect of the relations between knowledge, pluralism and a genuine economic democracy. Geoff Hodgson's comments are apposite when he says:

we cannot condemn the original socialist project simply on the basis of the excesses of the totalitarian regimes of the twentieth century. But the Soviet and Chinese experiments do tell us a great deal about the general problems with the design, particularly concerning central planning, and the role of property and markets in sustaining politico-economic diversity. To understand that experience we do need to understand the limitations of the original socialist project. If socialism is to survive at all it must overcome its congenital agoraphobia – which contains, literally, 'fear of markets'. It has to learn to inhabit open systems and open spaces. (Ibid.: 61)

Public ownership, planning and markets all have a role to play in the development of alternative economic thinking if we are to begin to tackle the collective economic and environmental problems that face us in the twenty-first century. Hodgson's 'impurity principle' is also relevant here; the idea that every 'socio-economic system must rely on at least one structurally dissimilar subsystem to function' (ibid.: 126). Just as capitalism needs non-capitalist forms of social relations to survive, so in a more socialized system there will still be a need for 'impure' forms of organization, such as, for example, some kinds of markets and some forms of private ownership. Hodgson, Burczak and others advocated forms of market socialism as a means of addressing these issues; with Burczak's worker-owned forms of social ownership operating in more competitive markets being one of the most innovative recent solutions to Hayek's critique of central planning and state ownership. One does not have to embrace fully the market-centric leftism of Burczak to recognize that this is fertile terrain for socialists to engage with – going beyond the older debates of the twentieth century. However, recognition of the 'impurities' of actually existing economies provides a compelling argument for economic democracy and pluralism in the development of new forms of public ownership.

Beyond twentieth-century utopias to an open and deliberative politics of public ownership

Reflecting on the hegemony of the new right in the 1990s, the late Paul Hirst argued that democracy was socialism's best answer to market fundamentalism of the right and the accommodation of the centre-left and social democracy to neoliberalism (Hirst 1997). Henry Ford famously quipped that 'the customer can have a car painted any colour that he wants so long as it is black' (Ford and Crowther 1926).

In the contemporary global economy, dominant institutions such as the IMF and the European Union seem to be thinking along similar lines; 'you can have any economy you want as long as it is privately owned and controlled'. Additionally, there should be tight fiscal rules that make it impossible to depart from a neoliberal straitjacket. As I have argued in previous chapters, markets and private property are no more a guarantee of democracy and individual freedom than state monopolies and central planning; both lead to exploitation and alienation of the majority of the population while achieving increased concentration and centralization of economic power over time. Against the oxymoron of the free market, the sanctity of private property rights and the negative freedom of Hayek's selfish individual, I have argued in this book for a set of strategies that begin to reshape the economy as a democratic and collective endeavour. In this respect, the best defence of socialism and public ownership should be its adherence to variety, pluralism, positive freedoms and deliberative decision-making in opposition to the faux choice of the 'free market'. Socialists need in this sense to accept that 'democratic socialism' will involve the principle of variety, and even that some forms of private ownership are necessary alongside public ownership.

The principles for public ownership enunciated in Chapter 7 attempt to take this heterodox approach forward, moving beyond the failings of past forms of public ownership rooted in social democratic and conventional Marxist thinking. These shared the basic weakness of being over-centralized and monolithic state entities that were far removed from the ordinary citizen, or revealed a productivist bias in favour of a disappearing industrial proletariat. Not surprisingly, few mourned the passing of these earlier forms.

The approach pursued here remains heavily informed and guided by a Marxist concern with class justice, recognizing the way the work of the mass of the world's population is appropriated by and on behalf of a small elite through the current economic system. While the current work is in the spirit of Marx it is probably not in the manner that many of his adherents, past and present, would choose or agree with. It casts anti-capitalistic thinking as an open and deliberative project rather than a set of prescriptive 'tablets of stone' to be handed down by a revolutionary vanguard (Cumbers and McMaster 2010). It is also an approach that seeks to work with the grain of accumulated and varied local knowledge, experience and insight, rather than applying a universal model or prescription imposed by central diktat (Hodgson 1999; Burczak 2006).

Having highlighted the flaws in both free market and centralized state socialist utopias in delivering greater economic democracy and participation, I have argued here for the importance of institutional variety and a politics of tolerance over more prescriptive or top-down models of public ownership. This requires a commitment to egalitarian values and principles that can at the same time be sensitive to different contexts in time and space. There is no 'off the shelf' nationalization model of public ownership that can be applied everywhere to retake the economy from elite interests; rather there is a need to work with existing and diverse collective and mutualist traditions in civil society to push forward an alternative economic project. The account of the emergence of the Danish wind power sector in the previous chapter illustrates the potential for harnessing older traditions of mutualism, associationalism and collective practice with contemporary progressive concerns, such as combating climate change. It also demonstrates how a more participatory model of public ownership that is deeply embedded within existing structures of civil society can be effective in mobilizing support for state policies and targets at the national scale.

This is an important departure for the left in recognizing affinity with very different forms of 'anti-capitalism', but, as the alter-globalization movement has shown us, practices of neoliberal capitalist enclosure pose a threat to a variegated terrain of already existing collective forms of ownership and economic decision-making. Older and even more conservative forms of cooperation and collective learning can be both learnt from and drawn upon in constructing more democratic forms of economic practice. The respect for diverse and alternative traditions of common ownership alongside a politics grounded in current practice rather than an idealistic future utopia unites perspectives as different as the 'commons' discourse discussed in Chapter 6, Neurath's anti-essentialist socialism and the pragmatism of John Dewey and institutional economists such as Thorstein Veblen. All were suspicious of grand revolutionary narratives but all also shared a dislike of elite institutions and a belief in grounded dialogue and engagement; instrumental over ceremonial values (Veblen 1990) in forging progressive structures.

A commitment to decentred and dispersed economic decision-making

Going beyond over-centralized past forms, I have also argued for forms of public ownership that are underpinned by a decentred and dispersed set of institutional arrangements. The Norwegian experience with North Sea oil is particularly interesting here. In challenging the power and knowledge of multinational oil companies, a national state oil company, Statoil, was tasked with the role of securing control and ownership of the country's resources on behalf of the nation. Although, as Chapter 8 indicated, Statoil became an increasingly powerful set of interests capable of capturing the national political agenda, there were some important democratic and deliberative safeguards constructed to embed the company within a context where wider societal and environmental concerns have influenced policy-making. The role of alternative institutional centres for knowledge construction such as the Petroleum Directorate and the country's parliament in holding the company's management to account on a regular basis have been critical in fostering a more active and engaged civil society around the issue of oil development.

The Norwegian example also shows the limits to a social democratic form of public ownership, which fails to take seriously questions of control and democratic renewal in the apparatus of state-owned enterprises. The capture of the oil public policy agenda by the oil-industrial complex in the 1990s, and the abandonment of wider social policies such as the moderate production agenda, the commitment to community and local economic development in favour of a national competitiveness agenda, shows the pitfalls of allowing 'commercial interests' to override 'political interference'. As both the Danish and Norwegian examples illustrate, the politicization of energy discourse led to vibrant and wide-ranging public debates and participation, which were able to challenge elite development agendas and pose alternatives. Both were the scene in short of Gramscian counter-hegemonic strategies. Although it is too early to assess the potential for more radical and democratic economic structures to evolve in the Latin American pink tide discussed in Chapter 5, it is clear that there is a similar desire to politicize and debate economic policy here.

Although both the Norwegian and Danish examples owe much to a particular kind of political economy and tradition such that their transferability to other kinds of state and societies, notably many countries in the global South, may be problematic, certain aspects are generalizable. In particular, a contested terrain of state–civil society–economy relations is important so that social movements struggle both through and beyond the state in the forging of discourses around collective ownership and non-capitalist forms of social relations. The Latin Americans working for radical social change do share these characteristics, as do many movements working for reform of public services in places such as South Africa (McDonald and Ruiters 2012). Both the Danish example in particular (the Norwegian case less so) and the Latin American cases also share the fusion of a modernist agenda around public ownership with respect for and indeed engagement of older traditions of collectivism and the 'common good'. Respect for different traditions that can both work through and beyond the state is a critical general lesson to be drawn here.

If the Norwegian case illustrates the importance of challenging the centralization of power and knowledge in forms of state-owned enterprise, the Danish case hints at the potential for diverse forms of public ownership and a genuine pluralism of political associations. I have argued strongly here, echoing Neurath and O'Neill, not for one definitive form of public ownership, but that a range of collective forms can and should coexist. These will provide sources for different perspectives and positions that can create the kind of agonistic politics that Mouffe insists is critical to a more radical democracy. They would also encourage a range of different identities and loyalties within people; an interesting element of the saturation of different forms of public ownership in the Danish case – municipal consumer cooperatives, producer cooperatives and state-owned enterprises – is the extent to which individuals will belong to more than one form, which one might expect to have an important role in preventing the entrenchment of oppositional and vested interests in public policy discourse.

Like many of the more recent commons and autonomous writers, Neurath was wary of the centralizing tendencies of one form of public ownership – particularly linked to the central state apparatus – and was therefore a strong believer in a multiplicity of forms of socialism and collective ownership, as revealed by his plans for the Bavarian economy in the post-revolutionary situation in 1918. Neurath's writings generally are incredibly insightful and forward thinking in his advocacy of the kind of diverse solidarity-based economy that would chime with many in the anti-capitalist movement today (O'Neill 2003). He advocated a non-market but decentralized version of socialism founded upon overlapping associations of self-government where power was dispersed rather than held in a single authority, although there would remain the need for some central coordination (ibid.). A critical element in this schema was the need for 'economic tolerance that can support several non-capitalist forms of economy simultaneously' (Neurath 1920: 397, cited in O'Neill 2006: 71).

Continuing to struggle 'in and against' the state

Celebrating diversity, pluralism and decentred forms of public ownership should not, however, mean lionizing local, decentralized and autonomous spaces – uncontaminated by engagement with a 'corrupt' state – as the only terrain for developing an anti-capitalist politics of cooperation and solidarity. There is a yearning for a 'new localism' on both the left and right (Featherstone et al. 2012), and the 'state' as a space for political action seems to have few defenders in the current climate. The leftist strands of localism, particularly those converging around a trans-local commons, have claimed the democratic high ground for themselves by emphasizing the importance of a prefigurative politics of direct democracy and grassroots participation in response to the centralizing tendencies of Marxism-Leninism and social democracy.

While the underlying ethos of participation and democratization within the commons discourse outlined in Chapter 6 is appealing, there remains a 'fuzziness' in its approach to the more practical issues of how we construct economic institutions and structures that might seriously challenge existing capitalist social relations. There is also a tendency in some accounts to dismiss engagement and contestation of capitalist and state structures for perspectives that seek to work outside of capitalist social relations. This leads to a rejection of the state and traditional forms of public ownership as a suitable terrain for constructing alternatives. In contrast I have argued here for a continuing politics 'in and against the state' (London Edinburgh Weekend Return Group 1980) as a way to theorize the possibilities for developing forms of public ownership that combine the need for higher-level regulation with the commons promise of a more democratic and participatory politics.

Nineteenth- and twentieth-century social movements achieved many progressive gains through targeting the state as a sphere for political actions, particularly in the areas of welfare, labour and women's rights. While it is too early to make a definitive comment regarding the implications for a more radical democratic politics, we can similarly record that the evidence from Venezuela and Bolivia so far suggests that capturing the state for left agendas – through nationalization policies – has already delivered considerable progress, in terms of reclaiming control over the economy from foreign and domestic elites, and redistributing income from rich to poor. My analysis of Norway's experience with state ownership in the oil industry shows the possibilities for more democratic forms of governance to develop within national-level state-owned structures, if there is a commitment to encase them within a deliberative and decentred political institutional framework. Arguably, though, this needs a pre-existing and diverse civil society.

Clearly, though, and despite such caveats, the state remains too important a space of contemporary economy life for the left to be disengaged from it. Instead, as Hilary Wainwright has argued, there is a need for radical democracy to begin to contest and reclaim state spaces from those on the right who have constructed their own discourses around the perceived failings of the public realm (Wainwright 2003). The rescaling of state forms in recent years in response to processes of globalization provides opportunities here in the shape of devolution programmes that transfer power to sub-national scales, even though to date this has usually led to regressive competitiveness agendas at city and regional scales. Nevertheless, some of the most interesting and novel forms of public ownership and partnership are being constructed at the municipal state level, through the public–public partnership ideas reported in Chapter 5 that forge alternative and horizontal trans-local connections in opposition to the 'top-down' IMF- and World Bank-imposed models of privatization. Similarly, there are examples of considerable public sector innovation at the local scale, notably the municipal-cooperative model of ownership piloted in the Copenhagen Mittelgrunden offshore wind development. Such examples offer a way forward in beginning to construct alternative discourses around reclaiming public ownership and to an extent they can sidestep regressive neoliberal state processes at the national scale. However, they act as beacons for a broader counter-hegemonic project rather than an alternative beyond the state.

Remaking the case for public ownership

It is becoming increasingly apparent that the current economic system is not fit for purpose. If we accept the premise that the primary task for an economy is to allocate resources to safeguard human existence in a way that is sustainable in harmony with our planet, while at the same time ensuring that the benefits of economic activity are distributed as evenly as is possible, it is clear that the current system is failing. My aim in this book has been to argue that one of the most important reasons for this is that the economy is dominated by capitalist practices and in particular a form of capitalism known as neoliberalism. Neoliberalism is characterized by three elements: private ownership, unregulated markets and increasingly exploitative employment relations. Taken together, these are creating an increasingly imbalanced and uneven economy which is socially divisive, politically toxic and environmentally unsustainable.

However, we are also living through a period when more and more people are beginning to question 'the system'. Increased public awareness of the disparities between wealthy elites and the ordinary citizen, and the knowledge that these elites dominate decision-making in the global economy, are resulting in growing demand for change, as evident in the alternative globalization movements and more recently in growing street protests around the world at austerity policies and the entrenched power of financial interests (Mason 2012). Yet the left still seems to be long on critique and short on alternative proposals.

To begin to address this situation, I have argued that we need to revisit public ownership as a concept; collective decision-making and the idea of the 'common good' should return to the forefront of discussions about the economy. However, the other overriding theme in the book is that we need also to reclaim public ownership from both its detractors and those who continue to use it in an undemocratic manner for particular interests in appropriating our common wealth. A reconstituted concept of public ownership, framed around economic democracy and public participation in economic decision-making, is vital to this task.

At the core of my argument here is that our ideas about public ownership need to be radically rethought to be relevant to the changing global economy of the twenty-first century. This will – as our Danish case illustrates – involve a rethink of the relations between geographical scales, providing organizational structures that enhance local democracy but retaining the commitment to broader patterns of equity and distributive justice at the national and international scales. It means accepting the need for higher-level coordination in some areas of economic life if we are to develop effective solutions to some of the bigger questions facing humanity, such as finding a collective rather than a market-based answer to the devastation of rapid global warming. Hopefully, I have demonstrated that, against the received wisdom in governing circles, democratic public ownership is not only an increasingly urgent requirement but also a practical possibility in the years ahead.

Notes

Introduction

1 *Daily Telegraph*, 12 October 2008.

1 The post-1945 legacy

1 With the exception of steel, subsequent Conservative governments left Labour's nationalization programme intact until 1979, and even carried out a few nationalizations of their own as pragmatic solutions to specific industrial crises.

2 See Joan Robinson's devastating critique (Robinson 1969 [1933]) of the consequences of oligopoly and the subsequent need for public ownership of key industries.

3 By way of example, Saville quotes a letter from Labour minister (and future party leader) Hugh Gaitskell to his counterpart Herbert Morrison in 1949 in response to a trade union proposal: 'to the effect that TU representatives should be placed on the Boards with the right of members to recall such TU representatives as and when considered necessary is a more extreme example of syndicalist tendencies than anything yet put forward' (1993a: 59).

4 After the minister responsible for the nationalization programme, Herbert Morrison.

5 Attlee, with a private education at Haileybury school, before going on to university at Oxford (Thomas-Symonds 2010), being the most obvious.

6 Fishman describes Shinwell's House of Commons appearances of the time as being 'marked by an air of self-confident, almost complacent, triumphalism' (1993: 63).

7 See instead the vast literature that developed in the 1970s and 1980s around the problems of British economic decline, deindustrialization and the fundamental structural tensions between finance and productive capital (e.g. Williams et al. 1983; Fine and Harris 1985; Green 1989).

8 Figures varied slightly, for different nationalizations: Bank of England shareholders were given a total of around £58 million based on the 12 per cent dividend return over the previous twenty years, compared to the figure for the mines, which was based on fifteen years of average annual rent (Saville 1993a: 48).

9 As the British negotiator, only weeks before his death, Keynes was well aware of the consequences for the government's domestic plans (Saville 1993b). With his loss, there were few with the stature or ability to contest this foreign policy 'lock-in' which was to lead to continued military expenditure the country could ill afford and of course the sanctioning of the country's own atomic weapons capability (Mortimer 1993).

10 To provide an example, it was estimated that the mining industry alone required £200 million of catch-up investment (Saville 1993a: 48).

11 Although it is important

to record that public or common ownership at all geographical scales, from the municipal and city government, to individual states, to the federal state, have remained a fundamental but often embattled part of the US economy. The classic example of the survival of a public corporation against all odds is Amtrak, which was first created by Richard Nixon's administration in 1972. Even at its creation, the chips were firmly stacked against it, evident in the subsequent revelation that Nixon had planned to use nationalization to shut down the network after a couple of years (Loving Jr 2009). However, Amtrak has survived and even seen its passenger numbers increase over the longer term, from 16.6 million in 1972 to 28.7 million by 2008. Passenger numbers rose for six years in a row up until 2008, but there is still entrenched opposition to its growth as an alternative to the increasingly unsustainable US model of individualized automobile transport.

12 Perhaps the most extreme case was the Renault car company, which was taken into public ownership as a punishment for the owner, Louis Renault, who was accused of collaborating with the Germans. Renault's assets were confiscated and he died in prison before he was able to face charges, although it was later admitted that there was no firm evidence against him.

13 For example, Bull (computers), Thomson (electronics and telecommunications) (Hall 1987).

14 In 1947, the CDU announced in its Ahlen programme that the '"age of the unrestricted rule of capitalism" was over and conceded the need to "socialize the primary industries, iron and coal"' (Schneider 1991: 234). Two years earlier, in Cologne in June 1945, there had been calls for a 'true Christian Socialism' (ibid.: 239).

15 There is not the space to review all the different variations of state ownership in the communist countries after 1945 so the review here will focus on particularly prominent examples that exemplify the different forms of ownership followed. Cuba is an obvious omission, where everything was nationalized after 1968, including the smallest businesses and even street vendors selling hamburgers. There are now moves afoot for some liberalization under Raúl Castro, with plans to move one fifth of the workforce into the private sector ('Man in the news: Raul Castro', *Financial Times*, 17 September 2010). Tanzania is another obvious omission, with Nyrere's quest for a self-reliant African model ('Ujamaa') of socialism, but one in which Western models of centralized state ownership and collectivization triumphed over indigenous practices (Ibhawoh and Dibua 2003).

2 The neoliberal onslaught

1 For a good succinct overview see Harvey (2005). Peck and Tickell (2002) also give a useful account of the changing mutations of neoliberalism as a political project.

2 For a selection of views on these issues, see London CSE Group (1980), Schwarz (1981), Hodgson (1982), Kilpatrick and Lawson (1980), Hyman and Elger (1981).

3 The Solidarity Wage system, developed in the 1950s, was seen as a critical ingredient of what some labelled the Swedish model of social democracy of maintaining low inflation, full employment and economic growth and reducing income inequality from the 1950s into the

late 1980s. See Pontusson (1994) and Meidner (1993) for further details.

4 A quantitative analysis by Bowles et al. (1989) shows quite dramatically how the Reagan-era policies reversed the post-war trend of declining underlying capitalist power. See in particular Figure 4, p. 125.

5 Lister (2011: 1) cites a meeting at the Institute of Economic Affairs, which Hayek helped to found in the 1950s, shortly after Margaret Thatcher had become leader of the Conservative Party, when in response to another member's suggestion that they should 'adopt a moderate, pragmatic approach' she apparently held up a copy of Hayek's *Constitution of Liberty* and declared, 'This is what we believe' (ibid.).

6 Using figures from the National Accounts, Glyn (1989) shows that for manufacturing (where union strength resided) the relationship between profits and wages was reversed when comparing the periods 1973–79 and 1979–87. In the first period, profits, as a share of total income, were falling by an average 9.9 per cent per annum (!), while the share of wages was rising by 1.5 per cent per annum. In the latter period, the respective figures were 8.4 per cent per annum and –1.5 per cent.

7 In the decade after privatization (1984) employment was reduced from 238,000 to 156,000 (Pedersini 1999: 21). In the late 1990s the organization continued to haemorrhage jobs at an estimated rate of 5,000 per year (*Independent*, 10 November 2000, www.independent.co.uk/news/business/news/bt-to-float-four-divisions-in-biggest-shakeup-since-1984-privatisation-623435.html).

8 Credited to Harold Macmillan, Conservative prime minister in the 1950s, during a speech to the House of Lords criticizing Thatcher's policies in 1985.

3 Coming to terms with Hayek

1 The analysis draws from arguments made at greater length elsewhere about socialist economics more generally (see especially Cumbers and McMaster 2012).

2 Hodgson (1999) is especially good on this point. See Chapters 2 and 3 in particular.

3 It is important to distinguish this approach from earlier market socialists who engaged with Hayek and his colleague Von Mises in what became known as the socialist calculation debate. Both Von Mises and his opponents, notably Lange and Taylor, were engaging with the feasibility of socialism within a neoclassical equilibrium framework regarding the abilities of central planners to accurately replace the price mechanism with socialist accounting devices. Hayek was forced to respond to this with his arguments about tacit knowledge, which actually took him away from the neoclassical school at the same time as destroying the arguments of the first generation of market socialists (see Hodgson 1999; O'Neill 2003, 2006).

4 In reality, as Hodgson himself implicitly recognizes in his review of socialist economics, there has always been a wide range of thinking on both the forms of common ownership that might be adopted and the attitude towards markets, although certainly the idea of completely planned economies with no or limited role for markets was the dominant form of socialism for much of the twentieth century (Hodgson 1999: ch. 2).

5 For example, in a response to

comments on one of his papers, he notes: 'There are not just organizational limits to the knowledge that could be passed on to a centralized planning board, but epistemological limits. Much practical or tacit knowledge is embodied in use and cannot in principle be articulated in a propositional form that could be passed on to a single body. Any mechanism of coordination must allow actors to effectively use the particular practical knowledge that they possess. However, this is consistent with the claim that there are coordinating decisions at non-local levels that can and should be made in the absence of complete knowledge' (O'Neill 2002: 158).

4 Financial crisis

1 This was to be part of a wider approach within the union movement to build a social partnership with employers, although it was a particularly one-sided relationship given the weakness of the unions and the position of the employers in the labour market. Mills and others like him didn't seem to appreciate the scale of the vicious class war being fought at the time. Only the prospect of Labour winning the 1997 general election brought some employers back towards any kind of discourse of partnership, although there were few gains for workers (e.g. Cumbers 2005).

2 Short for 'there is no alternative' to the free market and deregulation in the face of global competition. The famous phrase credited to Margaret Thatcher, of course.

3 A quote attributed to former Labour minister and long-time confidant of Tony Blair, Peter (now Lord) Mandelson.

4 The essential argument underpinning the then Chancellor's, Gordon Brown's, support for private investment into public projects was that it would help reduce the Public Sector Borrowing Requirement as part of his aim to cut total public debt. This, as Sawyer and O'Donnell (1999: 14) note, was a 'false view' (see also Heald 1997) in that under most public–private schemes the 'public sector avoids the outlay of capital expenditure on the school (or hospital) in the present only to incur renting or leasing costs of the school (hospital) for many years to come'. See Shaoul (1999), Pollock (2005), Treasury Select Committee (2011) for a range of devastating critiques of the PFI initiative from across the political spectrum.

5 The latest data available reveal that in the second quarter of 2010 the party received £3.2 million, of which £2.65 million came from trade unions, £178,234 from private individuals and the rest from companies and mutual organizations.

6 Another similarity with Thatcherism was New Labour's mixture of free market liberalism in the economy, an authoritarian populism with regard to its criminal and social policy and its appeal to British imperialist instincts in its foreign and defence policy (Hall 2011).

7 An international comparative study by Dieter Helm (1994) found little evidence, outside the telecommunications sector, that consumers in privatized utilities had fared any better than their counterparts in other countries where services remained in the public sector, while some studies of the electricity sector have even suggested that prices would have fallen by between 10 and 20 per cent without privatization, the

implication being that companies have made monopoly rents from the process (Branston 2000; Newbery and Pollitt 1997).

8 Reported in the *Guardian*, 22 January 2011, available at www.guardian.co.uk, accessed 22 November 2011.

9 BBC News, 17 February 2008, news.bbc.co.uk/1/hi/business/7249575.stm, accessed 21 July 2009.

10 *Observer*, 9 August 2009, www.guardian.co.uk/business/2009/aug/09/banking-credit-crunch, accessed 10 August 2009.

11 House of Commons Treasury Select Committee, *Mortgage Arrears and Access to Mortgage Finance. Fifteenth Report of Session 2008–09*, Stationery Office, London, 2009.

12 *Guardian*, 7 August 2009, www.guardian.co.uk/business/2009/aug/07/royal-bank-of-scotland-return-to-profits, accessed 10 August 2009.

13 *Spiegel Online*, 4 February 2008, accessed 31 May 2011.

14 Ibid.
15 Ibid.
16 Ibid.

17 Lord Adonis, Labour transport minister, cited in the *Guardian*, 1 July 2009, www.guardian.co.uk/business/2009/jul/01/east-coast-rail-statement, accessed 21 July 2009.

18 *Guardian*, 16 October 2002.

19 Reported in the *Guardian*, 17 November 2011.

5 Public ownership in Latin America

1 In Uruguay, following a public referendum, water privatization has actually been made illegal, as it has in the Netherlands.

2 After Simón Bolívar, the nineteenth-century hero of the independence struggle against Spain in Latin America.

3 Initially, Chávez and other military officers from a younger generation not prepared to carry out government orders against the protesters initiated a failed coup attempt in 1992, and on his release from jail Chávez successfully campaigned for the presidency (Robinson 2008).

4 data.worldbank.org/, accessed 20 November 2011.

6 Alternative globalizations

1 'Commoning' as a verb refers to the social practices through which commons are produced and reproduced, and is important in denoting the collective work and the alternative value practices underpinning that work (De Angelis 2007; Linebaugh 2008).

2 International Cooperative Alliance website, accessed 1 July 2010.

3 Like many other contemporary anti-capitalist theorists (e.g. De Angelis 2007; Douzinas and Žižek 2010), Hardt and Negri prefer the term communism to socialism, despite its twentieth-century associations with totalitarian state government. They argue, however, that 'Sometimes when a concept has been so corrupted, it seems one ought to abandon it and find another way to name what we desire. But, instead ... we find it better to struggle over the concept and insist on its proper meaning. At a purely conceptual level we would begin to define communism this way: what the private is to capitalism and the public to socialism, the common is to communism' (2009: 273).

4 Whether one agrees with their broader analysis of a new stage of capitalism around biopower and knowledge production, where the

Facebook and Twitter generation seem to have replaced the industrial proletariat as the gravedigger of capitalism, is another matter. See the recent excellent paper by Silvia Federici (2010) on this subject.

5 For a good selection of critiques, see the special issue of the journal *Capital and Class* (85, 2005, pp. 13–42).

6 Castells is the classic text here in emphasizing how globalization has recast the spatiality of social relations (Castells 1996, 1997, 1998). For him, a 'space of places' is giving way to a 'space of flows' where locally and territorially defined societies around the nation-state are being superseded by more global and delocalized networks of association. Another influential theorist, John Urry, has gone even farther in emphasizing a 'shift from a heavy solid modernity to one that is light and liquid and where speed of movement of people, money, images and information is paramount' (Urry 2004: 110).

7 I have developed a critique of this discourse with others elsewhere. See Cumbers et al. 2008a and b; Routledge and Cumbers 2009.

8 The civil unrest and uprising against the neoliberal policies of the government in 2001.

7 Remaking public ownership

1 The Swedish social democrats famously allowed their own capitalists to retain control of the ownership of firms – including the vast holdings of the Wallenberg family – in return for an extensive redistributive taxation system and welfare state. The Rehm-Meidner plan of the 1970s as outlined in Chapter 2 challenged this class compromise, of course.

2 Although the lack of political will on the mainstream left internationally, both before and after the financial crisis and current recession, to properly engage with distributional justice in these issues is telling about the power and entrenched pro-business discourse of political elites.

3 See instead, for a selection of views, Adaman and Devine 1996, 2001; Bowles and Gintis 1993; Cockshott and Cottrell 1993; De Martino 2000; Hodgson 1999, 2005; Mandel 1986; Nove 1983; Wainwright 1994.

4 As an aside, an important point that emerges from this discussion is that both markets and competition are notoriously under-theorized both by Marxist and socialist economists and the mainstream. Both are socially constructed and as such operate according to social norms, interpersonal relations, trust, social contract, moral obligations, rules, customs, etc. At a very simplistic level we need to differentiate between competition for purely personal gain and that which in a Schumpeterian sense has a broader social purpose (e.g. technological innovation, discovery). For an interesting discussion of these issues, see Rosenbaum (2000).

5 Competition would also imply the need for winners and losers, and for some firms to go bust, as well as for jobs to be lost. Such market-based approaches should therefore be complemented by decent welfare provision, including minimum income standards, retraining and macroeconomic measures – among them job creation schemes such as state-led public works – but there is not the space to discuss such broader issues to do with a socialist or solidarity economy here.

8 Norway's oil bonanza

1 The UK currently has a figure of 36.0, compared to an OECD average of around 32, while Norway has a figure of 25.8 (UNDP 2009). On the Gini index, the higher the figure, the greater the level of inequality in a country.

2 The UK had a Gini index rating of 0.28 in the mid-1970s and 0.33 in the 1980s, while Norway (no figures are available for the 1970s) recorded a figure of 0.24 in the mid-1980s (UNDP 2009).

3 One of the effects of this is that the political right has traditionally been extremely fragmented, compared to its situation in many countries, with separate political parties representing agrarian, business and Christian interests. This gave the Labour Party a period of governing hegemony from the 1940s through to the early 1980s (Mjoset et al. 1994).

4 The Norwegianization policy was also facilitated by a successful skills and training policy so that by the mid-1980s high-level engineers were being graduated from Trondheim's technical college and the two main geology departments at Oslo and Bergen universities had successful development research and education programmes in oil-related areas (Ryggvik 2010: 43).

5 Initially the government had sought to secure an influence through increasing the state ownership to 50 per cent in the already existing company Norsk Hydro, which had already expanded from its background in the water, chemical and metallurgical industries into the North Sea by the late 1960s (Ryggvik 2010).

6 See www.statoil.com, accessed 3 June 2011.

7 The US oil companies Mobil and Phillips were the two key players in the early years of Norwegian oil activities from the 1960s. Mobil in particular played a dominant role in oil and gas extraction to the extent that when the Norwegian government sought to recruit US oil expertise, it deliberately recruited from outside Mobil (Ryggvik 2010).

8 Over half of the workforce is unionized, compared to around 27 per cent in the UK, 11.9 per cent in the USA and 19.1 per cent in Germany, while over three-quarters of workers are covered by collective bargaining agreements (MacKinnon and Cumbers 2011).

9 Although in 1980 Norway suffered its worst offshore accident when the semi-submersible accommodation platform the *Alexander L. Kielland* was severely damaged in bad weather, leading to the loss of 123 lives.

10 Typified by its powerful general secretary for most of the 1980s and 1990s, Lars Anders Myrhe, who had a background as a geologist without ever having worked on the rigs (see Routledge and Cumbers 2009: ch. 6).

11 Thirteen died in accidents between 1980 and 1990, about one tenth of the figure in the earlier period, despite much higher overall working hours (Ryggvik 2010: 72).

12 At the time of writing (November 2011), unemployment is at 3.2 per cent compared to an OECD average of 8.5 per cent.

13 *For Velferdsstaten* in Norwegian.

9 Danish wind power

1 Indeed, there was a considerable reorganization of relations between central and local government during the 1970s involving a

considerable devolution of power to the latter.

2 See Mitchell's insightful analysis of the networks assembled around particular energy discourses as part of broader development agendas (Mitchell 2009).

3 Danish government sources suggest as many as 35,000 'wind engines' operating at this time (Kruse and Maegard 2008: 132).

4 A key development was the decision in the 1980s by the California state government to encourage wind power, which then became an important market for Danish turbine manufacturers.

5 Source: Danish Wind Turbine Owners Association.

6 Ibid., www.dkvind.dk/eng/publications/lacour_dv.pdf, accessed 20 October 2011.

7 One consequence of this has been a highly flexible labour market by northern European standards, although supported by generous welfare and training provision, known as 'flexicurity' (Anderson and Mailand 2005).

8 Economic liberalism has also run alongside an increasing nationalism and social conservatism, particularly in immigration policy, which has become one of the most hardline in Europe since 2001.

9 To the extent that he became general secretary of NATO on leaving office in 2009.

10 The reverse appears to be true in the calamitous decision of the UK government to drastically cut its feed-in tariff for solar energy (taken in October 2011 with just two months before it was due to be applied and with no broader public consultation) at a time when the industry was still in its infancy. This appears to have been prompted more by private utility lobbying and the 'austerity' economic policies of the Conservative–Liberal Democratic coalition.

Bibliography

Adaman, F. and P. Devine (1996) 'The economic calculation debate: lessons for socialists', *Cambridge Journal of Economics*, 20: 523–37.

— (2001) 'Participatory planning as a deliberative democratic process: a response to Hodgson's critique', *Economy and Society*, 30: 229–39.

Amin, A. (2005) 'Local community on trial', *Economy and Society*, 34(4): 612–33.

Amin, A. and D. Thomas (1996) 'The negotiated economy: state and civic institutions in Denmark', *Economy and Society*, 25: 255–81.

Amin, A., R. Hudson and A. Cameron (2002) *Placing the Social Economy*, London: Routledge.

Amsden, A. (1989) *Asia's Next Giant: South Korea and Late Industrialization*, Oxford: Oxford University Press.

Andersen, P. H. and I. Drejer (2008) 'Systemic innovation in a distributed network: the case of Danish wind turbines, 1972–2007', *Strategic Organization*, 6(1): 13–46.

Anderson, P. (2009) 'A new Germany?', *New Left Review*, 57: 5–40.

Anderson, S. (1992) *North Sea Oil and State Policy: A Comparison of the UK, Norway and Denmark*, Oxford: Oxford University Press.

Anderson, S. K. and M. Mailand (2005) 'The Danish flexicurity model: the role of the collective bargaining system', Paper compiled for the Danish Ministry of Employment, Department of Sociology, University of Copenhagen.

Arestis, P. and M. Sawyer (2001) 'The economic analysis underlying the "Third Way"', *New Political Economy*, 6: 255–78.

Armstrong, P., A. Glyn and J. Harrison (1991) *Capitalism since 1945*, Oxford: Blackwell.

Åsard, E. (1982) 'American unions and industrial democracy: the "Business Unionism" thesis re-examined', *Statsvetenskaplig Tidskrift*, 3: 155–64.

Bakker, K. (2003) 'From public to private to ... mutual? Restructuring water supply governance in England and Wales', *Geoforum*, 34(3): 359–74.

Barchesi, F. (2003) 'Communities between commons and commodities. Subjectivity and needs in the definition of new social movements', *The Commoner*, 6.

Bass, B. M. and V. J. Shackleton (1979) 'Industrial democracy and participative management: a case for a synthesis', *Academy of Management Review*, 4(3): 393–404.

Bayliss, K. (2002) 'Privatization and poverty: the distributional impact of utility privatization', *Annals of Public and Cooperative Economics*, 73(4): 603–25.

Bernstein, E. (1993 [1899]) *The Preconditions of Socialism*, English trans., Cambridge: Cambridge University Press.

Beynon, H. and H. Wainwright (1979)

The Workers' Report on Vickers, London: Pluto.

BIS (2004) 'Bank failures in mature economies', Basel Committee on Banking Supervision, Working Paper no. 13, Bank of International Settlements, Basel.

Blackburn, R. (1999) 'The new collectivism: pension reform, grey capitalism and complex socialism', *New Left Review*, I/233: 3–65.

Bliss, B. (1954) 'Nationalisation in France and Great Britain of the electricity supply industry', *International and Comparative Law Quarterly*, 8: 277–90.

Bohm, S., A. Dinerstein and A. Spicer (2010) '(Im)possibilities of autonomy: social movements in and beyond capital, the state and development', *Social Movement Studies*, 9(1): 17–32.

Bowles, S. and H. Gintis (1993) 'A political and economic case for the democratic enterprise', *Economics and Philosophy*, 7: 75–100.

Bowles, S., D. M. Gordon and T. E. Weisskopf (1989) 'Business ascendancy and economic impasse: a structural retrospective on conservative economics, 1979–1987', *Journal of Economic Perspectives*, 3: 107–34.

Boyer, R. (1987) 'The current economic crisis: its dynamics and its implications in France', in G. Ross, S. Hoffman and S. Malzacher (eds), *The Mitterrand Experiment*, Cambridge: Polity Press.

Bramble, T. (2006) 'Another world is possible: a study of participants at Australian alter-globalization social forums', *Journal of Sociology*, 42(3): 289–311.

Branston, J. R. (2000) 'A counterfactual price analysis of electricity privatisation in England and Wales', L'Institute Discussion Paper 7, Universities of Birmingham, Ferrara and Wisconsin-Milwaukee.

Brenner, N. (1998) 'Between fixity and motion: accumulation, territorial organization, and the historical geography of spatial scales', *Environment and Planning D: Society and Space*, 16(4): 459–81.

— (2004) *New State Spaces*, Oxford: Oxford University Press.

Brenner, R. (2005) *The Economics of Global Turbulence*, London: Verso.

Brown, G. (1997) 'Foreword', in *Partnerships for Prosperity: The Private Finance Initiative*, London: Treasury Taskforce.

Brummer, A. (2009) 'Mr Brown's bankers', *New Statesman*, January, www.newstatesman.com/economy/2009/01/government-banks-bankers, accessed 15 September 2009.

Burczak, T. (2006) *Socialism after Hayek*, Ann Arbor: University of Michigan Press.

Caffentzis, G. (2004) 'A tale of two conferences: globalization, the crisis of neoliberalism and question of the commons', Talk prepared for the Alter-Globalization Conference, 9 August, San Miguel de Allende, Mexico.

— (2009) 'A tale of two conferences: globalization, the crisis of neoliberalism and question of the commons', *The Commoner*, 13.

Callaghan, G., M. Danson and G. Whittam (2011) 'Community ownership and sustainable economic development', *Scottish Affairs*, 74: 79–100.

Callaghan, J. (2000) 'Rise and fall of the alternative economic strategy: from internationalisation of capital to "globalisation"',

Contemporary British History, 14: 105–30.

Callari, A (2009) 'A methodological reflection on the "thick socialism" of Socialism after Hayek', *Review of Social Economy*, 67(3): 367–73.

Castells, M. (1996) *The Rise of the Network Society*, Oxford: Blackwell.

— (1997) *The Power of Identity*, Oxford: Blackwell.

— (1998) *End of Millennium*, Oxford: Blackwell.

CCLC (1977) *A Reply to Bullock*, London: City Company Law Committee.

Chang, H.-J. (2006) 'Industrial policy in East Asia – lessons for Europe', Paper prepared for the EIB Conference in Economics and Finance on 'An industrial policy for Europe?', Luxembourg.

— (2007) *State-owned Enterprise Reform*, New York: UNDESA.

— (2009) 'Under-explored treasure troves of development lessons – lessons from the histories of Small Rich European Countries (SRECs) in 2009', in M. Kremer, P. van Lieshoust and R. Went (eds), *Doing Good or Doing Better – Development Policies in a Globalising World*, Amsterdam: Amsterdam University Press.

Chang, H.-J. and R. Rowthorn (eds) (1995) *The Role of the State in Economic Change*, Oxford: Clarendon Press.

Chodor, T. (2009) 'Venezuela's Bolivarian Revolution: a counterhegemonic response to neoliberalism?', Paper presented to the Australasian Political Studies Association Annual Conference, Sydney, 27–30 September.

Cleaver, H. (1979) *Reading Capital Politically*, Brighton: Harvester.

Clift, B. (2001) *The Jospin way*, *Political Quarterly*, 72(2): 170–9.

Clifton, J., F. Comín and D. D. Fuentes (2003) *Privatisation in the European Union: Public Enterprises and Integration*, Dordrecht: Kluwer.

Coates, K. and T. Topham (1972) *The New Unionism: The Case for Workers' Control*, Nottingham: Spokesman.

— (1975) *Shop Stewards and Workers' Control*, Nottingham: Spokesman.

Cockshott, P. and A. Cottrell (1993) *Towards a New Socialism*, Nottingham: Spokesman.

Cole, G. D. H. (1920) *Guild Socialism: A Plan for Economic Democracy*, New York: Frederick A. Stokes.

Collinson, P. (2011) 'Sale of Northern Rock leaves the public dangling on the hook', *Guardian*, 17 November.

Compass/NEF (2010) *Better Banking: A Manifesto to Re-organise the UK Banking System to Serve and Strengthen the British Economy through Structural Reform*, London: Compass.

Conquest, R. (1986) *The Harvest of Sorrow: Soviet Collectivization and the Terror-Famine*, Oxford: Oxford University Press.

Conservative Party (1979) *Conservative Manifesto 1979*, London: Conservative Party.

— (1983) *Conservative Manifesto 1983*, London: Conservative Party.

Cook, J., S. Deakin and A. Hughes (2001) 'Mutuality and corporate governance: the evolution of the UK building societies following deregulation', Working Paper 205, ESRC Centre for Business Research, University of Cambridge.

Crotty, J. (2009) 'Structural causes of the global financial crisis: a critical assessment of the

"New Financial Architecture"', *Cambridge Journal of Economics*, 33: 563–80.
Cumbers, A. (2000) 'The national state as mediator of regional development outcomes in an era of globalisation: a comparative analysis of the UK and Norway', *European Urban and Regional Studies*, 7(3): 237–52.
— (2004) 'Embedded internationalisms: building trans-national solidarity networks in the British and Norwegian trade union movements', *Antipode*, 36(5): 829–50.
— (2005) 'Genuine renewal or pyrrhic victory? The scale politics of trade union recognition in the UK', *Antipode*, 37(1): 116–38.
— (2007) 'The fictitious commodity', *Variant: Special Issue on the Oil Economy*, 28, Spring, pp. 16–18.
— (2012) 'North Sea oil, the state and divergent development in the United Kingdom and Norway', in J. A. McNeish and O. Logan (eds), *Flammable Societies: Studies on the Socio-economics of Oil*, London: Pluto.
Cumbers, A. and J. Farrington (2000) 'Keeping privatisation on track: the active state, the unwilling investor and the case of rail freight in the UK', *Area*, 32(2): 157–67.
Cumbers, A. and R. McMaster (2010) 'Socialism, knowledge, the instrumental valuation principle and the enhancement of individual dignity', *Economy and Society*, 39(2): 247–70.
— (2012) 'Revisiting public ownership: knowledge, democracy and participation in economic decision-making', *Review of Radical Political Economics*, forthcoming.
Cumbers, A., D. MacKinnon and J. Shaw (2010) 'Labour, organisational rescaling and the politics of production: union renewal in the privatised rail industry', *Work, Employment and Society*, 24(1): 127–44.
Cumbers, A., C. Nativel and P. Routledge (2008a) 'Labour agency and union positionalities in global production networks', *Journal of Economic Geography*, 8(2): 369–87.
— (2008b) 'The entangled geographies of global justice networks', *Progress in Human Geography*, 32(2): 183–200.
Cunningham, M. (1993) 'From the ground up? Labour governments and economic planning', in J. Fyrth (ed.), *Labour's High Noon: The Government and the Economy 1945–51*, London: Lawrence and Wishart.
Cunninghame, P. (2008) 'Reinventing an/other anti-capitalism in Mexico: the Sixth Declaration of the EZLN and the "other campaign"', in W. Bonefeld (ed.), *Subverting the Present, Imagining the Future: Insurrection, Movement, Commons*, New York: Autonomedia.
Curry, T. and L. Shibut (2000) 'The cost of the savings and loans crisis: truth and consequences', Federal Deposit Insurance Corporation, www.fdic.gov/bank/analytical/banking/2000dec/brv13n2_2.pdf, accessed 19 November 2011.
Davies, P. and Wedderburn of Charlton (1977) 'The land of industrial democracy', *Industrial Law Journal*, 6: 197–211.
De Angelis, M. (2005) 'PR like process! Strategy from the bottom-up', *Ephemera*, 5(2): 193–204.
— (2007) *The Beginning of History: Value Struggles and Global Capital*, London: Pluto.
De Martino, G. (2000) *Global*

Economy, Global Justice, London: Routledge.
— (2003) 'Realizing class justice', *Rethinking Marxism*, 15(1): 1–31.
— (2011) *The Economist's Oath: On the Need for Professional Economic Ethics*, Oxford: Oxford University Press.
DEA (Danish Energy Agency) (2007) *Danish Electricity Supply: Statistical Survey*, Copenhagen: Danish Energy Agency.
— (2010) *Danish Energy Policy 1970–2010*, Copenhagen: Danish Energy Agency
Devine, P. (1988) *Democracy and Economic Planning: The Political Economy of a Self- Governing Society*, Cambridge: Polity Press.
Douzinas, C. and S. Žižek (2010) *The Idea of Communism*, London: Verso.
Dowd, D. (2001) *Capitalism and Its Economics: A Critical History*, London: Pluto.
DTI (Department of Trade and Industry) (1998) *Conclusions of the Review of Energy Sources for Power Generation and Government Responses to Fourth and Fifth Reports of the Trade and Industry Committee*, Cm 4071, London: Stationery Office.
EEA (2004) 'Energy subsidies in the European Union, a brief overview', EEA Technical Report 1/2004.
Escobar, A. (2001) 'Culture sits in places: reflections on globalism and subaltern strategies of localization', *Political Geography*, 20(2): 139–74.
— (2008) *Territories of Difference: Place, Movements, Life, Redes*, Durham, NC: Duke University Press.
— (2010) 'Latin America at a crossroads', *Cultural Studies*, 24(1): 1–65.
Estrin, S. (1983) *Self-Management: Economic Theory and Yugoslav Practice*, Cambridge: Cambridge University Press.
— (1991) 'Yugoslavia: the case of self-managing market socialism', *Journal of Economic Perspectives*, 5(4): 187–94.
Featherstone, D., A. Ince, D. MacKinnon, K. Strauss and A. Cumbers (2012) 'Progressive localism and the construction of political alternatives', *Transactions of the Institute of British Geographers*, 37(2): 177–82.
Federici, S. (2010) 'Feminism and the politics of the commons', *The Commoner*, 14.
Fine, B. (1989) 'Denationalisation', in F. Green (ed.), *The Restructuring of the UK Economy*, London: Harvester Wheatsheaf.
— (1990) 'Scaling the commanding heights of public enterprise economics', *Cambridge Journal of Economics*, 14(2): 127–42.
Fine, B. and L. Harris (1985) *The Peculiarities of the British Economy*, London: Lawrence and Wishart.
Fine, B. and D. Milonakis (2009) *From Economic Imperialism to Freakonomics: The Shifting Boundaries between Economics and the Other Social Sciences*, London: Routledge.
Fine, B. and K. O'Donnell (1985) 'The nationalized industries', in B. Fine and L. Harris, *The Peculiarities of the British Economy*, London: Lawrence and Wishart.
Fishman, N. (1993) 'Coal: owned and managed on behalf of the people', in J. Fyrth (ed.), *Labour's High Noon: The Government and the Economy 1945–51*, London: Lawrence and Wishart.
Ford, H. and S. Crowther (1926) *My Life and Work*, New York: Doubleday.

Fukuyama, F. (1992) *The End of History and the Last Man*, London: Penguin.

Fyrth, J. (ed.) (1993) *Labour's High Noon: The Government and the Economy 1945–51*, London: Lawrence and Wishart.

Gamble, A. (1995) 'The crisis of conservatism', *New Left Review*, I/214: 3–25.

Gibson-Graham, J. K. (2006) *A Post-Capitalist Politics*, Minneapolis: University of Minnesota Press.

Glyn, A. (1989) 'The macro-anatomy of the Thatcher years', in F. Green (ed.), *The Restructuring of the UK Economy*, Chichester: Harvester Wheatsheaf.

— (1995) 'Social democracy and full employment', *New Left Review*, I/211: 33–55.

— (2006) *Capitalism Unleashed*, Oxford: Oxford University Press.

Glyn, A. and B. Sutcliffe (1972) *British Capitalism, Workers and the Profits Squeeze*, London: Penguin.

Goldman, M. I. (2003) *The Piratization of Russia: Russian Reform Goes Awry*, New York and London: Routledge.

Gorz, A. (1982) *Farewell to the Working Class: An Essay on Post-Industrial Socialism*, London: Pluto Press.

Gowan, P. (2009) 'Crisis in the heartland', *New Left Review*, 55: 5–29.

Gramsci, A. (1971) *Prison Notebooks*, New York: International Publishers.

Green, F. (ed.) (1989) *The Restructuring of the UK Economy*, Chichester: Harvester Wheatsheaf.

Hadjilambrinos, C. (2000) 'Understanding technology choice in electricity industries: a comparative study of France and Denmark', *Energy Policy*, 28: 1111–26.

Hall, D. and E. Lobina (2010) *Water Companies in Europe 2010*, Greenwich: Public Service International Research Unit.

Hall, D., J. Lethbridge, E. Lobina, S. Thomas and S. Davies (2003) 'The UK experience – privatised sectors and global companies', Paper presented at a conference on 'Privatisation experiences in Europe', CESinfo, Munich.

Hall, D., S. Thomas and V. Corral (2009) *Global Experience with Electricity Liberalisation*, Greenwich: Public Services International Research Unit.

Hall, D., E. Lobina and V. Corral (2010) *Replacing Failed Private Water Contracts*, Greenwich: Public Services International Research Unit.

Hall, P. A. (1987) 'The evolution of economic policy under Mitterrand', in G. Ross, S. Hoffman and S. Malzacher (eds), *The Mitterrand Experiment*, Cambridge: Polity Press.

Hall, S. (2003) 'New Labour's double shuffle', *Soundings*, 24: 10–24.

— (2010) 'Life and times of the first new left', *New Left Review*, 61: 177–96.

— (2011) 'The neoliberal revolution', *Soundings*, 48.

Hardt, M. and A. Negri (2009) *Commonwealth*, Cambridge, MA: Harvard University Press.

Harnecker, M. (2007) *Rebuilding the Left*, London: Zed Books.

Harstad, H. (2009) 'Globalization and the new spaces for social movement politics: the marginalization of labor unions in Bolivian gas nationalization', *Globalizations*, 6(2): 169–85.

Harvey, D. (1982) *The Limits to Capital*, Oxford: Blackwell.

— (2003) *The New Imperialism*, Oxford: Oxford University Press.

— (2005) *A Brief History of Neoliberalism*, Oxford: Oxford University Press.
— (2006) 'Neoliberalism as creative destruction', *Geografiska Annaler: Series B Human Geography*, 88(2): 145–58.
— (2010) *The Enigma of Capital*, London: Profile.
Harvie, D. (2000) 'Alienation, class and enclosure in UK universities', *Capital and Class*, 71: 103–32.
Hayek, F. (1944) *The Road to Serfdom*, Chicago, IL: University of Chicago Press.
— (1948) *Individualism and Economic Order*, Chicago, IL: University of Chicago Press.
Heald, D. (1997) 'Privately financed capital in public services', *Manchester School of Economic and Social Studies*, 65: 568–98.
Helm, D. (1994) 'British utility regulation: theory, practice and reform', *Oxford Review of Economic Policy*, 10.
Herod, A. (2001) *Labor Geographies: Workers and the Landscapes of Capitalism*, New York: Guilford.
Hetherington, P. (2003) 'Obituary: Joe Mills, the man who fixed it for Blair', *Guardian*, 9 January.
Heymann, M. (1999) 'A fight of systems? Wind power and electric power systems in Denmark, Germany, and the USA', *Centaurus*, 41: 112–36.
Hines, C. (2000) *Localization: A Global Manifesto*, London: Earthscan.
Hirst, P. (1994) *Associative Democracy: New Forms of Social and Economic Governance*, Cambridge: Polity Press.
— (1997) *From Statism to Pluralism*, London: UCL Press.
HM Treasury (2002) *Implementing Privatisation: The UK Experience*, London: HM Treasury.
Hodgson, G. (1982) 'Socialist economic strategy: a reply to Donald Schwarz', *Capital and Class*, 16: 127–30.
Hodgson, G. M. (1984) *The Democratic Economy: A New Look at Planning, Markets and Power*, Harmondsworth: Penguin.
— (1999) *Economics and Utopia*, London: Routledge.
— (2005) 'The limits to participatory planning: a reply to Adaman and Devine', *Economy and Society*, 34: 141–53.
— (2006) 'What are institutions?', *Journal of Economic Issues*, 15(1): 1–25.
Holloway, J. (2002) *Changing the World without Taking Power: The Meaning of Revolution Today*, London: Pluto.
— (2005) *Changing the World without Taking Power: The Meaning of Revolution Today*, 2nd edn, London: Pluto.
— (2010) *Crack Capitalism*, London: Pluto.
Hudson, R. (1989) *Wrecking a Region*, London: Pion.
— (2000) *Production, Places and Environment: Changing Perspectives in Economic Geography*, London: Longman.
Hughes, J. (1960) *Nationalised Industries in the Mixed Economy*, London: Fabian Society.
Hyman, R. and T. Elger (1981) 'Job controls, the employers' offensive and alternative strategies', *Capital and Class*, 15: 115–49.
Ibhawoh, B. and J. I. Dibua (2003) 'Deconstructing Ujamaa: the legacy of Julius Nyerere in the quest for social and economic development in Africa', *African Journal of Political Science*, 8(1): 59–83.
IEA (2006) *Energy Policies of IEA*

Countries – Denmark, Paris: International Energy Agency.

Jensen, I. K. (2003) *Mænd I Modvind* [Men Facing Headwinds], Copenhagen: Børsen.

Jessop, B. (2002) *The Future of the Capitalist State*, Cambridge: Polity Press.

Jones, C. and A. Murie (1999) *Reviewing the Right to Buy*, Birmingham: Birmingham University.

Kautsky, K. (1902) *The Social Revolution*, Chicago, IL: Charles Kerr.

Keen, S. (2011) *Debunking Economics*, revised and expanded edition, London: Zed Books.

Keynes, J. M. (1936) *The General Theory of Employment, Interest and Money*, London: Palgrave Macmillan.

Kilpatrick, A. and T. Lawson (1980) 'On the nature of industrial decline in the UK', *Cambridge Journal of Economics*, 4: 85–102.

King's Fund (2003) *Getting the Right Medicines? Putting Public Interests at the Heart of Health-related Research*, London: King's Fund.

Kornai, J. (1979) 'The dilemmas of a socialist economy: the Hungarian experience', Research Series no. GL12, Economic and Social Research Institute (ESRI).

Krohn, S. (2000) *Danish Wind Turbines: An Industrial Success Story*, Danish Wind Turbine Manufacturers Association, www.windpower.dk/articles/success.htm.

Krugman, P. (2009) 'Saved by big government', *Guardian*, 10 August.

Kruse, J. and P. Maegard (2008) 'An authentic story about how a local community became self-sufficient in pollution-free energy and created a source of income for the citizens', *The Commoner*, 13: 129–39.

Labour Party (1945) *Let Us Face the Future: A Declaration of Labour Policy for the Consideration of the Nation*, London: Labour Party.

Labour Party Manifesto for Scotland (1979) *The Better Way Forward*, Glasgow: Scottish Labour Party.

Lange, O. and F. M. Taylor (1938) *On the Economic Theory of Socialism*, Minneapolis: University of Minnesota Press.

Lauber, V. and E. Schenner (2011) 'The struggle over support schemes for renewable electricity in the European Union: a discursive-institutionalist analysis', *Environmental Politics*, 20(4): 508–27.

Lawson, N. (1992) *The View from No. 11: Memoirs of a Tory Radical*, London: Bantam.

Lefebvre, H. (1991) *The Production of Space*, Oxford: Blackwell.

Linebaugh, P. (2008) *The Magna Carta Manifesto: Liberties and Commons for All*, Berkeley: University of California Press.

Lister, A. (2011) 'The "mirage" of social justice: Hayek against (and for) Rawls', CSSJ Working Papers Series SJ017, Centre for the Study of Social Justice, Oxford University.

Lobina, E. (2000) 'Cochabamba – water war', *FOCUS on the Public Services*, 7(2): 5–10.

Lobina, E. and D. Hall (2001) *UK Water Privatisation: A Briefing*, Greenwich: Public Services International Research Unit.

— (2007) *Water Privatisation and Restructuring in Latin America*, Greenwich: Public Services International Research Unit.

London CSE Group (1980) *The Alternative Economic Strategy: A Response by the Labour Movement to the Economic Crisis*, London: CSE Books.

London Edinburgh Weekend Return Group (1980) *In and Against the State*, London: Pluto.

Loving, R., Jr (2009) 'Formula for fixing Amtrak', *Trains*, 69(3): 26–33.

Macfarlane, L. (1996) 'Socialism and common ownership: an historical perspective', in P. King (ed.), *Socialism and the Common Good*, London: Frank Cass.

MacKinnon, D. and A. Cumbers (2007) *An Introduction to Economic Geography: Globalisation, Uneven Development and Place*, London: Pearson.

— (2011) *An Introduction to Economic Geography: Globalisation, Uneven Development and Place*, 2nd edn, London: Pearson.

MacKinnon, D. and J. Shaw (2010) 'New state spaces, agency and scale: devolution and the regionalisation of transport governance in Scotland', *Antipode*, 46: 1226–52.

— (2011) 'Moving on with "filling in"?', *Antipode*, 42(5): 1226–52.

MacKinnon, D., A. Cumbers and J. Shaw (2008) 'Re-scaling employment relations: key outcomes of change in the privatised rail industry', *Environment and Planning A*, 40: 1347–69.

Magnusson, L. and J. Ottoson (2000) 'State intervention and the role of history – state and private actors in Swedish network industries', *Review of Political Economy*, 12(2): 191–205.

Mandel, E. (1986) 'In defence of socialist planning', *New Left Review*, I/159: 5–37.

Marshall, J. N., R. Willis and R. Richardson (2003) 'Demutualisation, strategic choice, and social responsibility', *Environment and Planning C: Government and Policy*, 21(5): 735–60.

Marshall, J. N., A. Pike, J. S. Pollard, J. Tomaney, S. Dawley and S. Gray (2012) 'Placing the run on the Rock', *Journal of Economic Geography*, 12(1): 157–81.

Marx, K. (1906) *Capital*, New York: Random House.

Maskell, P., H. Eskelinen, I. Hannibalsson, A. Malmberg and E. Varne (1998) *Competitiveness, Localised Learning and Regional Development: Specialisation and Prosperity in Small, Open Economies*, London: Routledge.

Mason, P. (2012) *Why It's Kicking Off Everywhere: The New Global Revolutions*, London: Verso.

Massey, D. (1984) *Spatial Divisions of Labour*, Basingstoke: Macmillan.

— (1993) 'Power-geometry and a progressive sense of place', in J. Bird, B. Curtis, T. Putnam, G. Robertson and L. Tickner (eds), *Mapping the Futures: Local Cultures, Global Change*, London: Routledge, pp. 59–69.

— (2004) 'Geographies of responsibility', *Geografiska Annaler B*, 86: 5–18.

— (2005) *For Space*, London: Sage.

— (2007) *World City*, Cambridge: Polity Press.

Mathers, A. and G. Taylor (2005) 'Contemporary struggle in Europe', *Capital and Class*, 85: 27–9.

McCarthy, J. (2005) 'Commons as counterhegemonic projects', *Capitalism Nature Socialism*, 16: 9–24.

McDonald, D. A. and G. Ruiters (eds) (2012) *Alternatives to Privatization: Public Options for Essential Services in the Global South*, London: Routledge.

McNeish, J. A. and O. Logan (eds) (2012) *Flammable Societies: Studies on the Socio-economics of Oil*, London: Pluto.

Meadows, D. H., D. L. Meadows, J. Randers and W. W. Behrens III (1972) *The Limits to Growth*, New York: Universe Books.

Megginson, W. L. and J. M. Netter (2001) 'From state to market: a survey of empirical studies of privatization', *Journal of Economic Literature*, 39: 321–89.

Meidner, R. (1993) 'Why did the Swedish model fail?', *Socialist Register*, 29: 211–28.

Meyer, N. I. and A. L. Koefoed (2003) 'Danish energy reform: policy implications for renewables', *Energy Policy*, 31: 597–607.

Miller, D. and W. Dinan (2000) 'The rise of the PR industry in Britain 1979–1998', *European Journal of Communication*, 15(1): 5–35.

Minns, R. (1996) 'The social ownership of capital', *New Left Review*, I/219: 42–61.

Mitchell, T. (2009) 'Carbon democracy', *Economy and Society*, 38(3): 399–432.

Mjoset, L., A. Cappelen, J. Fagerberg and B. S. Tranoy (1994) 'Norway: changing the model', in P. Anderson and P. Camiller (eds), *Mapping the West European Left*, London: Verso.

Moller, B. (2010) 'Spatial analyses of emerging and fading wind energy landscapes in Denmark', *Land Use Policy*, 27: 233–41.

Moore, H. L. and E. Mayo (2001) *The Mutual State and How to Build It*, London: New Economics Foundation.

Mortimer, J. (1993) 'The changing mood of working people', in J. Fyrth (ed.), *Labour's High Noon: The Government and the Economy 1945–51*, London: Lawrence and Wishart.

Moss, B. H. (1988) 'Industrial law reform in an era of retreat: the Auroux laws in France', *Work, Employment and Society*, 2(3): 317–34.

Mouffe, C. (2005) *On the Political*, London: Routledge.

Muet, P. A. (1985) 'Economic management and the international environment', in H. Machin and V. Wright (eds), *Economic Policy and Policy-making under the Mitterrand Presidency 1981–1984*, London: Frances Pinter.

Murrell, P. (1991) 'Can neoclassical economics underpin the reform of centrally planned economies?', *Journal of Economic Perspectives*, 5: 59–76.

NAO (2011) *The Financial Stability Interventions, Extract from the Certificate and Report of the Comptroller and Auditor General on HM Treasury Annual Report and Accounts 2010–11*, HC 984, July.

NEF (2009) *The Ecology of Finance: An Alternative White Paper on Banking and Financial Sector Reform*, London: New Economics Foundation.

Neurath, O. (1945) 'Physicalism, planning and the social sciences: bricks prepared for a discussion v. Hayek', Otto Neurath Nachlass in Haarlem 202 K.56, 26 July.

— (2003 [1920]) 'Total socialization', in T. E. Uebel and R. Cohen (eds), *Otto Neurath Economic Writings*, Dordrecht: Kluwer.

Newbery, D. and M. Pollitt (1997) 'The restructuring and privatisation of Britain's CEGB: was it worth it?', *Journal of Industrial Economics*, 45(3): 269–303.

Nolan, P. (1995) *China's Rise, Russia's Fall: Politics, economics and planning in the transition from Stalinism*, Basingstoke: Macmillan.

— (2001) *China and the Global Economy: National champions, industrial policy and the big business revolution*, Houndsmill: Palgrave.

North, P. (1998) 'Exploring the politics of social movements through "sociological intervention": a case study of local exchange trading schemes', *Sociological Review*, 46: 564–82.

— (2007) *Money and Liberation: The Micropolitics of Alternative Currency Movements*, Minneapolis: University of Minnesota Press.

— (2010) *Local Money*, Dartington: Green Books.

Notes from Nowhere (2003) *We Are Everywhere*, London: Verso.

Nove, A. (1980) 'The Soviet economy: problems and prospects', *New Left Review*, I/119: 3–19.

— (1983) *The Economics of Feasible Socialism*, London: George Allen and Unwin.

NPD (2009) *Facts 2009: The Norwegian Petroleum Sector*, Oslo: Norwegian Petroleum Directorate.

OECD (1998) 'Corporate governance, state-owned enterprises and privatisation', *Proceedings*, Organisation for Economic Co-operation and Development, Paris.

— (2000) *OECD Economic Surveys: Denmark*, Paris: Organisation for Economic Co-operation and Development.

— (2003) *Privatising State-owned Enterprises: An Overview of Policies and Practices in OECD Countries*, Paris: Organisation for Economic Co-operation and Development.

— (2008) *Growing Unequal?: Income Distribution and Poverty in OECD Countries*, Paris: Organisation for Economic Co-operation and Development.

Ohmae, K. (1990) *The Borderless World*, London: Collins.

O'Neill, J. (1998) *The Market: Ethics, Knowledge and Politics*, London: Routledge.

— (2002) 'Socialist calculation and environmental valuation: money, markets and ecology', *Science and Society*, 66: 137–51.

— (2003) 'Neurath, associationalism and markets', *Economy and Society*, 32: 184–206.

— (2006) 'Knowledge, planning and markets: a missing chapter in the socialist calculation debates', *Economics and Philosophy*, 22: 55–78.

— (2007) *Markets, Deliberation and Environment*, London: Routledge.

ONS (2010) *Share Ownership Survey 2008: Statistical Bulletin*, Newport: Office of National Statistics.

Orwell, G. (1982 [1941]) *The Lion and the Unicorn*, Harmondsworth: Penguin.

Palast G. (2000) 'Inside corporate America: an internal study reveals the price "rescued" nations pay: dearer essentials, worse poverty and shorter lives', *Observer*, Business section, 8 October.

Palma, G. (2009) 'The revenge of the market on the rentiers: why neo-liberal reports of the end of history turned out to be premature', *Cambridge Journal of Economics*, 33: 829–66.

— (2010) 'Why has productivity growth stagnated in most Latin American countries since the neo-liberal reforms?', Cambridge Working Papers in Economics (CWPE) 1030, University of Cambridge.

Panitch, L. and S. Gindin (2009) 'From global finance to the nationalization of the banks: eight theses on the economic crisis', *The Bullet: Socialist Project: E bulletin*, 189, www.socialist

project.ca/bullet/bullet189.html, accessed 9 May 2012.
Pannekoek, A. (1947) 'Public ownership and common ownership', *Western Socialist*, November.
Parker, D. (2004) 'The UK's privatisation experiment: the passage of time permits a sober assessment', CESIfo Working Paper 1126, Munich.
Peck, J. and N. Theodore (2007) 'Variegated capitalism', *Progress in Human Geography*, 31(6): 731–72.
Peck, J. and A. Tickell (2002) 'Neoliberalizing space', *Antipode*, 34(3): 380–404.
Pedersen, O. (2006) 'Denmark's negotiated economy', in J. L. Campbell, J. A. Hall and O. K. Pedersen (eds), *National Identity and a Variety of Capitalism: The Case of Denmark*, Montreal: McGill University Press.
Pedersini, R. (1999) 'Privatisation and industrial relations', DSS Papers SOC 2-0, European Industrial Relations Observatory (EIRO), Brussels.
Polanyi, K. (1944) *The Great Transformation: the Political and Economic Origins of Our Time*, Boston, MA: Beacon.
Pollock, A. (2005) *NHS Plc: The Privatisation of Our Health Care*, London: Verso.
Pontusson, J. (1994) 'Sweden – after the Golden Age', in P. Anderson and P. Camiller (eds), *Mapping the West European Left*, London: Verso.
Prychitko, D. (2002) *Markets, Planning and Democracy: Essays after the collapse of communism*, Cheltenham: Edward Elgar.
Rancière, J. (2001) 'Ten theses on politics', *Theory and Event*, 5(3).
Resnick, S. and R. Wolff (1994) 'Between state and private capitalism: what was Soviet "Socialism"?', *Rethinking Marxism*, 7(1): 9–30.
Robinson, J. (1969 [1933]) *The Economics of Imperfect Competition*, Basingstoke: Macmillan.
Robinson, W. I. (2008) *Latin America and Global Capitalism: A Critical Globalization Perspective*, Baltimore, MD: Johns Hopkins University Press.
Rogow, A. A. and P. Shore (1955) *The Labour Government and British Industry 1945–51*, Oxford: Clarendon Press.
Rosenbaum, E. F. (2000) 'What is a market: on the methodology of a contested concept', *Review of Social Economy*, 58(4): 455–82.
Ross, G. (1987) 'From one left to another: "Le Social" in Mitterrand's France', in G. Ross, S. Hoffman and S. Malzacher (eds), *The Mitterrand Experiment*, Cambridge: Polity Press.
Ross, G. and J. Jenson (1994) 'France: triumph and tragedy', in P. Anderson and P. Camiller (eds), *Mapping the West European Left*, London: Verso.
Ross, G., S. Hoffman and S. Malzacher (eds) (1987) *The Mitterrand Experiment*, Cambridge: Polity Press.
Routledge, P. and A. Cumbers (2009) *The Entangled Geographies of Global Justice Networks*, Manchester: Manchester University Press.
Rowthorn, R. (1989) 'The Thatcher revolution', in F. Green (ed.), *The Restructuring of the UK Economy*, London: Harvester Wheatsheaf.
Rutherford, M. (1983) 'Review: the politics of Thatcherism', *Marxism Today*, July, pp. 43–4.
Ryggvik, H. (2010) *The Norwegian Oil Experience: A Toolbox for Managing Resources?*, Oslo:

Centre for Technology, Innovation and Culture.

Ryland, E. (2010) 'Danish wind power policy: domestic and international forces', *Environmental Politics*, 19(1): 80–5.

Sadler, D. (2001) 'The political economy and regional implications of energy policy in Britain in the 1990s', *Environment and Planning C: Government and Policy*, 19: 3–28.

St Meld (1973/74) *Petroleumsvirksomhetens plass i det norske samfunnet* [The role of petroleum activities in Norwegian society], White Paper no. 25, Oslo: Ministry of Finance.

Saville, R. (1993a) 'Commanding heights: the nationalisation programme', in J. Fyrth (ed.), *Labour's High Noon: The Government and the Economy 1945–51*, London: Lawrence and Wishart.

— (1993b) 'Introduction', in J. Fyrth (ed.), *Labour's High Noon: The Government and the Economy 1945–51*, London: Lawrence and Wishart.

Sawyer, M. and K. O'Donnell (1999) *A Future for Public Ownership*, London: Lawrence and Wishart in association with UNISON.

Schneider, M. (1991) *A Brief History of the German Trade Unions*, Bonn: J. H. W. Dietz.

Schumacher, E. (1973) *Small Is Beautiful: Economics as if People Mattered*, London: Abacus.

Schwarz, D. (1981) 'The eclipse of politics: the alternative economic strategy as socialist strategy', *Capital and Class*, 13: 102–13.

Scottish Government (2009) *An Oil Fund for Scotland: Taking Forward Our National Conversation*, Edinburgh: Scottish Government.

Sejersted, F. (1993) *Demokratisk kapitalisme*, Universitetsforlaget Oslo.

Seyfang, G. (2006) 'Sustainable consumption, the new economics and community currencies: developing new institutions for environmental governance', *Regional Studies*, 40: 781–91.

Shaoul J. E. (1999) 'The looking glass world of PFI', *Public Finance*, 29 January–4 February.

Soerensen, H. C., L. K. Hansen, K. Hammarlund and J. H. Larsen (2003) 'Experience with and strategies for public involvement in offshore wind projects', Seminar on National Planning Procedures for Offshore Wind Energy in the EU, Institute for Infrastructure, Environment and Innovation, Brussels, 5 June.

Spronk, S. and J. Webber (2007) 'Struggles against accumulation by dispossession in Bolivia: the political economy of natural resource contention', *Latin American Perspectives*, 34(2): 31–47.

Stephens, M. (2009) *The Government Response to Mortgage Arrears and Repossessions. Housing Analysis and Surveys Expert Panel 6*. Commissioned by the Department for Local Government and Communities, London.

Stevens, R. (2004) 'The evolution of privatisation as an electoral policy 1970–90', *Contemporary British History*, 18: 47–75.

Sturmthal, A. (1952) 'The structure of nationalized enterprises in France', *Political Science Quarterly*, 67: 357–77.

Swyngedouw, E. (2009) 'The antinomies of the postpolitical city: in search of a democratic politics of environmental production', *International Journal of Urban and Regional Research*, 33(3): 601–20.

Thomas-Symonds, N. (2010) *Attlee: A Life in Politics*, London: I. B. Tauris.

Thompson, P. (2004) *Skating on Thin Ice: The Knowledge Economy Myth*, Glasgow: Strathclyde University Press.

Tickell, A. (1998) 'Privatisation, employment and windfall tax', *Area*, 30: 83–90.

Toke, D. (2011) 'Ecological modernisation, social movements and renewable energy', *Environmental Politics*, 20(1): 60–77.

Trانæs, F. (2001) 'Danish wind energy cooperatives', Danish Wind Turbine Manufacturers Association (DWTMA), www.windpower.dk , accessed 15 November 2011.

— 'Danish wind energy cooperatives', Part 1, http://ele.aut.ac.ir/~wind/en/articles/coop.htm, accessed 11 June 2012.

Treasury Select Committee (2011) *Private Finance Initiative*, Seventeenth Report, London: House of Commons.

UNDP (2009) *Human Development Report 2009*, New York: United Nations Development Programme.

Urry, J. (2004) 'Small worlds and the new "social physics"', *Global Networks*, 4(2): 109–30.

Vartainen, J. (1995) 'State and structural change: what can be learnt for the successful late industrialization', in H.-J. Chang and R. Rowthorn (eds), *The Role of the State in Economic Change*, Oxford: Oxford University Press.

Veblen, T. B. (1990) *The Place of Science in Modern Civilization and Other Essays*, intro. by W. J. Samuels, New Brunswick: Transaction Publishers (originally published by Viking Press, New York, 1919).

Waddams Price, C. and R. Hancock (1998) 'Distributional effects of liberalising UK residential utility markets', *Fiscal Studies*, 19(3): 295–319.

Wade, R. (1990) *Governing the Market: Economic Theory and the Role of Government in East Asian Industrialization*, Princeton, NJ: Princeton University Press.

Wahl, A. (2010) 'How new social alliances changed politics in Norway', in A. Bieler and I. Lindberg (eds), *Global Restructuring, Labour and the Challenges for Transnational Solidarity*, London: Routledge.

Wainwright, H. (1994) *Arguments for a New Left: Answering the Free Market Right*, Oxford: Blackwell.

— (2003) *Reclaim the State*, London: Verso.

Warhurst, C. and P. Thompson (2006) 'Mapping knowledge in work: proxies or practices?', *Work, Employment and Society*, 20(4): 787–800.

Webber, J. (2010) 'Venezuela under Chávez: the prospects and limitations of twenty-first century socialism, 1999–2009', *Socialist Studies*, 6(1): 11–44.

Weisbrot, M., R. Ray and L. Sandoval (2009a) *The Chávez Administration at 10 Years: The Economy and Social Indicators*, Washington, DC: Center for Economic and Policy Research.

Weisbrot, M., R. Ray and J. Johnston (2009b) *Bolivia: The Economy during the Morales Administration*, Washington, DC: Center for Economic and Policy Research.

Weiss, L. (1998) *The Myth of the Powerless State*, Ithaca, NY: Cornell University Press.

Whyman, P. (2004) *An Analysis of the Economic Democracy Reforms in Sweden*, Lampeter: Edwin Mellen Press.

Wicken, O. (2007) *The Layers of National Innovation Systems: The Historical Evolution of a National Innovation System in Norway*, Oslo: Centre for Technology, Innovation and Culture.

Williams, K., J. Williams and D. Thomas (1983) *Why Are the British Bad at Manufacturing?*, London: Routledge & Kegan Paul.

Williams, R. (1961) *The Long Revolution*, London: Chatto and Windus.

Wilpert, G. (2007) *Changing Venezuela by Taking Power: The History and Policies of the Chávez Government*, London and New York: Verso.

Woolfson, C., J. Foster and M. Beck (1997) *Paying for the Piper: Capital and Labour in Britain's Offshore Oil Industry*, London: Mansell.

Woolfson, C., J. Foster and M. Beck (1993) *Paying for the Piper*, London: Mansell.

Wray, R. (2009) 'The rise and fall of money manager capitalism: a Minskian approach', *Cambridge Journal of Economics*, 33: 807–28.

Wright, E. O. (2010) *Envisioning Real Utopias*, London: Verso.

Žižek, S. (1999) *The Ticklish Subject: The Absent Centre of Political Ontology*, London: Verso.

Zwerdling, D. (1980) *Workplace Democracy. A Guide to Workplace Ownership, Participation, and Self-Management Experiments in the United States and Europe*, New York: Harper Colophon.

Index

Abbey National company, 104
Abu Dhabi, 102
accumulation by dispossession, 126
Adaman, F., 69
agonism, 137, 173, 191, 216
agoraphobia (market fear) of the left, 67, 211, 212; countering of, 70–3
agriculture, 30; collectivization of, 31; traditional practices of, 129
Aguas Bonaerense SA (ABSA) company, 113
Aguas del Tunari (ADT) company, 108
AIG insurance company, 99
air traffic control, partial privatization of, 88
Alliance and Leicester company, 104
alter-globalization movement, 123–41, 214; failure of, 138
alternative economic strategies, 3–6; in Latin America, 108–22
Alternative Economic Strategy (AES), 43
Amersham International, privatization of, 54
Anderson, P., 26–7
Anglo-American Council on Productivity, 15
anti-capitalist politics, resurgence of, 124–6
Appleyard, Adam, 3
Arctic, oil development in, 188
Argentina, 131
Argentinazo movement, 138
Aristotle, 211
Asset Protection Scheme (UK), 99
associated producers, use of term, 76
Attlee, Clement, 11
Austria, 27

Autonomous Communities (Mexico), 130
autonomy, 134, 135, 156, 160, 217; as site of political struggle, 137–8; disempowering aspects of, 141; engagement with the state, 138; (im)possibility of, 136–9; spaces outside capitalism, 128

Bad Godesberg Declaration, 26
Balfour Beatty company, 52
Bank for International Settlements (BIS), 100
Bank of England: independence of, 85, 87; nationalization of, 13, 14, 18
banking: community banks, 105; crisis of, 1–2; green banks, 105
banks: in global markets, 56; nationalization of, 59, 99–100 (in UK, 96–9, 100, 102)
Banque Nationale de Paris (BNP), 96
Bear Stearns bank, 99
Bernstein, Eduard, 152
Bevan, Aneurin, 17
Bevin, Ernest, 17
biopower, concept of, 133–4
Blair, Tony, 86, 89, 90, 204
Bohm, S., 137–8
Bolivarian participatory process, 113–16
Bolivarian Revolution, 4, 114, 120, 135
Bolivia, 108, 113, 119, 120, 217; autonomous movements in, 138; economic growth of, 118; nationalization in, 116–18
Bradford and Bingley company, 1, 97
Branson, Richard, 96–7, 102, 103
Brazil, 113
British Energy, privatization of, 56
British Gas, privatization of, 53

245

British National Oil Corporation (BNOC), 44; privatization of, 20
British Telecom, 51; privatization of, 53, 55, 56; proposed renationalization of, 96
Brittan, Leon, 89, 204
Brown, Gordon, 2, 85, 86, 89, 102
Brundtland, Gro Harlem, 191
Building Societies Act (1986) (UK), 104
Burczak, Theodore, 70–3, 80, 123, 148, 149, 163, 170, 212
bureaucracy, 40, 43; of centralized planning, 29
Bush, George W., 2, 204
buttonholing machine, invention of, 30

Callari, Antonio, 76
Cambridge Political Economy Group, 44
Campaign for the Welfare State (Norway), 189
Capital Issues Committee, 17
capitalism: changing value system of, 123; commons as external to, 126; varieties of, 74, 157
capitalist exploitation *see* exploitation, capitalist
Carlsberg, Johan, 178
centralization, 150, 216; of planning, 29, 40, 63–7, 76, 211 (flaws of, 69–70)
Charbonnages de France, 24
Chávez, Hugo, 4, 114–16, 119–21, 135
Cheltenham & Gloucester company, 104
Chicago school of economists, 40
Chile, 113; privatization in, 46
China, 36, 63, 100; economic model of, 212; state ownership in, 28–32
Cholderton Water company, 57
Christian Democrat Union (CDU) (Germany), 26, 91
Churchill, Winston, 11
cities, networks of, 156
Citrine, Walter, 15
climate change, 125, 126, 164, 166, 188

Clinton, Bill, 90
Co-operative company, 105
coal industry: in France, 24; in UK (nationalization of, 14, 16, 17, 19, 43; strike in, 22)
Cochabamba (Bolivia), water issues in, 108–9, 110, 117
Cole, G. D. H., 158
collective ownership, 68, 72, 107; elimination of, 36
collectivization of agriculture, 28, 31
commanding heights of the economy, 149–50, 166, 190
commercial freedom, use of term, 186
Commerzbank, 99
Committee of Inquiry on Industrial Democracy, 42–3
commodification, rollback of, 125
common ownership, use of term, 6–8
common resources, appropriation of, 80
commoning, resurgence of, in global North, 131
commons, 122, 146, 151–2, 151; as model of ownership, 128; discourse of, 123–41; emergence of agenda, 126–30; external to capitalism, 126, 141; global, 123, 127; practice of, 130–2, 139–41; reclaiming of, 137; trans-locality of, 127
commons thinking, limits of, 136
Communal Councils (Venezuela), 115
communism, 13, 23, 25, 29, 41; as economic model, 12; state ownership under, 28–33
Community Councils (Venezuela), 121
competition, 164, 208; as human trait, 163
Concession Law (1909) (Norway), 178
Conference of Socialist Economists (CSE), 44
Conservative Party (Norway), 175, 185, 186, 189
Conservative Party (UK), 47, 49, 54, 89, 90

cooperation, ethos of, 206–8
cooperatives, 7, 77, 116, 137, 164, 167, 170, 171, 193, 198, 199–201; numbers of, 131–2; of consumers, 166; of producers, 166; of wind turbine owners in Denmark, 197
Coordinadora de Defensa del Agua y la Vida (Cochabamba), 111
Copenhagen Energy company, 206
corruption, 119, 121
council housing, sale of, 48
counter-hegemonic strategies, 215
credit crunch, 96
credit unions, 104–5, 137
Cripps, Stafford, 15
cross-subsidization of low income groups, 51, 170

Danish Wind Turbine Owners Association, 197
Dansk Olie og Naturgas (DONG) company, 198, 209
Darling, Alistair, 1, 97, 100
De Angelis, Massimo, *The Beginning of History*, 136
debt, cancellation of, 125
decentralization, 150–1, 156, 159, 162–3, 167, 170, 174, 177, 179, 190, 194, 198, 199, 202; economic, 68, 214–16; of public ownership, in Denmark, 192–209
decommodification, 127
democracy, 5, 68, 71, 77–9, 107, 122, 162, 169; crisis of, 4; deliberative, in Norwegian oil industry, 173–91; direct, 120; economic, 15, 26, 28, 30, 43, 71, 118–21, 123, 145, 150, 154–5, 209, 214; in the workplace, 41, 42; limits of post-Hayekian vision of, 73–7; participatory, 115
democratic deficit under state ownership, 36
democratization from below, 127
demutualization, in UK, 104, 105
de-nationalization, 39
Denmark, 4, 28; Energy Package, 195, 196; National Energy Plan, 194; oil and gas resources, 192, 193–4; wind power sector in, 192–209, 214, 219
depoliticization of economic questions, 92–3
Devine, P., 69
devolution, political, 160
Dewey, John, 214
dialogue, importance of, 154–5
dictatorships, in Latin America, 110
Diggers, 151
division of labour, 162; spatial, 21
Drop the Debt Campaign, 58
dual strategy of radical change, criticized, 135
Durbin, Evan, 15

East Asian countries, state-owned enterprises in, 33–5
Ecuador: nationalization in, 113; privatization in, 57–8
education: management of, 170; marketization of, 127
ejido common land (Mexico), 130; repeal of laws, 139
electoral cycle, problem of, 32
electricity: planability of, 31; privatization of, 51
electricity industry, 170; in Denmark, 198; in France, nationalization of, 23; in Norway, 178–9; in UK, nationalization of, 21
ELKRAFT association (Denmark), 198
ELSAM association (Denmark), 198
employee ownership, 48–9
enclosure of commons, in England, 129; struggle against, 126
Energy Act (1999) (Denmark), 202
energy policy, 31; in Europe, 89
Enlightenment, aspirations of, 211
environmental sustainability, 75, 183, 191, 201
Erhard, Ludwig, 26
ethical code for economists, 75
European Commission: and renewable energy, 206; electricity liberalization programme, 202
European Union (EU), 59, 88–9, 213; energy markets in, 89; energy

sector, 101; policy on renewable energy, 204; Single Market agenda, 164, 201, 202
exodus, concept of, 141
exploitation, capitalist, 74, 128; basis of, 72, 77

Fanny Mae mortgage company, 99
Federici, Silvia, 129, 131
feed-in tariff (FIT), 202–5, 207–8
fictitious commodities, 169
financial and economic crisis, 3, 36, 85–107; and return of public ownership, 96–100; in UK, 105
financial capital, 18, 23, 34; beneficiary of privatization, 53; ownership of, 169
financial services, social exclusion from, 104
Financial Services Authority (UK), 98
Fine, Ben, 20, 39, 50
Finland, 27
five-year plans, 29, 34
Fjell, Olav, 187
Ford, Henry, 212
Fordism, 13
forests, privatization of, 95
France, 63, 66; nationalization in, 23–6; privatization in, 90, 92; renewable energy in, 205
France Telecom, privatization of, 92
Fraser, Douglas, 41
Freddy Mac insurance company, 99
freedom of information, 125
Friedman, Milton, 40
friendly societies, 103–4
full state ownership (FSO), 166–7

García Linera, Alvaro, 117, 121
gas industry: in Bolivia, drive to renationalization of, 116; in France, nationalization of, 23; in UK, nationalization of, 21
Gaulle, Charles de, 23, 24
George, Henry, 178
Germany: banking in, 99; FIT scheme in, 205,
207–8; nationalization in, 26–7; privatization in, 91
Gini index of inequality, 175
Glass-Steagall Act (1933) (USA), 90
global governance institutions, 159, 164
globalization, alternative *see* alter-globalization movement
GNER company, 101
Goldman Sachs, 99
Goodwill Agreements (Norway), 175
Goodwin, Fred, 3
government deficits, 1–2
Government Pension Fund - Global (Norway), 175
Gramsci, Antonio, 141
guild socialism, 152–3, 158

Halifax company, 104
Hallsworth, Joseph, 15
Hardt, Michael, 131, 133–4, 147
Harvey, David, 38, 124, 126, 158–9
Hatfield rail disaster, 52, 53, 95
Hayek, Friedrich von, 5, 36, 40–1, 49, 61, 72–3, 79, 80, 123, 150, 162, 164, 213; coming to terms with, 62–81; *The Road to Serfdom*, 63
Hayekian concerns, addressed from the left, 67–70
HBOS bank, 1, 97
health and safety, in Norwegian oil sector, 184–5
health care, management of, 170, 189
Heath, Edward, 47
Hirst, Paul, 212
hjemfallrett laws (Norway), 178
Hodgson, Geoff, 64, 66–7, 68–9, 71, 74, 77, 147, 153, 155, 162, 211–12
Holloway, John, 132–3; *Changing the World without Taking Power*, 134–5
Honduras, privatization in, 58
housing, regulation of, 169
Huancayo (Peru), sanitation project in, 113
Hubbard, Richard John, 187
Human Development Index, 173
Humphrys, John, 93

Hungary, 30, 32
Hutton, Will, 2
Hyndley, Lord, 17
Hypo Real Estate company, 99

ignorance, problem of, 64
Import Substitution Model, 58
impurity principle, 212
indigenous peoples, 17; control of local resources, 130; land ownership practices of, 131; movements in Bolivia, 138; struggles of, 129
individualization of ownership, 72
Indymedia, 127
innovation, 70, 153-4; problem of, 134; rate of, 79
intellectual property rights, 79, 126
International Energy Agency, 192
International Monetary Fund (IMF), 38, 57-8, 125, 213; resistance to, 111
iron and steel industry, nationalization of (UK), 13
Istituto per la Ricostruzione Industriale (IRI), 91
Italy, privatization in, 90-1

Japan, 33, 34
Johl, Johannes, 195
John Lewis partnership, 170
Johnsen, Arve, 179
Johnson Matthey bank, nationalization of, 100
Jospin, Lionel, 90, 92
justice: appropriative, 8, 71, 74, 80, 123, 148, 163, 188, 207, 208; class justice, 145-50, 213; distributive, 71, 146, 163, 164; productive, 163; social, 107, 145-50, 211

Kautsky, Karl, 154
Keynes, John Maynard, 146, 154
Keynesianism, 40, 133
Khrushchev, Nikita, 30
Klein, Naomi, 93
knowledge: distribution of, 65; problem of, 134; promotion of, 153-4; tacit, 65

Kohl, Helmut, 91
Korea, 33-4
Krugman, Paul, 2

Labour Party (Norway), 178, 179, 184, 186, 189, 191
Labour Party (UK), 11, 14, 44, 47, 77, 85, 147; Clause 4, 15, 86 see also New Labour
la Cour, Paul, 195, 197
land: ownership of, 169; in Norway, 176; in Scotland, 160
Lange, Oskar, 15
Latin America, alternative political economy in, 1, 108-22; privatization in, 107 see also pink tide, in Latin America
Lawson, Nigel, 54
Lehman Brothers, 1, 99
Lend Lease programme, 18
LETS schemes, 137
Lewis, Russell, 47
life expectancy, in Africa, 59
living wage campaigns, 161
local labour, employed by multinationals, 120
local or municipal ownership (LMO), 166-7
localism, 156, 177, 179, 205, 217; in wind turbine ownership in Denmark, 196-7, 208; limits of, 162, 201, 209
localization, of production, 164
Locke, John, 71
London: as global city, 55; shift of headquarters to, 21
London Passenger Transport Board, 16
London Underground, funding of, 102
Long Term Capital Management hedge fund, 100

Major, John, 52
managers, benefit from privatization, 52
Mandel, Ernest, 75-6
Mandelson, Peter, 89

market economy, 7, 154, 155, 163, 211, 212, 213; failure of, 127; in socialist economy, 75
market socialism, 70–3, 170
Martino, George de, 148–9, 188
Marx, Karl, 77–8, 129, 146, 211, 213
Marxism, 41, 45, 67–8, 69, 70–3, 128, 130, 148, 150, 152, 153, 154, 213
Massey, Doreen, 55
maternity and paternity rights in Scandinavia, 140
Meidner, Rudolf, 45
mesas técnicas (Bolivia), 120
Mills, Joe, 85–6
Misicuni hydro-electricity project (Bolivia), 110
misiones (Venezuela), 116
Mittelgrunden Wind Farm (Denmark), 206, 218
Mitterrand, François, 25
MNC Suez company, 112
Model Municipality project (Norway), 189
modernization, 14–17, 30, 128, 129, 176, 178, 179, 180; liberal, rebellion against, 111
Monnet, Jean, 24
Morales, Evo, 4, 116–18
Mouffe, C., 216
Movimiento al Socialismo (MAS) (Bolivia), 117, 120–1
multi-polar polities, 151
multinationals, negotiation with, 177–8
mutualism, 155, 161, 171, 177; history of, 103–6

nation-state, 157; as site of struggle, 156
National Coal Board, 15, 19, 22
National Express rail sector, nationalization of, 101
National Health Service (NHS) (UK), 7, 14, 20, 160
National Union of Mineworkers (NUM), 15
nationalization, 5, 11–12, 93, 147, 217; as remedy for failing competitiveness, 17; as solution for extraordinary events, 97; as temporary state, 101–2; British experience of, 13–22; contested from the left, 140; critiques of, 150; failure of, myths about, 94; in Bolivia, 116–18; in Ecuador, 113; in France, 23–6; in Germany, 26–7; in UK, failure of, 35; of banks, 99–100 (in UK, 96–9, 100, 102); of Norwegian oil, 167; single-model, 214; unpopularity of, 44 *see also* renationalization
Nationwide company, 105
natural resources, sovereignty of, 116–18
Negri, Antonio, 131, 133–4, 147
neoclassical economics, 3, 211
neoliberalism, 4, 5, 6, 37, 68, 75, 185, 201, 204, 207, 208, 213; and social democracy, 88–92; as class control project, 39–46; constitutive elements of, 218–19; contesting of, 187–90; contradictions of, 100–3; in China, 32; in Latin America, 110–11; onset of, 38–61; opposition to, 124; rollback of, 109–13
Neurath, Otto, 78, 79, 81, 152, 154–5, 157–8, 200, 214, 216
New Labour, 86, 95, 100, 101, 103, 160; and privatization, 88–90; relationship with neoliberalism, 87, 106
Nippon Steel company, 34
NORDPOOL market, 203
North American Free Trade Agreement (NAFTA), 130
Northern Rock company, 3, 103, 104; nationalization of, 1, 96–7; reprivatization of, 102, 105
Northern Rock (Asset Management), 102
Norway, 27–8, 120, 140; electoral geography of, 182; industrialization in, 176; nationalism in, 181; oil-industrial complex in, 185–7; oil industry in, 173–91, 214–15, 217

(nationalization of, 167); rejection of EU membership, 181, 191
Norwegian model of oil development, 173, 174–6, 177
Nove, Alex, 31, 64–5, 75, 163; *The Economics of Feasible Socialism*, 171
nuclear power: in Denmark, 194–5; investment in, 21
Nuclei of Endogenous Sustainable Development (Venezuela), 116
Nustad, Terje, 174

O'Neill, John, 78–9, 81, 154, 158, 200, 216
occupation of factories, 13
Occupy Wall Street movement, 94
odelsov regulation (Norway), 177
OFS union (Norway), 185
oil and gas industry: in Bolivia, nationalization of, 117; in Siberia, 31; North Sea, 44, 49, 50; tax evasion of, in Venezuela, 115 *see also* Denmark *and* Norway
oil dependency, in Denmark, 193
oil prices: collapse of, 185, 186; rise of, 193
Olive Tree Alliance (Italy), 90–1
Organisation for Economic Co-operation and Development (OECD): index of product market regulation, 59; report on Demark, 202
Organization for Renewable Energy (OVE) (Denmark), 196
Orwell, George, 7
Osborne, George, 106
Ostrom, Elinor, 127
over-concentration of power, 146
Owen, Robert, 131
ownership, variable geographies of, 157

Pacific LNG company, 117
Palast, Gregory, 58
Palme, Olaf, 44
Pannekoek, Anton, 6
Paragraph 10 (Norway), 180; repeal of, 187

partial state ownership (PSO), 166–7
participatory forms of governance, 145, 150, 173, 174, 200, 214
partition of the sensible, 93
patenting: of living organisms, 125; of seeds, campaigning against, 127; of wind turbine prototypes, 207
PDVSA company, 114–15, 119, 120
Pérez, Carlos Andrés, 114
Peru, export of natural gas, 117
Petroleum Directorate (Norway), 183–4, 190, 215
Phaleas of Chalcedon, 151
pink tide, in Latin America, 109, 111, 215
Pinochet, Augusto, 40
planning: decentralized, 78; democratic participatory, 69 *see also* centralization, of planning
Plato, 151
pluralism, 77–9, 200, 217; importance of, 154–5
Pohang Steel Company, 34
Poland, 30
Polanyi, Karl, 169
political interference, use of term, 186
post-political era, 93–4, 106
poverty, reduction of, 118, 169
Powell Duffryn company, 17
primitive accumulation, 38, 74; concept of, 128–9
private, opposition to, 7–8
private finance initiative (PFI), 88, 102, 110
private owners, compensation of, 18
private ownership, 39, 40, 67, 68, 74, 75, 103, 147, 163, 208; uncontested as concept, 106
private property, 7; relation to democracy, 48; rights of, 41
privatization, 75, 87; and New Labour, 88–90; as enclosure of commons, 126; beneficiaries of, 52–5; contested politics of, 92–6; critiques of, 38–9, 103; failure of, 58; globalization of, 55–7;

in Chile, 46; in Latin America, 107; in Russia, 59, 62; in UK, effects of, 50–2; mixed outcomes of, 94; of banks, in Korea, 34; of water industry, 108 *see also* Cochabamba; politics of, 38–61; promotion of, 54–5; rebellion against, 109, 111; resistance to, 95–6, 189; reversal of, 109; role of left parties in, 90; scaled up as policy paradigm, 57–9; under Margaret Thatcher, 46–50
Prodi, Romano, 91
projects for social emancipation, 160
property rights, resistance to, 79
public ownership, 1–8, 77–9; as state ownership, 11–37; democratically controlled, 164, 172; democratized and deliberative, 145–55; diversity in, 81; forms of, 3; Hayekian critiques of, 63–7; in Latin America, 108–22; in twenty-first century, 162–71; of water resources, 112–13; open and deliberative, 212–14; perceived shortcomings of, 94; remaking and rescaling of, 145–7; remaking case for, 218–19; return of, 96–100; spatiality of, 155–62; support for, 95; use of term, 6–8; variegated forms of, 164, 167
Public Services International Research Unit, 51
public spending cuts, 4

Quality Municipality Project (Norway), 189

rail industry, in UK: nationalization of, 19; privatization of, 53, 54 (leads to problems, 101); renationalization of, 89, 95
Railtrack company, 53, 88
Rancière, Jacques, 85, 93
Rasmussen, Anders Fogh, 204
raw materials, global demand for, 118
Reagan, Ronald, 46, 100

redistribution of income, 146–7, 166, 188
Reduced Emissions on Degradation and Deforestation (REDD), 188
renationalization, 89, 95, 118–21
Renault, 23, 24
renewable energy: discourse of, 200–6; in Denmark, 192–209
repossession of homes, 98–9
resource allocation, 70; problem of, 29
respect, need for, 214, 216
Ridley, Nicholas, 47
right to the city movement (USA), 161
Roosevelt, F. D., 23
Ross, Wilbur, 102
Rowthorn, Bob, 39
Royal Bank of Scotland, 1, 3, 97, 99
Russia, 101; privatization in, 59, 62

Salstjobaden Agreement, 28
Sánchez de Lozada, Gonzalo, 117
Sandler, Ron, 103
Savings and Loans company, 100
scalar fix, 159–60
scalar politics, of renewable energy in Denmark, 200–6
Schroeder, Gerhard, 91
Schumpeter, Joseph, 12
Scottish National Party, 103
self-determination, 134
self-employment, 163
self-governance of communities, right to, 130
self-valorization, working-class, 161
Shinwell, Manny, 16, 17
Singapore, 34
single-solution theory, 79
Smith, Adam, 43
SNCAM company, 23
Social Democrat Party (Germany), 26, 91, 205
Social Democratic Party (Sweden), 44
social ownership, in Yugoslavia, 32
social problems, calculated in monetary terms, 79
socialism, 8, 13, 23, 25, 43, 47, 58,

63–4, 69, 72, 78, 152, 157, 163, 212; actually existing, 80; alternative model of, 66, 87; critique of, 64, 136; democratic, 213; economic organization of, 77; for the rich, 100–3; in one country, 170; incompatible with biopolitical production, 133; model of, 158; municipal, 21; parliamentary road to, 11; possibility of, 171; post-Hayekian view of, 73–7; twenty-first century, 113–16 *see also* market socialism *and* state socialism

Socialist Left party (Norway), 182
socialization, 14–17
solidarity, 80, 129, 155, 211, 217; translocal politics of, 131, 141
Solidarity Wage system (Sweden), 45
Spain, renewable energy in, 205
spatial fix, 159
spatial imaginary, 155–7, 161–2
speculation, 62, 169
Stalin, Joseph, 28, 30, 31
state: as sphere for political action, 217; engagement with, 136–40; fetishism of, 158; in and against, 217–18; in, against and outside of, 139–41, 139; left strategy for, 132–3; non-engagement with, 141; reclaiming spaces of, 218; rediscovery of, 85–107, 85; rescaling of forms of, 218; role of, 40, 156, 193, 196, 198, 209; winning of state power, 134
state capitalism, 29
state ownership, 119; critique of, 35–7, 140; in East Asian countries, 33–5; of Norwegian oil industry, 173–91; reconstituted forms of, 141; under communist regimes, 28–33
state socialism, 6–7
Statoil company, 174, 179, 185–6, 215; Articles of Association, 180; establishment of, 175, 182; governance framework of, 183;

operates as multinational, 186; partial privatization of, 186–7; regulation of, 190
sterling, maintaining value of, 19–20
strikes, 27, 48; in Bolivia, 108; in Norway, 184
Stuhlmann, Alexander, 100
sub-prime sector, 99
Summers, Larry, 90
supranational forms of governance, 159, 164
surplus, social: allocation of, 149; production of, 148
Sweden, 27–8, 46, 140

Taiwan, 33–4
Tanzania, IMF policies in, 58
tax havens, dismantling of, 125
Temasek company, 34
Terje, Leif, 187
Thatcher, Margaret, 20, 22, 38, 40, 46, 100
Thatcherism, 60, 86; as counter-revolution, 39; privatization project of, 46–50
Third Way, 89
Three Mile Island accident, 194
tiger economies of Asia, 33, 35
Tobin Tax, 125
tolerance, 151–3
toxic assets, 97, 99
tradable green certificates (TGC), 202–4
trade unions, 12, 23–4, 26, 27, 40, 44–5, 85, 86, 113, 138, 180, 186, 189; attack on, 49; defeat of, 124; demonization of, 48; grassroots, 185; in Denmark, 193; in Norway, 184, 190
transport, public, management of, 170
Tredegar Medical Aid Society, 160
Trondheim, model municipality project in, 189
Tvind school (Denmark), windmill, 194, 196

Umunna, Chuka, 105

unemployment, 25, 49, 50, 52, 99, 114, 187
Union of Municipal and General Employees, 189
Union of Soviet Socialist Republics (USSR), 12, 12, 36, 57, 63; collapse of, 204; economic model of, 13, 32, 157, 163, 212; inefficiencies in, 64; resource allocation in, 70; state ownership in, 28–32
United Autoworkers Union (UAW), 41
United Kingdom (UK), 2, 63, 95; banking nationalization in, 96–9; comparison with Norwegian oil sector, 174–5; private ownership in, 103; total factor productivity in, 94
United States of America (USA), 2, 4, 18, 23, 100; banking nationalization in, 99
utilities, management of, 169–70

Veblen, Thorstein, 214
Venezuela, 113, 114, 119–21, 217; constitution of, 114; public ownership in, 121–2

wage-earner funds (WEFs), 44–5
wage relationship, 7; abolition of, 72
Wainwright, Hilary, 218
Washington Consensus, 38, 57, 110
water, as commodity, 112–13
water industry, 170; exit of multinationals from, 113; privatization of, 51–2, 54, 57, 101, 108 (resistance to, 60)
Waterfall Law Controversy (Norway), 177–8
Webb, Beatrice, 15
Webb, Sidney, 15

Welfare State, 13, 14, 106, 157, 159, 189, 191, 194
Welsh Water/Dwyr Cymru company, 57
West LB bank, 99–100
Wilson, Harold, 20
wind farms: cooperative ownership of, 197; support for, 206
Winstanley, Gerrard, 151–2
women, at forefront of commoning processes, 131
Wootton, Barbara, 15
worker-managed firms, 71–2, 73, 116
worker-ownership of enterprises, 76, 77, 80, 212
workers' control, movement for, 43
workers' representation in companies, 23, 42, 173, 184–5
working class, 7; voters, alienation of, 94
working conditions, in renationalized industries, 119 *see also* health and safety
Working Environment Act (1977) (Norway), 184
World Bank, 38, 57, 110, 125, 127, 128, 169; revolt against, 109
World Social Forum (WSF): Bamako Appeal, 125; Porto Alegre meeting, 125
Wright, Erik Olin, 139, 160, 185

Yacimientos Petroliferos Fiscales Bolivianos (YPFB), 117; renationalization of, 117
Yugoslavia: economic model of, 157; public ownership in, 32–3; self-management in, 36

Zapatista movement (Mexico), 4, 111, 130–1; non-engagement with Mexican state, 138

About Zed Books

Zed Books is a critical and dynamic publisher, committed to increasing awareness of important international issues and to promoting diversity, alternative voices and progressive social change. We publish on politics, development, gender, the environment and economics for a global audience of students, academics, activists and general readers. Run as a co-operative, Zed Books aims to operate in an ethical and environmentally sustainable way.

Find out more at:

www.zedbooks.co.uk

For up-to-date news, articles, reviews and events information visit:

http://zed-books.blogspot.com

To subscribe to the monthly Zed Books e-newsletter, send an email headed 'subscribe' to:

marketing@zedbooks.net

We can also be found on **Facebook**, **ZNet**, **Twitter** and **Library Thing**.